THE ALIEN VISION
OF VICTORIAN POETRY

The Alien Vision of Victorian Poetry

Sources of
the Poetic Imagination in
Tennyson, Browning,
and Arnold

By E. D. H. Johnson

ARCHON BOOKS
Hamden, Connecticut
1963

COPYRIGHT, 1952, BY PRINCETON UNIVERSITY PRESS

[*Princeton Studies in English, No. 34*]

REPRINTED 1964 BY THE SHOE STRING PRESS, INC.
IN AN UNALTERED AND UNABRIDGED EDITION

LIBRARY OF CONGRESS CATALOG CARD NO.: 64-10457

PRINTED IN THE UNITED STATES OF AMERICA

FOREWORD

THIS book has resulted from the convergence of two distinct lines of inquiry. One was undertaken with the purpose of providing grounds for a critical revaluation of the poetry of the great Victorians: notably, Tennyson, Browning, and Arnold. The other originated in a desire to examine the relationship of the artist to society in the Victorian age.

Any random sampling of anthologies of Victorian poetry published over the last half century will reveal a remarkable uniformity in the choice of selections, despite the abundance and diversity of available material. Modern readers, it would seem, have uncritically accepted preferences passed on by previous generations, and in so doing have allowed their concepts of these poets and their work to be influenced by standards of taste very different from their own. The student who sets out to read right through Tennyson or Browning or Arnold can hardly fail to be surprised and gratified by the illuminations which await him on nearly every page. More importantly, he discovers as he goes along the necessity for revising his view of the artists in question to make room for hitherto unsuspected areas of originality, beauty, and power. And when read in full context, even those poems most staled by familiarity take on fresh meanings illustrative of neglected aspects of the writers' genius.

The prevalent tendency to hold up the poetry of Tennyson, Browning, and Arnold as a faithful mirror of the Victorian era has been responsible for a further historical fallacy in our thinking about these writers. Artists of their generation were the first to face the problem of communicating with a modern reading public little sensitive to the life of the imagination. A traditional view of the artist's social responsibilities led Tennyson, Browning, and Arnold to make a good many popular concessions, both in subject-matter and style; and an exaggerated notion of the extent of these concessions has implanted prejudices fatal to the serious study of their work. Yet the student who penetrates the blandly complacent surface of Victorian poetry does not have to probe very deep to come on evidence of a divided intent premonitory of the coming rift between society and its artists.

If sufficiently prolonged, the two methods of approach here outlined must eventually meet in a recognition that the qualities in Victorian poetry which accord least well with the conventional habits of mind of that age are precisely the ones most interesting to our own time. It follows that an attempt to reappraise these poets must inevitably take into account the circumstances under which the alienation of the artist has occurred. And conversely, any investigation of the origins of this alienation, as it is foreshadowed in Victorian poetry, cannot but involve a new and suggestive approach to the poets who most eloquently speak to us across their age.

My colleagues and friends, Donald A. Stauffer, Willard Thorp, and Alba H. Warren, have not only taken the time to read the manuscript of this book in its entirety, but have also helped me with suggestions at every stage in its writing. Richard P. Blackmur has also given me the benefit of his critical experience and wide knowledge of modern poetry. To all these I wish to express my deep appreciation for their generous and always helpful advice. And lastly, I should like to record my gratitude to Princeton University for the award of a Bicentennial Preceptorship and for the opportunity thus provided to devote myself to the completion of this work.

Princeton University
November, 1951

CONTENTS

INTRODUCTION ix

Tennyson

I. THE TWO VOICES 3
II. THE MASK OF CONFORMITY 12
III. SHADOW AND SUBSTANCE 21
IV. "THE HIDDEN WORLD OF SIGHT THAT LIVES BEHIND THIS DARKNESS" 59

Browning

I. "AND THEN I FIRST EXPLORED PASSION AND MIND" 71
II. "WITH THE WORLD AS STARTING POINT" 82
III. AUTHORITY AND THE REBELLIOUS HEART 91
IV. "MY HUNGER BOTH TO BE AND KNOW THE THING I AM" 137

Arnold

I. "THE DIALOGUE OF THE MIND WITH ITSELF" 147
II. POETRY AS MAGISTER VITAE 178
III. MYTH AND THE TIME SPIRIT 186
IV. "THE DEMAND FOR AN INTELLECTUAL DELIVERANCE" 205

CONCLUSION 215

INDEX OF POEMS 221

INTRODUCTION

THE important writing of the Victorian period is to a large extent the product of a double awareness. This was a literature addressed with great immediacy to the needs of the age, to the particular temper of mind which had grown up within a society seeking adjustment to the conditions of modern life. And to the degree that the problems which beset the world of a century ago retain their urgency and still await solution, the ideas of the Victorian writers remain relevant and interesting to the twentieth century. Any enduring literature, however, must transcend topicality; and the critical disesteem into which so much Victorian writing has fallen may be traced to the persistent notion that the literary men of that time oversubscribed to values with which our own time is no longer in sympathy. Yet this view ignores the fact that nearly all the eminent Victorian writers were as often as not at odds with their age, and that in their best work they habitually appealed not *to*, but *against* the prevailing mores of that age. The reader who comes to the Victorians without bias must be struck again and again by the underlying tone of unrest which pervades so much that is generally taken as typical of the period. Sooner or later he begins to wonder whether there is any such thing as a representative Victorian writer, or at any rate, whether what makes him representative is not that very quality of intransigence as a result of which he repudiated his society and sought refuge from the spirit of the times in the better ordered realm of interior consciousness. Since, however, any tendency to exalt individual awareness at the expense of conventionally established attitudes ran counter to the concept of the rôle of the artist which the Victorian age tried to impose on its writers, there resulted a conflict which has been too often ignored, but which must be taken into account in reaching any satisfactory evaluation of Victorian literature. This was a conflict, demonstrable within the work of the writers themselves, between the public conscience of the man of letters who comes forward as the accredited literary spokesman of his world, and the private conscience of the artist who conceives that his highest allegiance must be to his own aesthetic sensibilities.

Most Victorian writers still thought of themselves as men of letters in the full meaning of the term. Victorian literature was predominantly a literature of ideas, and of ideas, furthermore, brought into direct relation with the daily concerns of the reading public. To a degree now inconceivable the influential literary types of the nineteenth century were expository in character—the essay, tract, and treatise. The student who wishes to understand the Victorian world begins with such works as *Past and Present, The Stones of Venice, On Liberty, Culture and Anarchy*. The assumption that a writer's first responsibility is to get into close correspondence with his audience induced a great many of the original thinkers in the period to turn aside from their fields of special knowledge, to the end of making their theories more generally accessible. So Mill, Carlyle, Ruskin, Arnold, Morris, Huxley, after achieving distinction along specialized lines, gave up exclusive concentration on these in order to apply the disciplines they had mastered to subjects of the broadest human import. Or, to consider the novel, Dickens, George Eliot, Disraeli, Kingsley, Mrs. Gaskell, and Charles Reade all quite evidently chose themes with an eye to their social significance.

Yet, paradoxically, it becomes increasingly difficult to think of the great Victorians as other than solitary and unassimilated figures within their century. Deeply as they allowed themselves to be involved in the life of the times, familiarity seemed only to breed contempt. Their writings, inspired by a whole-hearted hostility to the progress of industrial culture, locate the centers of authority not in the existing social order, but within the resources of individual being. Nor was this procedure merely a reaction to the isolation which is traditionally visited on prophets without honor, although for many the years brought disillusionment and bitterness over the debacle of cherished programs of reform. The prestige of a Carlyle or Ruskin or Newman may almost be said to have risen in inverse proportion to the failure of their preach-

INTRODUCTION

ments. At the core of the malaise which pervades so much that is best in Victorian literature lies a sense, often inarticulate, that modern society has originated tendencies inimical to the life of the creative imagination. By mid-century the circumstances of successful literary production had begun to make demands on writers which strained to the breaking point their often very considerable capacities for compromise. Among novelists the careers of Dickens and Thackeray epitomize the all but intolerable difficulties of reconciling popular appeal with artistic integrity. A new generation, led by Rossetti and Swinburne, was to resolve the dilemma by an outspoken assertion of the artist's apartness; but for the writers who came of age in the 1830's and 1840's no such categorical disavowal of social commitment was admissible. As a result, there is recognizable in their work a kind of tension originating in the serious writer's traditional desire to communicate, but to do so without betraying the purity of his creative motive even in the face of a public little disposed to undergo the rigors of aesthetic experience. Even when, as was too often the case, their love of fame overcame their artistic restraint, traces of the initiating conflict remain imbedded in what they wrote; and it is these constantly recurring evidences of a twofold awareness which, perhaps more than any other trait, give its distinctive quality to the writing of the Victorian age.

In criticizing Victorian poetry it is necessary to keep this ambivalence in mind; and this is especially true for Tennyson, Browning, and Arnold, the poets who touched their period at the greatest number of points. The history of nineteenth-century English poetry records a gradual, but radical shift in the relationship of the artist to his public, with the three poets just mentioned occupying a position at dead center of the forces which were in opposition. A divorce between the artist and society first became conspicuous as an element of the Romantic movement; but even though they had to endure abuse or neglect, the Romantics did not in any sense think of themselves as abdicating the poet's traditional right to speak for his age. Blake, Coleridge, Wordsworth, Byron, Shelley,

INTRODUCTION

Keats were all, it is true, keenly sensitive to their generation's reluctance to pay attention to what they were saying, but they accepted isolation as a necessary consequence of their revolutionary program. That they should confess defeat, with the alternatives either of self-withdrawal or compromise, never seriously occurred to them. On the contrary, they declared open warfare on the prejudices which would dispossess them and continued to assert that the poet's vision is transcendently authoritative over all other agencies of intellectual and spiritual truth. Before the end of the century, however, the conflict thus resolutely engaged had been lost, and the artist had come to accept as a foregone conclusion his inefficacy as a shaping influence on the lives of his contemporaries. In compensation, he now espoused the aesthetic creed which goes by the name of art for art's sake, and with Pater and then Wilde as his apologists and Rossetti and Swinburne as his models, embraced his alienation from all but a coterie of initiates persuaded like himself to value the forms of art above its message.

Between the Romantics and the Pre-Raphaelites lie Tennyson, Browning, and Arnold, leading the poetic chorus of the great Victorian noonday. And by virtue of this midway position between the two extremes represented by the schools of poetry which came before and after, their work brings into sharp focus the choice which has been forced on the modern artist. In the common view, these mid-Victorian poets, either unable or unwilling to maintain the spirit of bellicose self-sufficiency which sustained their Romantic forbears, achieved rapprochement with their audience by compromising with the middle-class morality of the time, and in so doing deliberately sacrificed artistic validity. So flagrant a betrayal of the creative impulse, the argument then continues, provoked a reaction in the following generation, whereby the pendulum swung back towards the belief that art is and must be its own justification irrespective of ulterior motive. But this version of the poetic situation in the nineteenth century gravely misrepresents the real meaning of an endeavor on which Tennyson, Browning, and Arnold were alike engaged. For each

INTRODUCTION

of them was ultimately seeking to define the sphere within which the modern poet may exercise his faculty, while holding in legitimate balance the rival claims of his private, aristocratic insights and of the tendencies existing in a society progressively vulgarized by the materialism of the nineteenth and twentieth centuries. Thus it came about that the double awareness, which so generally characterized the Victorian literary mind, grew almost into a perpetual state of consciousness in these poets through their efforts to work out a new aesthetic position for the artist.

The literary careers of Tennyson, Browning, and Arnold present a number of striking parallels which, since their poetic endowments were so divergent, can only be explained in terms of influences impingeing on them from the outside. In the early manner of each there is an introspective, even a cloistral element which was later subdued in an obvious attempt to connect with contemporary currents of thought. Of the three, Tennyson succeeded most quickly in conforming to the Victorian ideal of the poet as popular bard; his reward was the laureateship as Wordsworth's successor. Browning's progress in public favor was more gradual, but the formation of the Browning Society in 1881 signaled his eventual arrival within the select company of Victorian idols of the hearth. Less versatile in poetic range, Arnold became a full-fledged man of letters and won the prestige of the Oxford Professorship of Poetry only after turning to prose; and it is perhaps worth pondering whether his inability to bring his poetry into closer accord with the demands of the age does not account for the fact that he has attracted a greater amount of serious critical attention in recent years than either Tennyson or Browning.

The Victorian writer, of course, had to acclimate himself to a reading public vastly bigger in size and more diverse and unpredictable in its literary requirements than any that had existed hitherto. There is something astonishing, even slightly appalling, in the unselective voracity with which the Victorians wolfed down *In Memoriam* and Bailey's *Festus*, *The Origin of Species*, and Samuel Smiles' *Self-help*, the novels

INTRODUCTION

of Dickens and the tales of Harriet Martineau. The ill success of their first volumes early awakened Tennyson, Browning, and Arnold to a realization that under existing conditions originality was no passport to artistic acclaim. The critics were for the most part hostile; but it was the disapprobation of intimate friends which carried the greatest weight. For while the poets might turn a deaf ear to the voice of the age as it spoke through the weekly and monthly journals which had feebly replaced the Edinburgh and Quarterly Reviews as arbiters in literary matters, the well-intended strictures of a Hallam or Elizabeth Barrett or Clough were another matter. And friends and foes were at one in their insistence that the poets take a broader view of their responsibilities as men of letters. In general, their work drew reproof on three counts, one major and two incidental thereto. It was unduly introspective and self-obsessed, and as a result it was too often obscure in content and precious in manner. All three faults are chargeable to immaturity; but as attributed indiscriminately to Tennyson, Browning, and Arnold, they carry additional implications suggestive of the tyranny which the age was to exercise over its artists. For the invariable inference in the attacks on these poets is that their faults could easily be remedied by more attention to normal human thoughts and activities, and correspondingly by less infatuation with their own private states of being.

The experiments in the narrative and dramatic modes to which Tennyson, Browning, and Arnold turned so early in their careers were certainly undertaken out of a desire to counteract objections of this kind. Yet it is apparent from the vagaries of their critical reputations that they were never sure enough of their audience to be able to estimate its response with any degree of reliability. The appearance of a *Maud* or *Sordello* or *Empedocles on Etna*, interspersed among more admired efforts, is continuing evidence that the best will in the world could not compensate for temperamental variances with prevailing tastes which went much deeper than the authors themselves always recognized. That they should have professed impatience with the often obtuse and

INTRODUCTION

ill-considered estimates of their poetry is not in itself surprising; but it is to be noted that as time went on they tended increasingly to transfer this resentment to the reading public at large. In their later days Tennyson and Arnold would have agreed with Browning's statement in *Red Cotton Night-Cap Country* about "artistry being battle with the age/ It lives in!" There is, of course, an element of the disingenuous in such professions of disdain for popular favor; and their assumed indifference cannot disguise the fact that all three poets were keenly sensitive to the fluctuations of their literary stock. In this respect they were no more than exhibiting an awareness natural to men of letters possessed of an inherent belief in the instrumentality of literature as a social force.

Yet again, the conventional explanation does not cover the facts; and we are brought back to the dichotomy which emerges from any close analysis of the relations between the artist and society in the Victorian period. The hallmark of the literary personalities of Tennyson, Browning, and Arnold alike is a certain aristocratic aloofness, a stubborn intractability which is likely to manifest itself at just those points where the contemporary social order assumed automatic conformity with its dictates. Thus, their refusal to be restricted by current suppositions is less often a subterfuge to cover a fear of failure than a forthright avowal of the artist's independence from societal pressures whenever these threaten to inhibit the free play of his imaginative powers. Tennyson, Browning, and Arnold never went to the lengths of the poets who came after in disassociating themselves from their audience. On the other hand, there is a fundamental error in the prevalent notion that they uncritically shared most of the foibles that, rightly or wrongly, are attributed to the Victorians. Such an opinion overlooks that quality of double awareness which we are now to investigate as the crux of the Victorian literary consciousness.

With these remarks as a starting point, it is proposed in the ensuing chapters to survey the artistic careers of the three poets, testing for each in turn the truth of the following statements. (1) In their youthful poems Tennyson, Browning, and Arnold revealed the habits of mind, the emotional and intellectual leanings, the kinds of imaginative vision—in other words, the native resources at the disposal of each. (2) Subsequently, from a desire to gain a wide audience for their work and hence to play an influential part in the life of the times, all three poets showed a willingness to make concessions to literary fashions with which they were temperamentally out of sympathy. (3) Resolved, nevertheless, that conformity should involve as little artistic loss as possible, Tennyson, Browning, and Arnold perfected remarkable techniques for sublimating their private insights without materially falsifying the original perceptions at the heart of their creative impulse. (4) The identification of these insights, along with the recognition of their concealed but vivifying action within poems ostensibly concerned with subjects of different and sometimes contradictory import, draws attention to the true centers of poetic intent in Tennyson, Browning, and Arnold, and thus provides a basis for reassessing their total achievement.

Tennyson

The deep has power on the height,
  And the height has power on the deep;
They are raised for ever and ever,
  And sink again into sleep. . . .

A deep below the deep,
  And a height beyond the height!
Our hearing is not hearing,
  And our seeing is not sight.

      THE VOICE AND THE PEAK

TENNYSON

I

THE TWO VOICES

Throughout his life Tennyson was subject to trance-like fits of abstraction in which the veil of sensory appearances seemed to draw aside and the inner life of things to stand revealed. It was largely on the testimony of such fleeting intuitions that the poet based his faith in spiritual being as the ultimate reality. A friend, Mrs. Marian Bradley, wrote that Tennyson remarked, after reading the Grail Idyll aloud: "Yes, it is true. There are moments when this flesh is nothing to me, when I feel and know the flesh to be the vision, God and the spiritual the only real and true—depend upon it, the spiritual is the real, it belongs to one more than the hand and the foot." The records of the poet's life contain many statements of a like nature; for instance, near the end of his life Tennyson told an acquaintance: "Sometimes as I sit here alone in this great room I get carried away out of sense and body, and rapt into mere existence, till the accidental touch or movement of one of my own fingers is like a great shock and blow and brings the body back with a terrible start." Yet Tennyson had inherited his full measure of the family's black blood with its susceptibility to prolonged periods of moroseness and depression. When these were on him, he distrusted all irrational promptings from the beyond as delusory snares, and tended to fall back for support on more conventional religious ideas.

Since Tennyson's temperament was at all times and to an

unusual extent characterized by a variability between the extremes of exaltation and despair, it is small wonder that the enigma of human consciousness with its conflicting intuitions should from the outset appear as a dominant motif in his poetry. Already in his earliest writing a polarity is observable, represented by two kinds of poetry, one showing a morbid preoccupation with the artist's subjection to his times, the other marked by a refusal to accept any such restriction. Thus, among Tennyson's Juvenilia one group of poems, prevailingly pessimistic and low-spirited in tone, exhibits a paralyzing sense of insecurity with regard to the outside world. The opening lines of the rejected *Perdidi Diem* sound a typical note:

> I must needs pore upon the mysteries
> Of my own infinite Nature and torment
> My Spirit with a fruitless discontent . . .

More explicit is the *Supposed Confessions of a Second-rate Sensitive Mind* in which the poet reproaches himself for having abandoned the "common faith" bequeathed by his mother. He speaks of his "gloomed fancy" and makes significant reference to his "damned vacillating state" and to "our double nature." As if in guilty acknowledgment of the penalty attached to denial of God, he cries: "I am void,/ Dark, formless, utterly destroyed."

In a contrary mood, however, Tennyson is aggressively disposed to repudiate the world and to seek immunity from its disturbances in the depths of his own imaginative being. The most arresting early example of such self-withdrawal is the poem entitled *The Mystic*, omitted after the 1830 volume. Possession of the visionary power has set the central figure apart from his fellows: "How could ye know him? Ye were yet within/ The narrower circle." While one hesitates to make out a case for Tennyson as in any sense a true mystic,* this poem written before he was twenty-one is pene-

---

* It may be noted in this connection, however, that the levels of intuitive awareness in Tennyson's poetry, as identified in the third section of the present chapter, very closely conform to the categories

trated with strange insights and shows remarkable grasp of the experiences which it purports to describe. In his condition of "still serene abstraction" the mystic transcends the boundaries of normal being and stands outside the limitations of time and space:

> He often lying broad awake, and yet
> Remaining from the body, and apart
> In intellect and power and will, hath heard
> Time flowing in the middle of the night,
> And all things creeping to a day of doom.

Another poem, published in 1830 but not thereafter, ascribes equal authority to the revelations of the individual imagination. This is Οἱ ῥέοντες, based, as its title indicates, on the Heraclitean doctrine of flux:

> All thoughts, all creeds, all dreams are true,
>   All visions wild and strange;
> Man is the measure of all truth
>   Unto himself. All truth is change.
> All men do walk in sleep, and all
>   Have faith in that they dream:
> For all things are as they seem to all,
>   And all things flow like a stream.
>
> There is no rest, no calm, no pause,
>   Nor good nor ill, nor light nor shade,
> Nor essence nor eternal laws:
>   For nothing is, but all is made.
> But if I dream that all these are,
>   They are to me for that I dream;
> For all things are as they seem to all,
>   And all things flow like a stream.

That the youthful Tennyson lived more intensely in his dreams than in the world around him is apparent from such

---

of mystical experience analyzed by William James in his *Varieties of Religious Experience*. Likewise, the four characteristics of the mystical habit of mind listed in Bertrand Russell's essay, "Mysticism and Logic," might be illustrated by innumerable passages from Tennyson.

a work as the prize poem *Timbuctoo*, which incorporates
material from a still earlier poem, *Armageddon*. Here the
imaginative faculty is symbolized by the Seraph, whose function it is to "visit his eyes with visions." And to the vision of the
fabled city thus vouchsafed the poet ecstatically gives himself
up, deliberately postponing until the end of the poem any
recognition of discrepancy between the actual and the ideal.
The most remarkable passage in *Timbuctoo*, however, is
the following in which Tennyson again undertakes to present
a version of the mystical experience, but now in such a way
as to infer that the seer and the poet have a common source
of inspiration:

> I felt my soul grow mighty, and my spirit
> With supernatural excitation bound
> Within me, and my mental eye grew large
> With such a vast circumference of thought,
> That in my vanity I seem'd to stand
> Upon the outward verge and bound alone
> Of full beatitude. Each failing sense,
> As with a momentary flash of light,
> Grew thrillingly distinct and keen. I saw
> The smallest grain that dappled the dark earth,
> The indistinctest atom in deep air,
> The Moon's white cities, and the opal width
> Of her small glowing lakes, her silver heights
> Unvisited with dew of vagrant cloud,
> And the unsounded, undescended depth
> Of her black hollows. The clear galaxy
> Shorn of its hoary lustre, wonderful,
> Distinct and vivid with sharp points of light,
> Blaze within blaze, an unimagin'd depth
> And harmony of planet-girded suns
> And moon-encircled planets, wheel in wheel,
> Arch'd the wan sapphire. Nay—the hum of men,
> Or other things talking in unknown tongues,
> And notes of busy life in distant worlds
> Beat like a far wave on my anxious ear.

TENNYSON

> A maze of piercing, trackless, thrilling thoughts,
> Involving and embracing each with each,
> Rapid as fire, inextricably link'd,
> Expanding momently with every sight
> And sound which struck the palpitating sense,
> The issue of strong impulse, hurried through
> The riven rapt brain. . .

The volume of poetry published in 1832 affords grounds for a still clearer differentiation between the two opposing tendencies manifested in the tentative compositions of extreme youth. Thus, Tennyson's lapses into self-doubt provide the theme of *The Two Voices* with its dramatic representation of a "divided will." Although the voice of faith eventually carries the day, it is the voice of doubt which may well seem the more persuasive to modern readers. The poet's awareness of the interdependence between state of mind and artistic productivity underlies the whole debate. Because he has lost religious conviction, he feels that he can no longer devote his talent to the services of mankind as in other days, "When, wide in soul and bold of tongue,/ Among the tents I paused and sung." The first voice, denoting the materialism which has laid waste the human spirit, mocks the quest for spiritual absolutes:

> Much less this dreamer, deaf and blind,
> Named man, may hope some truth to find,
> That bears relation to the mind.

Playing on Tennyson's uncertainty about the mysterious ways of the mind, the Mephistophelean voice continues:

> If straight thy track, or if oblique,
> Thou know'st not. Shadows thou dost strike,
> Embracing cloud, Ixion-like. . .

In the shadow of suicidal despair the poet tries to controvert the tempter by appealing to the "mystic gleams" which, despite the inherent "baseness in his blood," have from time to time brought intimations of a controlling and beneficent purpose in life. But evidently Tennyson himself was not sufficiently convinced by this argument to make it the basis for affirmation. The poet quite simply has no internal resources equal to the task of vanquishing doubt. This is accomplished for him by the voice from outside which speaks for conventional Christian faith. Through intuitive sympathy with the pious church-bound family, as well as with the beauty of the natural world, the poet discovers a need to identify himself with the life around him. And in this way hope is reborn under sanctions which have traditionally given the individual release from a too oppressive sense of his limitations.

The artistic success of the 1832 volume, however, derives from poems which celebrate the life of the imagination. In the greater objectivity of these compositions and in the skill with which their creator has mastered new and complex techniques for the projection of theme, we can measure Tennyson's progress towards a clearer realization of his genius. There is present, for example, an increased complexity of meaning, conveyed not by explicit statement, but through structural and textural devices of considerable subtlety. The poet conceives many of his poems on a centrifugal or wheel-like principle, the crux of the situation being the hub around which, like spokes, the contributory actions are in constant rotation. Paradoxically, it is the apparent immobility of this hub in contrast to the encircling play of circumstances which holds the reader's attention focussed on the center. Tennyson began to experiment with this method as early as *Recollections of the Arabian Nights*, where we follow the poet into the heart of Haroun Alraschid's enchanted garden, led on by the song of the nightingale, or rather

> Not he, but something which possess'd
> The darkness of the world, delight,
> Life, anguish, death, immortal love,
> Ceasing not, mingled, unrepress'd,
>   Apart from place, withholding time...

A similar contrast between an outer, temporal, and shifting sphere of activity and an inner, timeless, and fixed core of apprehension is developed in other early poems, such as *The Hesperides* and *The Sea Fairies*. In its aesthetic implications this technique approximates very closely the concept of art as stasis.

Tennyson's increasing control over the formal elements in his poetry is observable in such a poem as *The Lady of Shalott*, where structure supplies the key to meaning. A spell has entranced the lady and confined her to one room in her remote and silent castle. As if to emphasize her isolation from all human affairs, we are made conscious of the unceasing flow of life around the island of Shalott. The road runs by, the aspens quiver, the waves run, the slow horses trail the heavy barges, the shallop flitteth. The condition of the lady's enchantment is that she shall sit all day weaving into a tapestry similitudes of the life of this outer world as reflected in a mirror. Her dedication to this unworldly task is brought into vivid contrast with the multifarious concerns of the wayfarers on the road to Camelot—the village-churls, the market girls, the troop of damsels, the abbot, the shepherd-lad, and the knights. Her web is the shadow of a shadow, presenting an idealized version of the actuality which will destroy her when she meets it face to face. For everything is changed by the arrival within the mirror of Lancelot's image. No longer able to endure an existence of make-believe, the lady turns to the window and so invokes the curse. At once the web floats free and the mirror cracks; these are, we realize, metaphors for the creative imagination which has been shattered by the intrusion of direct experience. Appropriately, the world which the lady enters has been drained of the color and animation lent by fancy; and the manner of her dying symbolizes the extinction of the vitalizing imagination within her.

The discrimination between two ways of life, the one of artistic detachment, the other of emotional involvement, is construed in more general terms in *The Lotos-Eaters*. Again the poet makes brilliantly effective use of contrast. The restless dark-blue sea which environs lotos-land reminds the mariners of their homes and families, of warfare, and of all the strenuous claims of social existence. Within the charmed circle, however, there is surcease from care. For the lotos-eaters, just as for the Mystic and the bewitched lady of Shalott, time and space have ceased to have any meaning; the mariners have come to "a land where all things always seem'd the same!" The fruit of the lotos induces a dreamlike state of irresponsibility in which "the inner spirit sings." The choric song itself is dramatic in conception. The odd stanzas, lyric and descriptive in quality, weave the spell of the lotos, while the even ones follow a rhetorical pattern suggestive of the conflict within the consciences of the speakers. Furthermore, the successive stanzas tend to increase in length as if to imply a growing recognition of all that is at stake. Then, after the swooning magic of the seventh stanza has taken the senses captive, the meter of the last stanza* changes (following the introductory invocation to the lotos) to express the final troubled moment of decision when the mariners make their choice not to return to the outside world.

Yet persuasively as Tennyson could present the ideal of individual self-fulfillment, it is apparent from other poems in the 1832 volume that he was not completely happy in this aesthetic position. Membership in the Cambridge "Apostles," and especially the selfless example of Hallam, had brought him into closer touch with the spiritual predicament of the Victorians. Did not his absorption in the beauties of literature and of the Somersby countryside amount to an egocentric evasion of the obligations which the age imposed on its promising young artists? Friends and critics were at one in their insistence that the imagination could not be allowed to remain a law unto itself, but must be submitted to a higher tribunal. The Paris of *Œnone* is lost through hearkening to Aphrodite's invitation to sensual self-gratification rather than to Pallas Athene's grave exhortation:

> Self-reverence, self-knowledge, self-control,
> These three alone lead life to sovereign power.
> Yet not for power (power of herself

---

* As rewritten for publication in 1842.

Would come uncall'd for) but to live by law,
Acting the law we live by without fear;
And, because right is right, to follow right
Were wisdom in the scorn of consequence.

The same voice sounds in *The Palace of Art* so insistently as to suggest a revision of the creed exemplified in *The Lady of Shalott* and *The Lotos-Eaters*. The dedication makes clear that this poem was intended to be a refutation of art for art's sake, though one can hardly fail to note that the attack on that concept is conducted in such equivocal terms as to leave some doubt about the poet's perfect good faith. Once again, as in *The Lady of Shalott*, the focus of attention is an isolated consciousness; but in *The Palace of Art*, unlike *The Lady of Shalott*, the reader sympathizes with the external forces which break in on the soul's self-possession.*

The soul's motive in alienating itself from the world is one of aristocratic disdain for humanity. This it frankly admits in such a way as to reveal a total absence of any sense of social responsibility:

O Godlike isolation which art mine,
    I can but count thee perfect gain,
What time I watch the darkening droves of swine
    That range on yonder plain.

The palace of art symbolizes the many-chambered life of the imagination, furnished with all the treasures of natural

* Tennyson's use of a planetary analogy illuminates not only the theme but the structural principle of this poem:

And 'while the world runs round and round,' I said,
    'Reign thou apart, a quiet king,
Still as, while Saturn whirls, his steadfast shade
    Sleeps on his luminous ring.'

A further variation of this metaphor occurs later on to convey the sense of stagnation resulting from the individual's loss of communication with the surrounding order of things:

A star that with the choral starry dance
    Join'd not, but stood, and standing saw
The hollow orb of moving Circumstance
    Roll'd round by one fix'd law.

beauty, myth (including Christianity), the arts, literature, and the accumulated learning of scientists and philosophers. To the soul, seclusion among its hoarded possessions seems justifiable because of the artistic response which they evoke. It sings, but sings alone, untroubled by the fact that there is no one to hear its song:

> No nightingale delighteth to prolong
> Her low preamble all alone,
> More than my soul to hear her echo'd song
> Throb thro' the ribbed stone. . .

But after three years of unruffled self-absorption, disillusionment sets in. Despair brings on "deep dread and loathing of her solitude," and then the spectres of incipient madness, portrayed by a series of powerful and disturbing images. Driven at length to expiate its guilt, the chastened soul returns to the world and communion with its kind; but the end of the poem remains somewhat ambiguous in its implications. The palace of art is not destroyed, but remains intact against the time when the poet will return, bringing others to enjoy its felicities. Presumably, then, we are to believe that Tennyson would not altogether discredit the life of the imagination, but rather would insinuate that the artist must become aware of the responsibility to communicate his insights.

II

THE MASK OF CONFORMITY

With the collection of poems published in 1842 Tennyson begins to assume his familiar guise as Victorian prophet. The dilemma of the divided will persists, but has become so overlaid by other concerns as to be all but unrecognizable to the reader not familiar with poet's habits of mind in their germinal state. The protagonist of *Locksley Hall* undergoes the same crisis of doubt that found subjective expression in *Supposed Confessions of a Second-rate Sensitive Mind* and *The Two Voices*; but now larger social implications are involved. To bring the theme home to his age, Tennyson embeds it in melodramatic narrative of a kind dear to his heart: namely, crossed love between lovers of unequal worldly station. Furthermore, the poem concludes on a very much more positive note than *The Two Voices*. After rejecting the temptation to sink into sensuality on an Eastern island,* the hero takes the more manly decision to join the army and fight for his country.

Such a poem as *Tithonus* indicates Tennyson's growing disposition to disguise his private thoughts under extrinsic layers of meaning. Although not published until 1860, *Tithonus* was contemporary in conception with *Ulysses*. This extraordinarily beautiful and moving treatment of classical myth is usually read as an utterance of its author's grief over Hallam's death; but, like *The Lady of Shalott*, it is also almost certainly a symbolic representation of Tennyson's aesthetic philosophy. Taken so, Eos stands for the Keatsian ideal of beauty which holds the poet in bondage. Tithonus remembers the first thrilling visitations of the creative impulse:

> Ay me! ay me! with what another heart
> In days far-off, and with what other eyes
> I used to watch—if I be he that watch'd—
> The lucid outline forming found thee; saw
> The dim curls kindle into sunny rings;
> Changed with thy mystic change, and felt my blood
> Glow with the glow that slowly crimson'd all
> Thy presence and thy portals, while I lay,
> Mouth, forehead, eyelids, growing dewy-warm
> With kisses balmier than half-opening buds
> Of April, and could hear the lips that kiss'd
> Whispering I knew not what of wild and sweet,
> Like that strange song I heard Apollo sing,
> While Ilion like a mist rose into towers.

* Tennyson habitually associated the East with laxity of will and self-indulgence. See, for example, *The Hesperides*, *Tithonus*, and *The Voyage*.

Now, weighed down by age (a metaphor, perhaps, for Tennyson's desolation over the loss of his friend), the speaker asks only that he be allowed to return to share the common lot of his fellowmen:

> Let me go; take back thy gift.
> Why should a man desire in any way
> To vary from the kindly race of men,
> Or pass beyond the goal of ordinance
> Where all should pause, as is most meet for all?

The general run of new poems published in 1842, however, does not require, nor indeed call for, such probing after ulterior meanings. Tennyson had been less inattentive to criticisms of his previous work than he pretended; and in his desire for a wider measure of recognition he was beginning to court the public. The direction in which he was tending is clear from new developments which now begin to manifest themselves in his writing. In the first place, whereas he had before viewed contemporary life in the subjective and individualistic terms of *The Two Voices*, he now made a determined effort to write poems of topical interest, realistic in situation and conventional in tone. These are the so-called English Idyls, sentimental narratives of domestic life. Along with *Locksley Hall*, but more obviously addressed to Victorian tastes, the 1842 volumes included the following poems in this manner: *The Gardener's Daughter, Dora, Audley Court, Walking to the Mail, The Talking Oak, Lady Clare, Edward Gray* and *The Lord of Burleigh*. Although now and then the more sombre and moody streak in Tennyson's temperament cropped up, it was kept subservient to the controlling tone of bland tractability. In *Walking to the Mail*, for instance, Sir Edward Head's spiritual malady, so similar to that portrayed in *Locksley Hall*, provides matter for no more than a passing comment, and that of a moralizing kind:

> No, sir, he,
> Vext with a morbid devil in his blood
> That veil'd the world with jaundice, hid his face
> From all men, and commercing with himself,

> He lost the sense that handles daily life—
> That keeps us all in order more or less—
> And sick of home went overseas for change.

A like change takes place in the conduct of many of the poems derived from the author's reading. Tennyson's uneventful life made him more reliant than most English poets on literary sources of inspiration; but as we have seen in the cases of *The Lady of Shalott, The Lotos-Eaters,* and *Tithonus,* his happiest use of myths or legends generally involved a reinterpretation of their original significance in terms of some private and highly personal insight. In the 1842 collection, however, the reworking is undertaken with a didactic intent. As a result, the poet's handling of traditional stories frequently appears by modern standards overly explicit and rather offensively moralistic. The titles of these poems too often bring to mind the edifying tag-lines which incorporate their themes. Thus, for example: *Morte d'Arthur* ("The old order changeth, yielding place to new"), *Godiva* ("So the Powers, who wait/ On noble deeds, cancell'd a sense misused"), *Sir Galahad* ("My strength is as the strength of ten,/ Because my heart is pure").

In this body of poetry, too, we begin to recognize the Tennyson who was to constitute himself the advocate and defender of so many of the Victorians' cherished shibboleths. In particular, that dream of progress towards an Utopian social order, which was so deeply ingrained in the age, keeps recurring throughout these poems: in *Morte d'Arthur, Locksley Hall, The Golden Year* (first published in 1846), *The Day-Dream, The Poet's Song.* Likewise, passing references to aesthetic matters (in *The Gardener's Daughter, The Day-Dream,* and *The Golden Year*) show Tennyson moving towards the Ruskinian positions that art is incidental to life, that beauty only shines in use, and that the artist is a product of his society. In her description of the proper ends of poetry Princess Ida of *The Princess* endorses that commingling of ethics and aesthetics which made for the highest artistic accomplishment in the eyes of the age:

> But great is song
> Used to great ends; ourself have often tried
> Valkyrian hymns, or into rhythm have dash'd
> The passion of the prophetess; for song
> Is duer unto freedom, force and growth
> Of spirit, than to junketing and love.

Yet, as Tennyson drew closer to the laureateship and popular recognition as the official poetic voice of Victorian England, doubts lingered in his mind—if not so much the old ones of his capacity to fill this rôle, then new and equally grave ones occasioned by a clearer comprehension of the compromises necessary to fame. In a mood half humorous, half bitter, the speaker in *Will Waterproof's Lyrical Monologue* contrasts the conditions of literary success in the nineteenth century to those pertaining in previous periods:

> Hours when the Poet's words and looks
>   Had yet their native glow,
> Nor yet the fear of little books
>   Had made him talk for show;
> But, all his vast heart sherris-warm'd,
>   He flash'd his random speeches,
> Ere days that deal in ana swarm'd
>   His literary leeches.

More biting are the lines in *Walking to the Mail* which castigate society for its callous and blundering disregard for originality of mind:

>   Well—after all—
> What know we of the secret of a man?
> His nerves were wrong. What ails us who are sound,
> That we should mimic this raw fool the world,
> Which charts us all in its coarse blacks or whites,
> As ruthless as a baby with a worm,
> As cruel as a schoolboy ere he grows
> To pity—more from ignorance than will.

The evolution of the poet's aesthetic theories between 1832 and 1850, his *annus mirabilis*, is best illustrated by *In*

Memoriam. Anyone at all familiar with the poetry of Tennyson knows something of the history and influence of this elegy, which traces the author's progress from grief-stricken despair over Hallam's death to an ultimate affirmation of faith which all Victorian England, from the Queen down, accepted as meeting the needs of the modern spirit. What is less generally recognized is that *In Memoriam* is also an intimate record of Tennyson's thinking about the nature and purpose of his poetry during the period of seventeen years in which the elegy from its start as a collection of random lyrics grew into a highly formalized apologia.

By 1850, the year when *In Memoriam* was published, Tennyson had relinquished for good and all the confessional tone that runs through so much of his youthful poetry, including the early sections of *In Memoriam* itself. In the Prologue to the poem, not written until 1849, the poet could say with the diffidence of hindsight: "Forgive these wild and wandering cries,/ Confusions of a wasted youth." On this evaluation, *In Memoriam* is the best commentary. The author passes through four readily identifiable stages of development in clarifying his artistic intent; and these stages are roughly equivalent to his psychological advance from unrestrained grief through emotional numbness to hesitant hope and the eventual recognition that bereavement has provided a basis for religious certainty.

At the outset the poet is too overcome by Hallam's loss to use poetry as anything but a means of release, though he does pause to wonder over the vagaries of the imagination which can convert every emotion into grist for its mill:

> What words are these have fallen from me?
> > Can calm despair and wild unrest
> > Be tenants of a single breast,
> Or Sorrow such a changeling be?

He writes without forethought, speaking of himself as "that delirious man"

> Whose fancy fuses old and new,
> And flashes into false and true,
> And mingles all without a plan.

By the nineteenth poem, however, a greater degree of objectivity has led to the discovery that the poetic impulse occurs only in moments of comparative detachment, such as follow on paroxysms of sorrow. As the artist regains control, he is increasingly reluctant to put his faculties at the disposal of undisciplined emotion. There is even a touch of scorn in the thirty-fourth poem with its reference to

> Fantastic beauty; such as lurks
> In some wild poet, when he works
> Without a conscience or an aim.

Tennyson now enters a phase when, personal suffering somewhat alleviated, he can scrutinize his aesthetic motives more closely. Hallam's death has opened up tragic depths within his consciousness and left a sense of inability to deal adequately in poetic terms with the profounder implications of the experience. He thinks of the Gospel story and concludes that the noblest expressions of spiritual truth are directly provocative of action:

> Tho' truths in manhood darkly join,
>   Deep-seated in our mystic frame,
>   We yield all blessing to the name
> Of Him that made them current coin;
>
> For Wisdom dealt with mortal powers,
>   Where truth in closest words shall fail,
>   When truth embodied in a tale
> Shall enter in at lowly doors.
>
> And so the Word had breath, and wrought
>   With human hands the creed of creeds
>   In loveliness of perfect deeds,
> More strong than all poetic thought. . .

By contrast his obsession with self in the name of art seems unworthy; he has "loiter'd in the master's field,/ And darken'd sanctities with song." Yet there remains the indisputable fact that poetry assuages his stricken feelings as no other outlet can: "But in the songs I love to sing/ A doubtful gleam of solace lives." This being true, he will continue to think of his muse as the unpretending handmaiden of a private impulse:

> If these brief lays, of Sorrow born,
>   Were taken to be such as closed
>   Grave doubts and answers here proposed,
> Then these were such as men might scorn.
>
> Her care is not to part and prove;
>   She takes, when harsher moods remit,
>   What slender shade of doubt may flit,
> And makes it vassal unto love;
>
> And hence, indeed, she sports with words,
>   And better serves a wholesome law,
>   And holds it sin and shame to draw
> The deepest measure from the chords;
>
> Nor dare she trust a larger lay,
>   But rather loosens from the lip
>   Short swallow-flights of song, that dip
> Their wings in tears, and skim away.

For this self-imposed limitation in scope Tennyson presents in the seventy-seventh poem additional historical justification. Since the modern age offers no themes comparable to those which inspired the masterpieces of the past, the contemporary poet cannot hope for lasting fame and may as well confine his art to his own individual concerns.

By the eighty-fifth poem, however, Tennyson has seen hope dawn; and concurrently he begins to wonder, though as yet without any great amount of confidence, whether his poetic insights are solely attributable to grief playing with symbols and "pining life" fed on fancies. The dream allegory of the one hundred and third poem, which has interesting affinities with *The Palace of Art*, sounds a new and altogether more ambitious note. Here the poet first confesses that his suffering has been largely self-regarding. He has made out of Hallam's memory an idol to be set up in the private shrine of the imagination and worshipped, with the poetic faculties, represented as maidens, presiding over the rites as votaries. But now to Tennyson, as to the hero in *Locksley Hall*, has come "a summons from the sea," in response to which he has gone out into the world, there to be greeted by the living presence of his friend grown to heroic size. As Tennyson boards the ship, so often for him a symbol of the active life, Hallam likewise admits the maidens, who have "gather'd strength and grace/ And presence, lordlier than before" in preparation for the nobler demands henceforth to be made of them. After this it is not surprising in the one hundred and eighth poem to find the author renouncing the self-absorbed and inconclusive brooding of the earlier lyrics, and embracing in exchange that concept of participation in the common lot for which Tithonus had yearned:

> I will not shut me from my kind,
>   And, lest I stiffen into stone,
>   I will not eat my heart alone,
> Nor feed with sighs a passing wind. . .
>
> What find I in the highest place,
>   But mine own phantom chanting hymns?
>   And on the depths of death there swims
> The reflex of a human face.
>
> I'll rather take what fruit may be
>   Of sorrow under human skies:
>   'T is held that sorrow makes us wise,
> Whatever wisdom sleep with thee.

His doubts superseded by a firm faith in human destiny, Tennyson could look back as an artist and find that he had not undergone his spiritual ordeal in vain:

> I trust I have not wasted breath:
>   I think we are not wholly brain,
>   Magnetic mockeries; not in vain,
> Like Paul with beasts, I fought with Death. . .

Confident that he has attained self-mastery, the poet is ready to go on to other things. The Epilogue to *In Memoriam* brings before us an emotionally mature Tennyson who has not only silenced the disputation of the two voices, but has also brought his poetry into tune with the spirit of the age— or so he chooses to believe. In this conviction he can pretend in retrospect to disown as either frivolous or ineffectual the promptings of an inner awareness so much at variance with what he now feels his poetic mission to be:

> No longer caring to embalm
>   In dying songs a dead regret,
>   But like a statue solid-set,
> And moulded in colossal calm.
>
> Regret is dead, but love is more
>   Than in the summers that are flown,
>   For I myself with these have grown
> To something greater than before;
>
> Which makes appear the songs I made
>   As echoes out of weaker times,
>   As half but idle brawling rhymes,
> The sport of random sun and shade.

III

SHADOW AND SUBSTANCE

We have now arrived at Tennyson's middle period, the time of the *Enoch Arden* volume and *Idylls of the King*, the time, in other words, when the poet produced the work for which the Victorians valued him most highly and by which the twentieth century judges him most harshly. For it has become the commonly accepted view that in order to establish his contemporary reputation Tennyson temporized with his age, sold, so to speak, his birthright for a mess of pottage. And certainly, as we have seen, he was not immune to the coercive pressures which Victorian society exerted on his artistic theory and practice. As early as 1834 an admiring friend, James Spedding, had observed with foreboding this hesitancy to stand on his own feet: "His frailty is that he has not faith enough in his own powers, which produces two faults, first that he does not give his genius full beat; and, secondly, that he seeks for strength not within but without, accusing the baseness of his lot in life and looking to outward circumstances for more than a great man ought to want of them, and certainly more than they will ever bring."

Yet there are evidences enough that, even during the years of his greatest prestige as Victorian man of letters, Tennyson held aloof from his age and continued to live most intensely within the world of his own mind. Since, however, the conscious artist took pains to sublimate any traces of his inner consciousness, the revelations of its operation must be sought not on the surface of his poetry, but rather in the modes of perception by which he illuminated subject-matter ostensibly selected for its popular appeal. The thoughtful reader, who approaches the poetry of the 1850's and the 1860's by way of what came before, can hardly fail to observe in this later work the recurrence of certain themes and an habitual reliance on certain formal devices which are at variance with the expressed content of the material. It is as though there brooded in the background a mind constantly alert to strange and disturbing implications in the most commonplace circumstances. Thus, many of the poems which seem to be indisputably the products of Victorian literary convention have an extra dimension which, once recognized, relates them to the deeper sources of the author's poetic vision.

One such manifestation of an ulterior purpose is the reappearance of the dream motif throughout Tennyson's poetry. From biographical records it is ascertainable that the poet was at all times subject in his sleep to extraordinarily vivid and suggestive dreams, and that this trait became more pronounced with age.* Furthermore, the poems themselves show

* In his account of Tennyson's last years, his grandson writes: "He

a knowledge of dream psychology unique in the period, and such as could only have been acquired through autoanalysis. Especially frequent and accurate are the notations relating to the intermediary processes between waking and sleeping. In *A Dream of Fair Women* the transition from idle musing to the world of dreams is described as follows:

> And then, I know not how,
> All those sharp fancies, by down-lapsing thought
>   Stream'd onward, lost their edges, and did creep
> Roll'd on each other, rounded, smooth'd, and brought
>   Into the gulfs of sleep.
> At last methought that I had wander'd far
>   In an old wood . . .

And at the end of the same poem the writer describes his reluctant return to actuality in this way:

> No memory labors longer from the deep
>   Gold-mines of thought to lift the hidden ore
> That glimpses, moving up, than I from sleep
>   To gather and tell o'er
> Each little sound and sight. With what dull pain
>   Compass'd, how eagerly I sought to strike
> Into that wondrous track of dreams again!
>   But no two dreams are alike.

The Vision of Sin suggests how the direction of a dream may be radically altered if the sleeper is partially aroused; and a line in *Mariana in the South* calls attention to the occasional phenomenon of self-consciousness in the dreaming mind: "Dreaming, she knew it was a dream." The following stanza from *The Two Voices* shows that Tennyson had likewise been impressed by the continuity of memory between dreams:

---

had strange dreams, too: 'Priam has appeared to me in the night,' he said one morning to Hallam. Sometimes his dreams were of fir woods, cliffs and temples; once of building a succession of gorgeous pagodas which reached right up to heaven; once that he was Pope of the world and had to bear all its sins and miseries on his shoulders."

> As here we find in trances, men
> Forget the dream that happens then,
> Until they fall in trance again...

The early sonnet *To* ____, ("As when with downcast eyes"), derives from the common experience that memories, originating in dreams, may linger in waking thoughts as familiar but only partially recoverable intimations; and the same notion occurs in *The Two Voices*:

> Moreover, something is or seems,
> That touches me with mystic gleams,
> Like glimpses of forgotten dreams—

Tennyson's close attention to the dream state would be less arresting if it were not clear that he intermittently attached a good deal of importance to the activities of the sleeping mind. Might not its very passivity at such times release the intuitive faculty and thus open up channels for the apprehension of truths of which the waking intellect is imperceptive? In *The Lover's Tale* the poet speaks of "delicious dreams, our other life"; and later in the same poem he writes, commenting on the interrelations between the hero's conscious view of his situation and the phantasmal dreams inspired by it:

> Alway the inaudible, invisible thought,
> Artificer and subject, lord and slave,
> Shaped by the audible and visible,
> Moulded the audible and visible.

The Higher Pantheism is still more explicit: "Dreams are true while they last, and do we not live in dreams?"* But it was in *In Memoriam* that Tennyson explored most fully the implications of dreams as a means of attaining to spiritual truths lying beyond the ken of ratiocination.

As early as the fourth poem of *In Memoriam* the poet introduces a concept of sleep as the sponsor of emotive being in contrast to the activities of the purposive mind. Full realiza-

---

* Compare also Οἱ ῥέοντες, quoted on page 5.

tion of Hallam's loss comes to him when he has given his "powers away" to sleep and his "will is bondsman to the dark"; but: "With morning wakes the will, and cries,/ 'Thou shalt not be the fool of loss.'" In dreams, however, the poet can also forget his loss; and he is thus led in the forty-third poem to equate sleep with death, "that still garden of the souls" situated outside time and space. Sleep, then, may be courted as a form of mystical experience which releases the dreamer from the trammels of corporeal existence. Nevertheless, Tennyson had finally to admit that his dreams took the form of nightmares as often as not, and that he could find only sporadic relief through them. The life of the sleeping mind presented another version of the problem of appearance and reality which continually tormented him. In the famous fifty-fourth, -fifth, and -sixth poems of *In Memoriam* the spectacle of the struggle for existence leaves us in doubt whether it is Nature in conflict with God which "lends such evil dreams," or whether it is not man himself who is "a monster then, a dream,/ A discord."

All of Tennyson's thinking about the nature of dreams and their significance for the waking life is finally brought to bear on his immediate situation in the four extraordinary lyrics of *In Memoriam* which begin with the sixty-eighth. Sleep, again called "Death's twin-brother," restores Hallam to Tennyson; but their communion is imperfect because the Hallam of the dream is troubled. The poet awakens to realize that this trouble has had its origin in his own mind and that, therefore, the dream itself, as an instance of thought transference, possesses only such validity as can be attached to any act of the creative imagination. A second dream, occupying the sixty-ninth poem, elaborates the idea that heartfelt grief isolates the sufferer from his fellows and subjects him to their contemptuous derision. Interestingly enough, this dream, although much more artificially wrought than the preceding one, compels the poet's belief in the truth of its testimony, apparently because its symbolism develops within an orthodox religious framework. The next lyric, almost surrealistic in its imagery, reverts to the earlier surmise that dreams are but a form of wish-fulfillment; but all uncertainty vanishes in the last stanza when the ugly welter of preceding visions is suddenly replaced by a mystic intimation of Hallam's spiritual presence:

> Till all at once beyond the will
> I hear a wizard music roll,
> And thro' a lattice on the soul
> Looks thy fair face and makes it still.

After this revelation the poet of the seventy-first lyric is no longer disposed to question the testimony of dreams. If sleep has such strong credit with the soul, then he will invoke its assistance to cancel time and to trace a magic circle within which he and his friend may continue to be together. Tennyson's eventual willingness after so much self-examination to rely on dreams as a source of spiritual certitude clarifies certain later affirmations in the poem, such as: "But in my spirit will I dwell,/ And dream my dream, and hold it true"; or:

> Strange friend, past, present, and to be;
> Loved deeplier, darklier understood;
> Behold, I dream a dream of good,
> And mingle all the world with thee.

It becomes apparent, then, that Tennyson located in the dream state one center of the life of the imagination, like others not always predictable in its operations, but ultimately rewarding as no exclusively objective awareness ever could be. Additional evidence in support of this contention is contributed by the long list of poems, from the very earliest to the latest of Tennyson's career, which in one way or another make use of dreams. During his formative period the traditional type of the dream-allegory strongly attracted the poet. *A Dream of Fair Women*, *The Day-Dream*, and *The Vision of Sin* are all ambitious experiments in this genre. Of these the last is the most successful and the most interesting for a variety of reasons. By representing the fantastic irrelevancies of the dreaming mind and by exploiting the vivid sense impressions which accompany this condition, the poet was able to say things which his audience would hardly have tolerated as undisguised statements of his own perceptions. One can hardly miss the erotic symbolism which plays through the first part of the poem; and the opening of the final section reveals a talent for the macabre which Tennyson too rarely displayed:

> The voice grew faint; there came a further change;
> Once more uprose the mystic mountain-range.
> Below were men and horses pierced with worms,
> And slowly quickening into lower forms;
> By shards and scurf of salt, and scum of dross,
> Old plash of rains, and refuse patch'd with moss.

By the same token the old rake's song in section four is a masterpiece of grotesque and mordant humor of a kind infrequently met in Victorian poetry and almost never in Tennyson's subsequent work:

> You are bones, and what of that?
>   Every face, however full,
> Padded round with flesh and fat,
>   Is but modell'd on a skull.
>
> Death is king, and Vivat Rex!
>   Tread a measure on the stones,
> Madam—if I know your sex
>   From the fashion of your bones.
>
> No, I cannot praise the fire
>   In your eye—nor yet your lip;
> All the more do I admire
>   Joints of cunning workmanship.
>
> Lo! God's likeness—the ground-plan—
>   Neither modell'd, glazed, nor framed:
> Buss me, thou rough sketch of man,
>   Far too naked to be shamed!

Although this kind of allegoric writing was later to fall into abeyance along with the other fanciful forms of the poet's early years, Tennyson's continuing reliance on the mechanism of dreams reveals the spectre of "otherness" which haunted his mind even when he most scrupulously masked its presence. The volume published in 1864 under the title of *Enoch Arden and Other Poems* is often cited as the work most illustrative of the author's final submission to Victorian literary conventions; and the three poems which stand first in this volume have come to seem prime examples of the weakness for complacent moralizing which so often spoiled Tennyson's attempts to treat domestic tragedy in a realistic way. It comes as something of a surprise, therefore, to find introduced into each of these poems an element of the supernatural, which is not only unrealistic, but is also in no way essential to the elucidation of the theme.

In *Enoch Arden* Annie's decision to marry Philip is motivated by her ironically misleading dream of Enoch sitting under a palm-tree, which she construes as meaning that her husband is dead and in heaven. In *Aylmer's Field* Leolin dreams of Edith's death, and on the basis of this evidence commits suicide before confirmation can reach him. The significant thing to observe in both incidents is that the poet makes the motivation of two sufficiently commonplace characters depend on an intuitive faculty which is not really in the nature of either. The principal actors in *Sea Dreams* are equally unremarkable; and the sensational plot in which they are entrapped would hardly hold our interest were it not for the two dreams which suggest, quite in excess of the expressed moral content of the theme, that man's sentient existence is only a reflex of his unconscious being. Tennyson had already shown in the second and third parts of *The Lover's Tale* unusual comprehension of the way in which dreams are shaped by stimuli provided by waking experience. In *Sea Dreams* the visions of the husband and wife are even more closely keyed to setting and situation. The crashing of a wave, the breaking of a glass, a child crying in the night assume momentous proportions in the depths of the sleeping mind. And despite the fact that the poet becomes overly explicit and so destroys the illusion in his anxiety lest the reader misinterpret the moral of the two dreams, the poem is noteworthy as a further example of its author's oblique approach to seemingly conventional material.

Dreams, however, were for Tennyson only one of several related manifestations of the mystery of man's inner being. In studies of minds unhinged by madness the poet found another way of sublimating his concern with the life of the imagination. For insanity has this in common with dream, that it releases the consciousness from active engagement in the affairs of the outer world and turns it inward on itself. Both dream and madness confuse truth and seeming; but whereas dream moves through seeming towards truth, madness reverses the process and becomes, in effect, an avenue of escape from the importunities of reality. Thus, dream usually appears in Tennyson's poetry as a condition in which the individual fulfills inherent needs of his nature; but madness is treated as a disease brought on by overexposure to harsh circumstance and expressing an inability to compensate. Through dreams outer and inner tensions are equalized; madness results from the failure to make any such adjustment.

The Tennysons were, of course, an extremely eccentric family; and the spectacle of erratic and often violent behavior which he had from childhood observed in his close relatives would in itself account for the poet's familiarity with mental aberration. Certainly his poetry shows an acquaintance with symptoms of insanity which is as uncommon in its period as the somewhat similar interest in dream psychology. During the summer of 1840, while he was resident at Beech Hill, Tunbridge Wells, Tennyson formed a friendship with Matthew Allen, who was doctor-in-charge of a neighboring asylum. Allen had gained considerable reputation for his enlightened ways of treating mental patients (one of whom had been the poet, John Clare); and it seems likely that through this association Tennyson had a chance to study abnormal behavior at first hand.

As early as his unpublished poem, *The Outcast*, Tennyson had used madness as a subject. And while there is no question of insanity in *Supposed Confessions of a Second-rate Sensitive Mind* or *The Two Voices*, the suicidal depression of the speakers in both poems suggests a state of neurasthenia bordering on derangement. The same lack of intellectual equilibrium characterizes the central figures in *Mariana* and *Locksley Hall*; and in *Aylmer's Field* actual imbecility is visited on the old baron as punishment for his inflexible pride. In these poems it may be observed that the madness, whether incipient or actual, is not directly the result of any congenital instability of mind so much as an outcome of the pressure of external events which have undermined the characters' powers of resistance.

More revelatory of Tennyson's true intent in exploring the theme of madness is *Maud*, which, despite its lukewarm reception, always remained the author's favorite among his poems. Here the protagonist's insanity is, significantly enough, a trait inherited from his father who had presumably killed himself in a fit of despondency. Throughout the first part of the poem Tennyson shows extreme skill in foreshadowing the dénouement of the second part. In his variability between moods of dejection and exhilaration, in his animosity against the social order counter-balanced by attempts to bolster his self-esteem, in his fascination with concepts of violence, madness, and death, the gathering emotional strain on the hero's temperament is dramatically evoked. Then with the killing of Maud's brother in "the red-ribb'd hollow behind the wood," the shadow, which symbolizes guilt, appears and dogs the murderer overseas and through fits of uncontrolled despair until his mind gives way. In the fifth section of Part Two, which is set in a madhouse, Tennyson shows his ability to deal with the nightmare visions of the disordered intellect. The hallucinations which parade before the speaker gather up and arrange in fantastic but meaningful patterns all the strands of his previous experience. And it is appropriately through the medium of his fevered imagination that the hero finally comprehends the nature of his transgression. Self-knowledge comes as a result of intuitive perception of the meaning of the rose symbol and of the kind of passion which it exemplifies: "It is only flowers, they had no fruits,/ And I almost fear they are not roses, but blood." After this the third part of *Maud*, in which the hero vows himself to further purgation through a life of action in the Crimean War, seems hardly more than a sop to Victorian sentimentalism, though it is to be feared that its inclusion is one more indication of the poet's readiness to let his notion of the poet's public rôle usurp the place of artistic sensibility.

In *Lucretius* madness becomes the agency for dramatizing not only the life of the imagination, but also the tragic reprisals enacted on the rational mind. There is unmistakable irony in Tennyson's choice of Lucretius to formulate his theme; for the champion of philosophic materialism might be supposed the least likely of all persons to fall victim to fanciful delusions. Driven frantic by his wife's philtre, Lucretius experiences three dreams, each of which calls for close interpretation. The first is a monstrous version of his own system, showing an atomistic universe in a chaotic state of flux. Here is symbolized the loss of control over the workings of the intellect. The second dream, which solicits the philosopher's senses through an orgiastic vision of Hetairai, "hired animalisms," represents the revenge of the flesh on one who had always minimized its claims. Lucretius then dreams of the naked loveliness of Helen of Troy, who stands for artistic beauty. The sword in this image is presumably the power of cold reason which threatens but is unable to subdue the aesthetic sense. In the lucidity of awakening Lucretius endeavors by rational methods to accommodate the meaning of these dreams within the limitations of the philosophy to which he has devoted his life. He fights a rear-guard action, retreating from one hard-won position to another and drawing ever closer to the despairing choice between confessed defeat and suicide. To Aphrodite as instigator of sexual license he opposes the more abstract concept of the goddess in her guise of Venus Genetrix. But his accustomed view of the gods as elevated beings, enjoying the "sacred everlasting calm" to which he aspires, is shot through with doubts as to whether the laws of nature are after all compatible with a celestial order. And even granting the existence of the gods, does not their very remoteness from human concerns leave the individual alone responsible for his fate? In defense of suicide, Lucretius considers the vicissitudes which render life intolerable; and he concludes, recalling the sensual riot of his dreams, that the "worst disease of all" is

> These prodigies of myriad nakednesses,
> And twisted shapes of lust, unspeakable,
> Abominable, strangers at my hearth
> Not welcome, harpies miring every dish,
> The phantom husks of something foully done,
> And fleeting thro' the boundless universe,
> And blasting the long quiet of my breast
> With animal heat and dire insanity.

For reassurance Lucretius turns to Nature whom in her aspect as lawgiver he has always worshipped, only to realize that she condones the excesses to which he is now tempted. He beholds with fascinated loathing a classical vision of lust triumphant—the rape of an Oread by a satyr. At first his sympathy goes out to the Oread as she flees her brutish pursuer, though the terms used to describe the nymph are significant of ulterior perceptions. There follow in quick succession moods of revulsion when the creature seems about to fling herself on him, and of relief when she is captured instead. At this point a sickening revelation of his interest in the scene is vouchsafed to Lucretius:

> Hide, hide them, million-myrtled wilderness,
> And cavern-shading laurels, hide! do I wish—
> What?—that the bush were leafless? or to whelm
> All of them in one massacre?

In vain he tries to disprove the conjurings of his heated imagination by calling on philosophy to show that the satyr is outside the natural order of being: "Twy-natured is no nature." This latest vision, coming on top of the preceding dreams, has opened his eyes all too clearly to the double nature of man. Self-recognition destroys for Lucretius the hope of ever recovering "the sober majesties/ Of settled, sweet, Epicurean life"; for

> now it seems some unseen monster lays
> His vast and filthy hands upon my will,
> Wrenching it backward into his, and spoils
> My bliss in being . . .

On the surface of this poem lies a moral teaching such as the age had come to expect from the author of *In Memoriam*: namely, that the unaided reason is not in itself strong or sure enough to discipline man's sensual nature.* In addition to its explicitly didactic purpose, however, *Lucretius* gives important bearings on Tennyson's aesthetic position at the most influential period in his career. The self-loathing which comes over the philosopher as a result of his madness, with its accompanying dreams and visions, destroys his confidence in his creative powers. Lucilia's potion has had a twofold effect:

> . . . for the wicked broth
> Confused the chemic labor of the blood,
> And tickling the brute brain within the man's
> Made havoc among those tender cells, and check'd
> His power to shape.

Hitherto it is for his writing that he has lived:

---

* Tennyson habitually uses animal imagery to suggest both the fierceness and the degradation of man's physical appetites. In *Saint Simeon Stylites* and *The Vision of Sin* the hallucinations following on loss of intellectual control torment the speakers with obscene visions, primarily bestial in nature. And throughout *In Memoriam* the poet's appeal to the evolutionary hypothesis calls up images expressive of the baser and more primitive passions:

> Arise and fly
> The reeling Faun, the sensual-feast;
> Move upward, working out the beast,
> And let the ape and tiger die.

See also the fifty-sixth and one hundred and twentieth lyrics of *In Memoriam*.

> For save when shutting reasons up in rhythm,
> Or Heliconian honey in living words,
> To make a truth less harsh, I often grew
> Tired of so much within our little life,
> Or of so little in our little life—

The thought of leaving his poem uncompleted at first dissuades Lucretius from suicide: "and if I go *my* work is left/ Unfinish'd." And even when the decision to kill himself is finally taken, there remains the consolation that his masterpiece will survive and be of benefit as long as there are men to read it:

> . . . till that hour,
> My golden work in which I told a truth
> That stays the rolling Ixionian wheel,
> And numbs the Fury's ringlet-snake, and plucks
> The mortal soul from out immortal hell,
> Shall stand.

Since he holds this faith in the validity of his creative impulse, why does Lucretius take self-extinction as the best way out of his situation? The answer to this question leads back to the problem posed by Tennyson in *Supposed Confessions of a Second-rate Sensitive Mind* and *The Two Voices*. Lucretius' madness is a metaphor for the mood of introspective depression which throughout his life harried Tennyson's attempts to fix his faith, but which he tried increasingly to sublimate in his poetry. Furthermore, the daring dreams and visions which emerge from Lucretius' inner consciousness had, as we have seen, their counterpart in the poet's own imagination. It follows, then, that Lucretius' despairing recognition of the incommensurable elements in his nature reflects the dilemma which Tennyson himself faced in presenting a view of human experience which would legitimatize his assumed function as Victorian sage and at the same time be faithful to his intuitive perceptions. Insofar as the poem represents the vagrant imagination in conflict with a settled system of philosophic thought, it illustrates the author's double awareness and the tensions resulting therefrom.

In the seventy-first poem of *In Memoriam* a third plane of irrational consciousness is, by implication, brought into relation with dream and madness: "Sleep, kinsman thou to death and trance/ And madness." Trance, as used here, denotes a form of mystical experience equivalent to the traditional concept of the visionary power as a faculty of the poetic imagination. It is like dream in that it annihilates any logical ideas of time or space or the interrelations between cause and effect. It is normally, however, a waking condition of the mind, and in this way akin to mental derangement. Reference was made in the opening of this chapter to Tennyson's recurrent fits of abstraction when he passed into a trance-like state and lost all sense of individual identity. Indeed, he seems on occasion to have been able to induce such "day-dreams." On one occasion he wrote: "A kind of waking trance I have frequently had, quite up from boyhood, when I have been all alone. This has generally come upon me thro' repeating my own name two or three times to myself silently, till all at once, as it were, out of the intensity of the consciousness of individuality, the individuality itself seemed to dissolve and fade away into boundless being, and this is not a confused state, but the clearest of the clearest, the surest of the surest, the weirdest of the weirdest, utterly beyond words, where death was an almost laughable impossibility, the loss of personality (if so it were) seeming no extinction but the only true life." In this connection it is perhaps significant that Tennyson discovered hypnotic powers in himself and successfully experimented with mesmerism.

As with sleeping dreams, therefore, Tennyson frequently introduces the vision or trance into his poetry for the purpose of suggesting an enlargement of experience beyond the more immediate implications of the matter in hand. But the same hesitancy to repose full confidence in extrasensory perceptions that we remarked in the poet's attitude towards dreams is also present in his treatment of visions. How could one be sure whether the revelation was a legitimate vision carrying supernatural authority, or whether it was not merely a self-imposed and superstitious delusion? For the fact that

Tennyson's senses played phantasmagoric tricks on him there is biographical evidence. His grandson tells how the poet would draw "the curious things which he said he often saw in the fire in the small hours of the morning—strange grim forms, half beast, half human." We are also told that in the highly nervous condition brought on by Charles Tennyson's death, the poet heard "perpetual ghostly voices."

In his poetry, however, such experiences, while described with extreme clarity, usually go with the workings of diseased imaginations. The fearsome hallucinations of the soul in *The Palace of Art* and of Saint Simeon Stylites are motivated in this way. On the other hand, the ultimate revelation that spirit is immortal comes to the poet of *In Memoriam* in a moment of trance-like exaltation quite obviously allied with true mystic vision. The ninety-fifth poem of the elegy describes how the poet was suddenly transfixed by a blinding apprehension of Hallam's presence, in comparison with which the testimony of the dream in the seventieth poem seems shadowy and inconclusive. The poet had lingered out-of-doors into the twilight. Left to himself, he was rereading his friend's letters when the illumination enveloped him:

> So word by word, and line by line,
>   The dead man touch'd me from the past,
>   And all at once it seem'd at last
> The living soul was flash'd on mine,
>
> And mine in this was wound, and whirl'd
>   About empyreal heights of thought,
>   And came on that which is, and caught
> The deep pulsations of the world,
>
> Æonian music measuring out
>   The steps of Time—the shocks of Chance—
>   The blows of Death.

And even though in the immediate aftermath the "trance/ Was cancell'd, stricken thro' with doubt," the more hopeful tone of the following lyrics leaves no doubt that for Tennyson this moment of insight was climactic and prepared the way for his subsequent attainment of religious faith. In passing, it is perhaps worthy of surmise whether, in greeting *In Memoriam* as an authoritative rebuttal to the modern spirit of scientific scepticism, the Victorian age ever seriously examined the nature of the evidence on which the laureate had erected his case. Certainly Tennyson's argument derives from a kind of imaginative awareness which his contemporaries had shown themselves little disposed to condone in his earlier poetry, and which in its implications could not but run counter to the dominant materialism of the times.

Although the psychological complexity of the vision tended to limit its poetic uses, as compared, for instance, with the devices of dream and madness, Tennyson often employed it for the purpose of opening up unexpected and disquieting perspectives through conventional material. A prophetic trance enables the protagonist of *Locksley Hall* to look into the future; and it is as the result of a similar visitation that the poet of *The Golden Year* celebrates his faith in the Victorian ideal of progress. More revealing in the present connection are the "weird seizures" under which the hero of *The Princess* suffers. They were not incorporated into the poem until the fourth edition, published in 1851; and since these additions are inappropriate either to the Prince's character or to the action and general tone of the poem, there has ever since been controversy about Tennyson's motives for including them. The initial lines describing the symptoms of these attacks show once more the poet's obsession with the enigma of appearance and reality as a central problem of knowledge. The Prince is speaking:

> There lived an ancient legend in our house.
> Some sorcerer, whom a far-off grandsire burnt
> Because he cast no shadow, had foretold,
> Dying, that none of all our blood should know
> The shadow from the substance, and that one
> Should come to fight with shadows and to fall;
> For so, my mother said, the story ran.
> And, truly, waking dreams were, more or less,

> An old and strange affection of the house.
> Myself too had weird seizures, Heaven knows what!
> On a sudden in the midst of men and day,
> And while I walk'd and talk'd as heretofore,
> I seem'd to move among a world of ghosts,
> And feel myself the shadow of a dream.

Three times the Prince undergoes these dream-like trances, in which "all things were and were not," while

> As in some mystic middle state I lay.
> Seeing I saw not, hearing not I heard...

Finally the trial of the tourney restores him to normalcy and allows him to accomplish his manhood through selfless union with the Princess Ida, herself regenerate.

Equally arbitrary is the faculty of second sight ascribed to Enoch Arden on his desert island:

> There often as he watch'd or seem'd to watch,
> So still the golden lizard on him paused,
> A phantom made of many phantoms moved
> Before him haunting him, or he himself
> Moved haunting people, things, and places, known
> Far in a darker isle beyond the line...

This sixth sense, released through isolation, informs Enoch that Annie has accepted Philip. Thereby the story gains a certain element of pathos; but we feel, nevertheless, that Enoch has been made a vehicle for conveying the author's own preoccupation with the spirit world.

Dream, madness, and vision are all essentially internal conditions of being. The mind regards itself; it is, so to speak, bemused by self-consciousness, and inhibited from translating its insights into action. Lucretius' suicide is the ultimate negation of the active life; and to a lesser extent all the vision-haunted characters in Tennyson's poetry exhibit a centripetal movement in their psychological processes. Their perceptions spin inward, isolating the core of consciousness from involvement in the outside world. Yet Tennyson was too much man of his time to put the life of contemplation above the life of doing; and in consequence we find in his poetry a fourth form of release, having its origin, like dream, madness, and vision, in the imagination, but, unlike the other three, more immediately productive of external consequences. When the poet undertakes to activate the mind's inner awareness, his characteristic method is the quest.

Again *The Two Voices* is the proving ground for a thematic device which was later to be elaborated. Recognizing man's native idealism, the voice of doubt derides the perennial search for intangible and unattainable truths. In reply the poet confesses ignorance of his goal, but finds reasons for optimism in the fact that there does after all exist in human nature an instinctual compulsion to fulfill itself through pursuing some sort of ideal. The language of the following passage is that of the spiritual pilgrim:

> I cannot hide that some have striven,
> Achieving calm, to whom was given
> The joy that mixes man with Heaven;
>
> Who, rowing hard against the stream,
> Saw distant gates of Eden gleam,
> And did not dream it was a dream;
>
> But heard, by secret transport led,
> Even in the charnels of the dead,
> The murmur of the fountain-head—
>
> Which did accomplish their desire,
> Bore and forebore, and did not tire,
> Like Stephen, an unquenched fire.

Tennyson was not to sound the full imaginative implications of the quest until late in his career; but his early poetry makes sufficient use of this motif to enable the reader to identify those aspects which principally commended it to the poet. The summons to the quest usually takes the form of a visionary flash of illumination, experienced most often while the recipient is in a state of trance-like exhilaration, though it may be vouchsafed through dream or even madness.

Thus, the hero of *The Princess* is started on his search for Ida by a voice mingling with the wind in the wild woods and announcing: "Follow, follow, thou shalt win." But success in the quest is incidental to the faith which motivates it. The prince's wanderings in *The Day-Dream*, Tennyson's version of the legend of the sleeping beauty, are thus described:

> He comes, scarce knowing what he seeks;
>   He breaks the hedge; he enters there;
> The color flies into his cheeks;
>   He trusts to light on something fair;
> For all his life the charm did talk
>   About his path, and hover near
> With words of promise in his walk,
>   And whisper'd voices at his ear.

Finally, although the quest involves its devotees in a life of strenuous activity, frequently productive of good to mankind, its true purpose is individual self-realization; and to this extent it is anti-social. Sir Galahad in the poem of that name succors distress wherever he encounters it; but his pursuit of the Grail is a lonely and entirely personal trial which requires the sacrifice of all worldly ties and communal pleasures.

All these elements are exemplified in two poems explicitly concerned with the quest: *Ulysses*, published in 1842 but written in the time of most intense grief over Hallam's death; and *The Voyage*, which appeared in the *Enoch Arden* volume of 1864. For Ulysses the whole purpose of life is the search for experience beyond the limits of proven achievement:

> Yet all experience is an arch wherethro'
> Gleams that untravell'd world whose margin fades
> For ever and for ever when I move.

The hero is an old man; but the gleam still beckons from beyond the horizon:

> And this gray spirit yearning in desire
> To follow knowledge like a sinking star,
> Beyond the utmost bound of human thought.

This poem is often taken as expressing a point of view directly contradictory to that embodied in *The Lotos-Eaters*. Actually the defeatism of *Tithonus* forms a more effective contrast; for Ulysses' final decision to give himself to a private vision is merely the counterpart in terms of action of the more passive self-obsession of the lotos-eaters. Furthermore, to read *Ulysses* as an intentional tribute to those solid public virtues most admired by the Victorians is wholly to misinterpret the author's central purpose. In setting out on further wanderings which have no clearly foreseen objective, the Greek hero is not restrained by any conventional scruples of duty either to his family or the people he rules. The character of Telemachus, as somewhat contemptuously alluded to, approximates much more closely the Victorian model of patriotic and domestic behavior. And the vaunted qualities of mind which will support Ulysses and his followers in their quest, the strength of "will/ To strive, to seek, to find, and not to yield," are here made to subserve a line of conduct which cannot be justified in any but the most individualistic terms.

The Voyage may be said to take up where *Ulysses* leaves off. The quest is its own *raison d'être*; and the chosen band which mans the ship is blithely indifferent to social responsibilities. The one sceptic in the crew, unable to maintain throughout a lifetime the self-sufficiency of his shipmates, commits suicide. If his death is a comment on the fate Tennyson conceived for Lucretius, then the perseverance of the others celebrates the dominance of mystic inward strength that supports the human spirit through the tribulations of earthly existence. And here it may be noted for future analysis that in his concept of the quest Tennyson was working towards a fusion of philosophy and aesthetics which would harmonize in a higher synthesis his underlying sense of alienation from Victorian society on the one hand and, on the other, his reluctance to give exclusive credit to the promptings of the artist's inner consciousness. For the dedicated seekers of *The Voyage* refuse to be stayed either by the sober household values of the North, or by the sensual exoticism of the East:

> At times a carven craft would shoot
>   From havens hid in fairy bowers,
> With naked limbs and flowers and fruit,
>   But we nor paused for fruit nor flowers.

The mysterious gleam which leads the ship on its endless quest has instilled in each member of the crew immaculate devotion to his individual vision:

> For one fair Vision ever fled
>   Down the waste waters day and night,
> And still we follow'd where she led,
>   In hope to gain upon her flight.
> Her face was evermore unseen,
>   And fixt upon the far sea-line;
> But each man murmur'd, 'O my Queen,
>   I follow till I make thee mine.'

Considered separately, the devices of dream, madness, vision, and the quest might not perhaps seem to furnish conclusive evidence of the operation of private insights within poems ostensibly addressed to a Victorian audience. When these motifs are taken together, however, it will be found that in one or another combination they characterize a neglected aspect of Tennyson's genius which is all-important to an adequate comprehension of his poetry. The truth of this statement may be tested by an examination of the *Idylls of the King*, the major creative effort of the poet's career, and one which occupied his thoughts for about fifty years from the first version of the *Morte d'Arthur*, written as early as 1835, to the publication in 1885 of *Balin and Balan*, the last of the Idylls. To the great majority of Victorian readers this work came to seem an heroic tribute to the values on which their society prided itself. Yet the modern reader may well be sensitive to overtones in the Idylls suggestive rather of the author's interior imaginative resources than of uncritical commitment to the manners and morals of the age.

To be sure, the Epilogue, addressed to Victoria, makes an overt appeal to the moralistic temper of the times. The Queen is asked to

> accept this old imperfect tale,
> New-old, and shadowing Sense at war with Soul,
> Ideal manhood closed in real man,
> Rather than that gray king whose name, a ghost,
> Streams like a cloud, man-shaped, from mountain peak,
> And cleaves to cairn and cromlech still . . .

And, indeed, when read, as is too often the case, on its most accessible level of interest, the *Idylls of the King* has something of the quality of a relic of Victorian sanctimony, redolent of habits of mind which the twentieth century does not share. In the conventional view the focal figure in the poem is an idealized ruler, composite of the moral earnestness of Hallam and the exemplary hearthside virtues of the Prince Consort. The adulterous passion of the Queen and Lancelot then becomes the principal agency for the downfall of Arthur's chivalric order, with each successive Idyll falling into place as a portrayal of the pernicious spread of the blight emanating from this pair. Marital disharmony (*The Marriage of Geraint* and *Geraint and Enid*), fratricide (*Balin and Balan*), overthrow of reason (*Merlin and Vivien*), misprision of innocence (*Lancelot and Elaine*), betrayal of faith (*Pelleas and Ettarre*)—through the perversion of the ideals on which it was founded a social order decays until in the last Idylls we witness its ultimate dissolution into chaos. The fact that the poem is so admirably shaped towards the exemplification of this theme certainly indicates that Tennyson wanted to invite just such a reading; and with this interpretation of the Idylls there is here no wish to quarrel. A modern audience, however, may be attracted to certain aspects of the poem's theme which are less conventional in their implications—may even be allowed to suspect that these aspects were the ones which most fully engaged Tennyson's own imagination.

There is no ignoring the sombre and doom-ridden atmosphere which from the very outset hovers over the *Idylls of the King.** This is *Götterdämmerung*. Of the ten poems

---

* The Idylls are here discussed in the order in which Tennyson finally arranged them. If, as seems certain, the over-all pattern of

entitled *The Round Table*, only the first, *Gareth and Lynette*, shows Arthur's knighthood in anything like its pristine health and vigor; and significantly, Gareth is very young, very naïf, and entirely new to the ways of the fellowship. With the two Idylls relating to Geraint and Enid the shadow of Guinevere's transgression begins to fall across the exploits of the knights, and it lengthens until all is dark. Much later, after she has fled from Camelot, the Queen dreams

> An awful dream, for then she seem'd to stand
> On some vast plain before a setting sun,
> And from the sun there swiftly made at her
> A ghastly something, and its shadow flew
> Before it till it touch'd her, and she turn'd—
> When lo! her own, that broadening from her feet,
> And blackening, swallow'd all the land, and in it
> Far cities burnt . . .

But the shadows that flit over Arthur's kingdom do not originate with the Queen's guilt; they were there from the first, lending an air of ambiguity to everything that happened. Tennyson shows great skill in establishing a tone of unreality. The very legitimacy of Arthur's title to the kingship is shrouded in dubiety. In *The Coming of Arthur* Bellicent bases her testimony on the vision which Bleys and Merlin saw; and final confirmation comes to Leodogran in the form of a misty dream. Thereafter, the reader first beholds Camelot through the eyes of Gareth and his companions. It seems a kind of Palace of Art, and the poet deliberately leaves in question whether it is real or existent only in the enchanted realm of the imagination:

> So, when their feet were planted on the plain
> That broaden'd toward the base of Camelot,
> Far off they saw the silver-misty morn

---

the poem did not clarify itself in the poet's mind until after he had made a considerable amount of progress, then we may likewise assume that the sections latest in actual date of composition were written for the purpose of supplying lacunae in the narrative or strengthening certain aspects of the theme which had come to seem important.

Rolling her smoke about the royal mount,
That rose between the forest and the field.
At times the summit of the high city flash'd;
At times the spires and turrets half-way down
Prick'd thro' the mist; at times the great gate shone
Only, that open'd on the field below;
Anon, the whole fair city had disappear'd.

   Then those who went with Gareth were amazed,
One crying, 'Let us go no further, lord;
Here is a city of enchanters, built
By fairy kings.' The second echo'd him,
'Lord, we have heard from our wise man at home
To northward, that this king is not the King,
But only changeling out of Fairyland,
Who drave the heathen hence by sorcery
And Merlin's glamour.' Then the first again,
'Lord, there is no such city anywhere,
But all a vision.'

Throughout the following Idylls the atmosphere thickens until, as though, in Merlin's words, man's passage were veritably from the great deep to the great deep and all in between a dream, the concluding actions are almost lost in obscurity. There is, for example, the strange immateriality of Guinevere's parting sight of the King:

>   . . . so she did not see the face,
>Which then was as an angel's, but she saw,
>Wet with the mists and smitten by the lights,
>The Dragon of the great Pendragonship
>Blaze, making all the night a steam of fire.
>And even then he turn'd; and more and more
>The moony vapor rolling round the King,
>Who seem'd the phantom of a giant in it,
>Enwound him fold by fold, and made him gray
>And grayer, till himself became as mist
>Before her, moving ghostlike to his doom.

And finally, there is the description of Arthur's last battle fought in a haunted mist so dense as to obliterate all distinction between the real and unreal:

> Nor ever yet had Arthur fought a fight
> Like this last, dim, weird battle of the west.
> A death-white mist slept over sand and sea,
> Whereof the chill, to him who breathed it, drew
> Down with his blood, till all his heart was cold
> With formless fear; and even on Arthur fell
> Confusion, since he saw not whom he fought.
> For friend and foe were shadows in the mist,
> And friend slew friend not knowing whom he slew;
> And some had visions out of golden youth,
> And some beheld the faces of old ghosts
> Look in upon the battle; and in the mist
> Was many a noble deed, many a base,
> And chance and craft and strength in single fights,
> And ever and anon with host to host
> Shocks, and the splintering spear, the hard mail hewn,
> Shield-breakings, and the clash of brands, the crash
> Of battle-axes on shatter'd helms, and shrieks
> After the Christ, of those who falling down
> Look'd up for heaven, and only saw the mist;
> And shouts of heathen and the traitor knights,
> Oaths, insult, filth, and monstrous blasphemies,
> Sweat, writhings, anguish, laboring of the lungs
> In that close mist, and cryings for the light,
> Moans of the dying, and voices of the dead.

Thus insisted on, mist and shadow become symbols of the misgivings which assail the knights vowed to the fulfillment of Arthur's vision. Addressing the seer, Gareth expresses the bewilderment of his followers, and perhaps his own:

> ... these, my men,—
> Your city moved so weirdly in the mist—
> Doubt if the King be king at all, or come

> From Fairyland; and whether this be built
> By magic, and by fairy kings and queens;
> Or whether there be any city at all,
> Or all a vision . . .

To which Merlin replies:

> And here is truth, but an it please thee not,
> Take thou the truth as thou hast told it me. . . .
> For there is nothing in it as it seems
> Saving the King; tho' some there be that hold
> The King a shadow, and the city real.
> Yet take thou heed of him, for, so thou pass
> Beneath this archway, then wilt thou become
> A thrall to his enchantments, for the King
> Will bind thee by such vows as is a shame
> A man should not be bound by, yet the which
> No man can keep; but, so thou dread to swear,
> Pass not beneath this gateway, but abide
> Without, among the cattle of the field.
> For an ye heard a music, like enow
> They are building still, seeing the city is built
> To music, therefore never built at all,
> And therefore built for ever.

To Balin, self-distrustful because of his madness, the rigors of the King's service seems too severe:

> Too high this mount of Camelot for me;
> These high-set courtesies are not for me.
> Shall I not rather prove the worse for these?

And the betrayed Pelleas raves: "we be all alike; only the King/ Hath made us fools and liars." Later Dagonet, the King's jester, jeers at Arthur in bitterness of spirit over the decline of the Round Table:

> . . . the king of fools!
> Conceits himself as God that he can make
> Figs out of thistles, silk from bristles, milk
> From burning spurge, honey from hornet-combs,
> And men from beasts—Long live the king of fools!

In the end, after the disintegration of all he has stood for, even Arthur gives way to self-doubt:

> Hearest thou this great voice that shakes the world,
> And wastes the narrow realm whereon we move,
> And beats upon the faces of the dead,
> My dead, as tho' they had not died for me?—
> O Bedivere, for on my heart hath fallen
> Confusion, till I know not what I am,
> Nor whence I am, nor whether I be king;
> Behold, I seem but king among the dead.

In their confusing of the ideal and the actual, the principal actors in the *Idylls of the King* lead a sort of double life. An ulterior meaning shadows their actions. They exist not only in the outer world of positive achievement, but also in an interior world of conflicting motives. It is the interaction between the two realms of consciousness which gives the poem its strange quality of intensity. Every action has its imaginative counterpart through the instrumentality of dream, madness, vision, and the quest. A list of the characters whose dreams, too numerous to catalogue, interpret critical passages in the Idylls would include: Leodogran, Enid, Lancelot, Elaine, Pelleas, Tristram, Guinevere, and Arthur. Inner stress induces madness in Balin and Pelleas, as well as Lancelot. In addition to the supernatural portents which attend the King's coming and passing, the vision of the Holy Grail, the phantom cup that comes and goes, is revealed with varying degrees of clarity to many of Arthur's knights. And the quest for the Grail is, of course, the very hallmark of fealty to the life of the imagination.

If a review of the Idylls be now undertaken with the foregoing observations in mind, there will be seen to emerge through the moral veneer which gave the poem its immediate appeal to the Victorian age a second and profounder theme. This theme, more consonant with Tennyson's habits of mind, reflects the under side of the author's twofold awareness, the side which faced away from society and towards his individual being as a creative artist. For it was in the depths of his own consciousness that Tennyson had finally to confront and struggle with the problem of appearance and reality which remorselessly obsessed his imagination. It is only when regarded in the light of this conflict that the full meaning of the *Idylls of the King* becomes manifest.

The poet hints at his intent as early as the opening lines to *Geraint and Enid*, where he departs from his usual practice in the Idylls and steps in front of the curtain:

> O purblind race of miserable men,
> How many among us at this very hour
> Do forge a lifelong trouble for ourselves,
> By taking true for false, or false for true;
> Here, thro' the feeble twilight of this world
> Groping, how many, until we pass and reach
> That other where we see as we are seen!

The initiating situation in this Idyll is Geraint's unfounded suspicion of his wife's fidelity, which grows out of her intimacy with Guinevere. Geraint, jealous by nature, is unwilling to believe in his own good fortune. His distrust is played off against the cynicism of Earl Doorm, the first of many characters in the Idylls wholly possessed by sensuality. Doorm tempts Enid with food, drink, and finally with fine raiment. Her rejection of the latter brings into play the theme of shadow and substance on which Tennyson was to work so many variations in the subsequent poems. For Enid's choice recalls not only the bedraggled condition in which Geraint first found her, but also the dream relating to her appearance at court, her actual presentation to Guinevere, and the Queen's gift of clothing.

A more tragic version of this conflict occurs in *Balin and Balan* which comes next after the Geraint and Enid story in the final ordering of the Idylls, although, significantly, it was the last of all to be written. The structure of this poem adroitly reinforces the irony of the central situation. Balin becomes Guinevere's knight as a means of averting further attacks of insanity; yet it is the disillusionment resultant on what Sir Garlon and Vivien tell him about the Queen's clandestine life that plunges him back into his final fatal derangement. In granting Balin permission to carry the Queen's device on his shield, Arthur says:

> Thou shalt put the crown to use.
> The crown is but the shadow of the king,
> And this a shadow's shadow, let him have it,
> So this will help him of his violences!

Subsequently, Balin's frantic flight from the court takes place after he has overheard Lancelot and Guinevere talking together. To Lancelot's account of his symbolic dream of the lily, token of innocence, the Queen opposes her waking choice of the rose, flower of physical passion. But it is Vivien whose cynical estimate of the Round Table finally opens Balin's eyes to the maddening actuality of his situation. Vivien (along with Gawain) is the clear-sighted advocate of the life of sensation in the *Idylls of the King*; and, as such, she symbolizes the materialistic threat which Earl Doorm and his kind offer to Arthur's order. This is the significance of her animistic hymn to the sun and its accompanying remark:

> This fire of heaven,
> The old sun-worship, boy, will rise again,
> And beat the Cross to earth, and break the King
> And all his Table.

The next Idyll, as its title, *Merlin and Vivien*, indicates, carries on the pattern of bringing into opposition two characters, one representing the inner integrity of spiritual being, the other the corrupting powers of the world. Vivien exerts the wiles of the flesh, not this time against the holy fanaticism of Arthur's knighthood, but against the authority of the intellect as vested in Merlin. The ensuing narrative presents interesting affinities with *Lucretius*; for both poems illustrate Tennyson's distrust of reason when it is not supported by some form of transcendental faith. Merlin knows that he cannot avert the fate which impends over Camelot. In deep despondency he has decided to withdraw from the court. The lines descriptive of his mental state Tennyson did not add until 1873, fourteen years after the first publication of *Merlin and Vivien* (at that time entitled simply *Vivien*), and furthermore, after the appearance of four Idylls concerned with later stages of the story:

> Then fell on Merlin a great melancholy;
> He walk'd with dreams and darkness, and he found
> A doom that ever poised itself to fall,
> An ever-moaning battle in the mist,
> World-war of dying flesh against the life,
> Death in all life and lying in all love,
> The meanest having power upon the highest,
> And the high purpose broken by the worm.

The symbol of Merlin's power is the spell bequeathed by a forgotten seer who had practised self-denial until

> to him the wall
> That sunders ghosts and shadow-casting men
> Became a crystal, and he saw them thro' it,
> And heard their voices talk behind the wall,
> And learnt their elemental secrets, powers
> And forces.

The victim of this spell loses all capacity to move and all sense of time, and is condemned forever to behold only that person who has enchanted him. In the apathy born of the realization that the Round Table cannot be preserved by wisdom of the mind, Merlin yields to the fascination of the arch-realist Vivien with her mocking comment: "Man dreams of fame while woman wakes to love." So the power lodged in the spell passes into her hands; and Merlin's bondage becomes a token of the failure of Arthur's ideal in its intellectual aspect.

Lancelot and Elaine is, of course, a reworking of *The Lady of Shalott* within a much wider context. Like the lady of the earlier poem, Elaine "lived in fantasy." The life of the imagination was her essential being; to shatter it would be to destroy her. As with the Lady of Shalott also, the symbol of Elaine's inner existence is a work of art, the case that she has embroidered for Lancelot's shield. Which is the more real, the battle-scarred shield emblematic of Lancelot's exploits in the great world beyond Astolat, or its fragile covering? Here Tennyson's use of detail is especially subtle. Elaine is awakened each morning by the *gleam* of the shield. She fashions its covering "fearing rust or soilure." To a truthful depiction of "all the devices blazon'd on the shield" she

> added, of her wit,
> A border fantasy of branch and flower,
> And yellow-throated nestling in the nest.

After Lancelot has returned to claim his shield, Elaine, like Mariana, lives on in her tower. Since her life depends on the delusion, she insists that it is her "glory to have loved/ One peerless, without stain."

The diamonds for which Lancelot is fighting operate symbolically against the main line of the story. Apparently so tangible and of such lasting beauty, they are no sooner found than lost; and possession of them is as unhappy as it is brief. Note the circumstances under which Arthur discovered the crown of the slain king:

> And Arthur came, and laboring up the pass,
> All in a misty moonshine, unawares
> Had trodden that crown'd skeleton, and the skull
> Brake from the nape, and from the skull the crown
> Roll'd into light, and turning on its rims
> Fled like a glittering rivulet to the tarn.
> And down the shingly scaur he plunged, and caught,
> And set it on his head, and in his heart
> Heard murmurs, 'Lo, thou likewise shalt be king.'

In Elaine's dream, as her brother narrates it to Lancelot, there is no holding onto the precious stone:

> . . . for, knight, the maiden dreamt
> That some one put this diamond in her hand,
> And that it was too slippery to be held,
> And slipt and fell into some pool or stream. . .

A dream strangely premonitory of the fact. For Guinevere in her jealous fury is to cast Lancelot's trophy of nine years' combat into the river at Camelot at precisely the moment when

> slowly past the barge
> Whereon the lily maid of Astolat
> Lay smiling, like a star in blackest night.

Among the Idylls *The Holy Grail* not only marks the turning point in the history of the Round Table, but also calls forth the author's deepest speculations on the nature of appearance and reality. The beauty of the poetry does not permit us to question the vision in which the Grail appears to Percivale's saintly sister; but there is something suspect in the knights' eagerness to dedicate themselves to the quest. Lancelot's motive is suggestive of the sensation-seeking of a declining order. Hitherto, his sense of guilt has inflicted intermittent spells of madness; now, intoxicated by the hope of purging his conscience, he undertakes the search as an individual enterprise. Certainly in Arthur's view the quest is a form of self-deluding lunacy for all but the chosen few. It represents an over-indulgence of man's spiritual nature as harmful in its way as the sensuality for which Vivien stands. In sadness of heart he predicts that his knighthood will "follow wandering fires/ Lost in the quagmire!" Guinevere's reaction is equally perceptive: "This madness has come on us for our sins."

Tennyson selects five knights whose experiences exemplify the ambiguity of the quest, though we are told that: "All men, to one so bound by such a vow,/ And women were as phantoms." Galahad and Gawain occupy the extreme positions. For the former the quest is the only reality and leads to beatification; for the latter it is a will-o'-the-wisp from which he soon turns back to earthly pleasures. Lancelot's way ends in frustration after exposing him to madness more humiliating than any he has yet known. Sir Bors' steadfast perseverance brings the desired vision, but his heart is never in the search. For him the brotherhood of the Round Table takes precedence over self-fulfillment. On his return to Camelot he refuses to speak of his experience, but goes straight to Lancelot and grasps his hand. Sir Percivale is the narrator and his adventure is most illuminating of all. Setting forth alone, he finds himself "thirsting in a land of sand and thorns," where all the pleasant things of this world turn to dust at his approach. At last under Galahad's guidance he consummates the quest; but in after years the episode which lingers in his memory is curiously at variance with the ordeal as a whole. For he recalls how he found his first love and longed to remain with her until he

> remember'd Arthur's warning word,
> That most of us would follow wandering fires,
> And the quest faded in my heart.

And even though he went on again in the wake of the vision, there is remarkably little solace in the recollection of temptation resisted:

> ... but one night my vow
> Burnt me within, so that I rose and fled,
> But wail'd and wept, and hated mine own self,
> And even the holy quest, and all but her...

To which his marveling auditor, the monk Ambrosius, adds a chorus-like comment from the point of view of those who, like himself, "want the warmth of double life," and "are plagued with dreams of something sweet/ Beyond all sweetness in a life so rich."

It is Arthur, however, who out of his weariness and sadness places the final evaluation on the quest for the Grail, recognizing in it a portent of the fading of his ideal of the perfect society. He confesses that he too is prone to visions such as dematerialize the phenomenal world. But such dreams, he says, do not belong to human life on earth, since they relate to a higher order of reality. Once man's work is done, however:

> Let visions of the night or of the day
> Come as they will; and many a time they come,

Until this earth he walks on seems not earth,
This light that strikes his eyeball is not light,
This air that smites his forehead is not air
But vision—yea, his very hand and foot—
In moments when he feels he cannot die,
And knows himself no vision to himself,
Nor the high God a vision, nor that One
Who rose again.*

After the quest for the Grail, the scene darkens rapidly, while the Round Table enters on the final stages of decline. *Pelleas and Ettarre* is a bitter companion piece to *Lancelot and Elaine*. By choosing a life of fantasy, and later death, Elaine retained her innocence; the actuality thrust on Pelleas destroys his innocence and reason together. For unlike Balin and Lancelot, Pelleas does not invite madness; it comes to him through circumstances over which he has no control. Lancelot's renunciation of Elaine is sorrowful, for his adultery only makes him more honorable in all his other conduct. Gawain, already identified in *Lancelot and Elaine* and *The Holy Grail* as the soulless materialist, is wholly cynical in his betrayal of Pelleas with Ettarre, who herself makes a mockery of chivalric love. Pelleas' disillusionment, then, becomes symptomatic of the overthrow of an entire social order. In his Lear-like frenzy he imagines that human nature has debased itself below the level of animals.

Of all the narratives in the *Idylls of the King*, *The Last Tournament*, not published until 1871, is perhaps most skillfully contrived to bring out the theme of shadow and substance. "The world/ Is flesh and shadow," says Dagonet; and the Tournament of the Dead Innocence mordantly em-

---

*Compare with these lines Tennyson's own statement, made in 1869: "Yes, it is true that there are moments when the flesh is nothing to me, when I feel and know the flesh to be the vision, God and the Spiritual the only real and true. Depend upon it, the Spiritual *is* the real: it belongs to one more than the hand and the foot. You may tell me that my hand and my foot are only imaginary symbols of my existence, I could believe you; but you never, never can convince me that the *I* is not an eternal Reality, and that the Spiritual is not the true and real part of me."

bodies his meaning. As with the diamonds in *Lancelot and Elaine*, the ruby carcanet has complex symbolic value. It is associated with "the maiden babe" who did not live after she was given into Guinevere's care. And it is won by Tristram for a last love-offering to Isolt of Lyonesse. Tristram's dream after his victory in the lists is filled with ironic implications:

> He seem'd to pace the strand of Brittany
> Between Isolt of Britain and his bride,
> And show'd them both the ruby-chain, and both
> Began to struggle for it, till his queen
> Graspt it so hard that all her hand was red.
> Then cried the Breton, 'Look, her hand is red!
> These be no rubies, this is frozen blood,
> And melts within her hand—her hand is hot
> With ill desires, but this I gave thee, look,
> Is all as cool and white as any flower.'
> Follow'd a rush of eagle's wings, and then
> A whimpering of the spirit of the child,
> Because the twain had spoil'd her carcanet.

Furthermore, the triangle of Mark, Isolt, and Tristram savagely parodies the situation obtaining among Arthur, Guinevere, and Lancelot, since Arthur could never have taken Mark's way, any more than Lancelot and Guinevere were capable of following the example of Tristram and Isolt in sacrificing all to love. That Lancelot, in the King's absence, should preside over this last tourney is a further irony in view of the combatants' behavior. We hear the death-knell of the Round Table when Tristram, who alone has fought bravely, rejoices with Isolt in the triumph of lawless passion over the unnatural restrictions imposed by Arthur on his knights:

>   The vows!
> O, ay—the wholesome madness of an hour—
> They served their use, their time; for every knight
> Believed himself a greater than himself,

And every follower eyed him as a God;
Till he, being lifted up beyond himself,
Did mightier deeds than elsewise he had done,
And so the realm was made. But then their vows—
First mainly thro' that sullying of our Queen—
Began to gall the knighthood, asking whence
Had Arthur right to bind them to himself?
Dropt down from heaven? wash'd up from out the deep?
They fail'd to trace him thro' the flesh and blood
Of our old kings. Whence then? a doubtful lord
To bind them by inviolable vows,
Which flesh and blood perforce would violate;
For feel this arm of mine—the tide within
Red with free chase and heather-scented air,
Pulsing full man. Can Arthur make me pure
As any maiden child? lock up my tongue
From uttering freely what I freely hear?
Bind me to one? The wide world laughs at it.
And worldling of the world am I, and know
The ptarmigan that whitens ere his hour
Woos his own end; we are not angels here
Nor shall be. Vows—I am woodman of the woods,
And hear the garnet-headed yaffingale
Mock them—my soul, we love but while we may;
And therefore is my love so large for thee,
Seeing it is not bounded save by love.

And finally, as a counterpart to the Tournament of the Dead Innocence, there is Arthur's sally against the Red Knight when his newly-sworn followers behave in a manner indistinguishable from that of the enemy for brute ferocity and abandonment to evil passions.

Throughout the greater part of the *Idylls of the King* Arthur is kept in the background, as if, in allowing his influence to be exerted indirectly, Tennyson had wished to explore alternative modes of behavior inspired by attraction to or repulsion from his example. Now in *Guinevere* and *The Passing of Arthur* the King moves into the forefront of the action that we may judge the reality of his personal dream as a way of life. By modern standards Arthur's treatment of the Queen may seem unendurably self-righteous; but this must not be allowed to close the reader's eyes to the King's discovery that, however wronged, he is still a man in love. Guinevere's betrayal has broken his heart and so tarnished his faith in the governing ideal of his life. No longer sustained by belief in the heavenly ratification of his mission, his mind is torn between vague and futile surmises. Either God is absent from the universe, or else mortal perceptions cannot fathom His purposes:

> ... for why is all around us here
> As if some lesser god had made the world,
> But had not force to shape it as he would,
> Till the High God behold it from beyond,
> And enter it, and make it beautiful?
> Or else as if the world were wholly fair,
> But that these eyes of men are dense and dim,
> And have not power to see it as it is—
> Perchance, because we see not to the close;—
> For I, being simple, thought to work His will,
> And have but stricken with the sword in vain,
> And all whereon I lean'd in wife and friend
> Is traitor to my peace, and all my realm
> Reels back into the beast, and is no more.

The altogether human suffering inflicted by the Queen has condemned Arthur, like so many of his subjects, to walk the shadow line between seeming and reality:

> Thro' this blind haze which, ever since I saw
> One lying in the dust at Almesbury,
> Hath folded in the passes of the world.

Gawain visits the King in dream; and his lament, "Hollow, hollow all delight," is a final comment on the life of the senses. But what is there to say for Arthur's vision after "that battle in the west/ Where all of high and holy dies away?"*

* The ruined chancel with its broken cross, symbolizing the undoing of Christianity, to which Bedivere bears the dying Arthur

Surely the return of Excalibur to the Lady of the Lake signifies that the time for heroic action has passed. One may well sympathize with Bedivere's sense of desolation as he watches the outward voyage of the funeral barge. If Camelot is a nobler vision of the Palace of Art, then the "island-valley of Avilion" becomes at one further remove a symbol of total alienation. And for all Tennyson's pious tribute in the Epilogue to Victoria's "crown'd Republic's crowning commonsense," the final impression left by the poem is one of tragic incompatibility between the life of the imagination and the ways of the world.

IV

"THE HIDDEN WORLD OF SIGHT THAT LIVES BEHIND THIS DARKNESS"

The *Idylls of the King* is, for the purposes of the present argument, the culminating achievement of Tennyson's artistic career, since the poet here conceived a work of major proportions which spoke home to his age and at the same time gave full expression to his own deepest intuitions. In none of his later writings do we to any like extent sense the operation of this double awareness. In fact, after about 1870 a deliberate split is observable in Tennyson's aesthetic intent. He continues to write poems in conformity with the prevailing tastes which he had exploited so successfully from the 1842 volume on. His invasion of the field of historical drama with *Queen Mary* in 1875 is perhaps the clearest evidence of his desire to reach as wide an audience as possible. On the other hand, in a return to and development of his earliest manner, he also produced a considerable number of poems anything

---

would seem to negate the withdrawal of Guinevere, Lancelot, and Percivale to an existence of religious seclusion.

but popular in nature, which are fully intelligible only if interpreted as projections of subjective states of mind. Whichever the category to which they belong, the poems published during the last two decades of Tennyson's life not only continue to employ the characteristic motifs of dream, madness, vision, and the quest, but do so in an even more highly selective way.

The pessimistic tone that darkens the concluding Idylls is strongly marked in the treatments of contemporary life which are the late counterpart of the English Idyls of the 1842 and *Enoch Arden* volumes. The poems in dialect are less humorous than their predecessors; and in such works as *The First Quarrel*, *The Wreck*, *Despair*, and *Forlorn* the melodramatic situations, as the titles suggest, usually have a gloomy outcome. The vigorously challenging tone of *Locksley Hall* has given way to the somewhat shrill petulance of *Locksley Hall Sixty Years After*. A comparison of the two poems indicates Tennyson's growing disquietude over the road Victorian England was travelling. The sentiments of the speaker in the latter have the querulous quality of a man driven almost frantic by the decay of those values which had seemed to guarantee social stability. And, indeed, madness in Tennyson's later poetry is almost invariably a condition directly attributable to environmental pressures. Among other examples, *Rizpah* is the most forceful study of insanity as a form of individual release from the harsh workings of external circumstance. In the same way, as may be shown in such poems as *In the Children's Hospital*, *Columbus*, *Despair*, and *Romney's Remorse*, the value of dreams resides in the solace which they bring to wounded sensibilities. Through sleep the sufferer escapes from actuality. Indeed, just as he tended increasingly to portray madness as an unproductive aberration, so the later Tennyson in those poems which celebrate the active life inclines to distrust the dream state as a form of self-indulgence. Saint Telemachus, tempted to the false asceticism of a Saint Simeon Stylites, hears a mystic voice, saying:

TENNYSON

> Wake
> Thou deedless dreamer, lazying out a life
> Of self-suppression, not of selfless love.

And Akbar feels that his dream of a universal church may by its very persuasiveness seduce him into complacency and so corrupt the will to act:

> The shadow of a dream—an idle one
> It may be. Still I raised my heart to heaven,
> I pray'd against the dream. To pray, to do—
> To pray, to do according to the prayer,
> Are, both, to worship Alla, but the prayers,
> That have no successor in deed, are faint
> And pale in Alla's eyes, fair mothers they
> Dying in childbirth of dead sons. I vow'd
> Whate'er my dreams, I still would do the right
> Thro' all the vast dominion which a sword,
> That only conquers men to conquer peace,
> Has won me.

On the other hand, a second body of poems proves that the ghostly promptings from the dark side of the human consciousness, which flicker through all Tennyson's work, visited the aging poet with greater and greater urgency. His need to believe in the existence of some controlling power outside the limitations of time and space had always been strong; towards the end of his life he was readier to accept the revelations of the inner mind, although its activities remained as much a mystery as ever to him. Furthermore, the impulse to give expression while there was yet time to the complex intuitions of the imagination overruled that concern for the artist's communicative function which had led to the sublimation of the deeper meanings in so much of his previous writing. As a result, the later volumes contain such remarkable poems as *The Ancient Sage* and *Vastness*, in which the pretense of objectifying theme through didactic narrative is dropped, and the author lets his imagination have its way in highly personal and often cryptic utterance.

TENNYSON

This poetry, as the voice of Tennyson's inner being, is shot through with visions of a transcendental kind. Nor is it surprising to find that the pilgrimage of the spirit towards ultimate truth presents itself, as often as not, under the aspect of a quest. The machinery of vision and the quest thus continues to motivate the themes of many of the later poems; and in the case of two of the most notable, *Merlin and the Gleam* and *The Voyage of Maeldune*, it prescribes the form. The first of these is a thinly disguised apologia for Tennyson's entire poetic career, viewed in terms of the generating impulses within each successive period. *The Voyage of Maeldune* is a broader allegoric representation of the life journey, rendered through symbols often perplexingly private. Analysis of these poems would only serve to explore ways of the imagination which have already been sufficiently travelled; but Tennyson's choice of the quest as a mode for embodying his profoundest spiritual convictions may suggest the inherently vitalistic habit of mind which is perhaps his strongest bond with the Victorian age. For in the quest, the active and contemplative life meet and are reconciled. It is the finite objective of revenge which holds Maeldune and his companions together and makes them persevere in their long and arduous journey, even though the wisdom garnered along the way invalidates the goal when it is at last in sight. And as Tennyson himself tells us in *Merlin and the Gleam*, the vision becomes all the more compelling after it has been challenged by sorrowful recognition of the disparity between shadow and substance, the actual and the ideal in this world:

>   Clouds and darkness
>   Closed upon Camelot;
>   Arthur had vanish'd
>   I knew not whither,
>   The king who loved me,
>   And cannot die;
>   For out of the darkness
>   Silent and slowly
> The Gleam, that had waned to a wintry glimmer

>   On icy fallow
>   And faded forest,
>   Drew to the valley
>   Named of the shadow,
>   And slowly brightening
>   Out of the glimmer,
> And slowly moving again to melody
>   Yearningly tender,
>   Fell on the shadow,
>   No longer a shadow,
>   But clothed with the Gleam.

The argument which emerges from the foregoing discussion should now be clear. Whether it be as an escape from actuality through dream or madness, or as an escape into higher truth through vision and the quest, the central emphasis in Tennyson's poetry develops from an inner rather than an outer awareness, from the life of the imagination rather than from a sense of responsibility to society. For the conflict between the appearance of the external world and the reality of the individual consciousness which we have found to be the real theme of the *Idylls of the King* runs through nearly all the more serious poems of Tennyson's later period. The aged protagonist of *Locksley Hall Sixty Years After* says: "All the world is ghost to me, and as the phantom disappears"; and the narrator of *The Sisters* elaborates this sentiment as follows:

>   My God, I would not live
> Save that I think this gross hard-seeming world
> Is our misshaping vision of the Powers
> Behind the world, that make our griefs our gains.

The fine poem, which Tennyson wrote on the birth of his son Hallam under the title of *De Profundis*,* originates in a like conviction that the world as we sense it shadows a higher

---

* The fact that the poet withheld until 1880 the publication of *De Profundis*, although it was presumably written in 1852, might well be construed as further evidence of his hesitancy in mid-career to reveal too openly the inner workings of his mind.

realm of spiritual being. The poet speaks of "that true world within the world we see,/ Whereof our world is but the bounding shore," and then continues, addressing his child:

> O dear Spirit, half-lost
> In thine own shadow and this fleshly sign
> That thou art thou—who wailest being born
> And banish'd into mystery, and the pain
> Of this divisible-indivisible world
> Among the numerable-innumerable
> Sun, sun, and sun, thro' finite-infinite space
> In finite-infinite Time—our mortal veil
> And shatter'd phantom of that infinite One,
> Who made thee unconceivably Thyself
> Out of His whole World-self and all in all—

But because such intimations from the recesses of the unconscious are intermittent, the dialogue between faith and doubt that we first overheard in *The Two Voices* goes on. It receives crowning expression in *The Ancient Sage*, the theme of which is "this double seeming of the single world." Here the voice of denial belongs to the young man who is, significantly, a lyric poet. The sage advises his disciple to take up a life of human service as a means of making "the passing shadow serve thy will," and so extirpating from his thoughts the "black negation of the bier." As for himself, the sage, who, of course, speaks for Tennyson, has attained to full self-reliance, and as a result passed beyond the need for outside support. He admits that the truth as he knows it cannot be proved, but neither can the position of his sceptical pupil:

> Thou canst not prove the Nameless, O my son,
> Nor canst thou prove the world thou movest in,
> Thou canst not prove that thou art body alone,
> Nor canst thou prove that thou art spirit alone,
> Nor canst thou prove that thou art both in one.
> Thou canst not prove thou art immortal, no,
> Nor yet that thou art mortal—nay, my son,

> Thou canst not prove that I, who speak with thee,
> Am not thyself in converse with thyself,
> For nothing worthy proving can be proven,
> Nor yet disproven.

But the sage, we find, has known mystic revelations of a kind which Tennyson himself experienced, and through them he has come to place unshakable trust in the imagination as the highest of human faculties:

> If thou wouldst hear the Nameless, and wilt dive
> Into the temple-cave of thine own self,
> There, brooding by the central altar, thou
> Mayst haply learn the Nameless hath a voice,
> By which thou wilt abide, if thou be wise,
> As if thou knewest, tho' thou canst not know;
> For Knowledge is the swallow on the lake
> That sees and stirs the surface-shadow there
> But never yet hath dipt into the abysm,
> The abysm of all abysms, beneath, within
> The blue of sky and sea, the green of earth,
> And in the million-millionth of a grain
> Which cleft and cleft again for evermore,
> And ever vanishing, never vanishes,
> To me, my son, more mystic than myself,
> Or even than the Nameless is to me.

Yet the imagination not only conceives, it also shapes; and so it is that for Tennyson inner awareness finally becomes allied with the artistic act as well as with the apprehension of philosophic truth. The source of all true inspiration is within the intuitional consciousness of the individual. This sense of the immateriality of the outward show, of the strangeness and mystery that always lie just under the appearance of things, of the unknowableness of the human mind in its instinctual perceptions is the germinal impulse in virtually all of Tennyson's best poetry. Hence his uneasy conviction that the age with its obsessive materialism could not really supply him the materials with which to work; hence also his recognition of the subterfuges that were necessary in order to get Victorian society to listen to his message.

For these reasons Tennyson's genius was most at home when employed on traditional legends of proven narrative and moral interest, which could yet be made exemplificatory of deeper implications for the reader who cared to look below the surface. Two comparatively late poems of this kind best illustrate the author's final aesthetic position. One is *Demeter and Persephone*. On first reading, this retelling of the familiar myth of the seasons seems hardly more than a rather tender rendering in elegiac terms of maternal devotion, consonant with the Victorian tendency to idealize domestic relationships. Yet it will be noticed on closer analysis that it is only in the first access of grief, when she thinks of her daughter as irretrievably lost, that Demeter suspends her generative function. Persephone, appearing in dream, explains that her periodic withdrawal from the phenomenal world to the nether region of shadows does not really involve a loss, but is mysteriously necessitated by the process of creation:

> The Bright one in the highest
> Is brother of the Dark one in the lowest,
> And Bright and Dark have sworn that I, the child
> Of thee, the great Earth-Mother, thee, the Power
> That lifts her buried life from gloom to bloom,
> Should be for ever and for evermore
> The Bride of Darkness.

When interpreted in this way, *Demeter and Persephone* becomes a symbolic representation of Tennyson's entire poetic career. Beneath his artistic productivity lay dark depths of consciousness on communion with which, rather than on any external stimulus, depended his will to create.

Tiresias, which Tennyson kept by him for many years before he decided to publish it in 1885, yields insight of a different kind into the poet's dispute with Victorian society. The prophet of the "song-built" city begins by lamenting the decline of his powers:

> These eyes, now dull, but then so keen to seek
> The meanings ambush'd under all they saw,
> The flight of birds, the flame of sacrifice,
> What omens may foreshadow fate to man
> And woman, and the secret of the Gods.

As with Tithonus, Tiresias' suffering is attributable to a vision of unearthly beauty. His punishment, however, entails loss of the faculty to compel belief through his art. The outraged goddess has decreed: "Henceforth be blind, for thou hast seen too much,/ And speak the truth that no man may believe." To his son Tiresias confesses that the vision still survives on the inner eye. The tragedy of his blindness is not that he cannot see what lies outside him, but that he is unable to share with the outer world the clarity of his interior perceptions:

> Son, in the hidden world of sight that lives
> Behind this darkness, I behold her still,
> Beyond all work of those who carve the stone,
> Beyond all dreams of Godlike womanhood,
> Ineffable beauty, out of whom, at a glance,
> And as it were, perforce, upon me flash'd
> The power of prophesying—but to me
> No power—so chain'd and coupled with the curse
> Of blindness and their unbelief who heard
> And heard not . . .

So "this power hath work'd no good to aught that lives"; and the poet's impotent desire to influence the lives of his contemporaries has left him helpless victim to

> The grief for ever born from griefs to be,
> The boundless yearning of the prophet's heart—

Like Ulysses and like the Ancient Sage, Tiresias hands over the responsibility to act in society's behalf to less imaginative youth. In so doing he accepts his isolation with its burden of private intuitions. And the reasons which he gives epitomize the choice which the Victorian age sooner or later imposed on all its true artists, however earnestly they might seek grounds for compromise:

> Virtue must shape itself in deed, and those
> Whom weakness or necessity have cramp'd
> Within themselves, immerging, each, his urn
> In his own well, draws solace as he may.

Browning

*But Art,—wherein man nowise speaks to men,
Only to mankind,—Art may tell a truth
Obliquely, do the thing shall breed the thought,
Nor wrong the thought, missing the mediate word.
So may you paint your picture, twice show truth,
Beyond mere imagery on the wall,—
So, note by note, bring music from your mind,
Deeper than ever e'en Beethoven dived,—
So write a book shall mean beyond the facts,
Suffice the eye and save the soul beside.*

        THE BOOK AND THE RING

BROWNING

I

"AND THEN I FIRST EXPLORED PASSION AND MIND"

In order to trace the operation of a double awareness in Browning's poetry, allowance must at the outset be made for three complicating factors which do not occur in a parallel study of Tennyson. Browning was a much more original artist than the laureate. Whereas Tennyson was content to locate his themes in a familar context, whether literary or relating to contemporary life, and, generally speaking, to present this material in conventional forms, Browning naturally inclined to recondite subject-matter and to experimental methods. Secondly, Tennyson's habit of mind was introspective, with the result, as we have seen, that the matrices of interest in his poetry are comparatively few and easy to identify. Browning, on the other hand, combined with greater intellectual self-confidence a multiple curiosity about man's external relationships. Tennyson could never have written as Browning did in the Epilogue to *Pacchiarotto, with Other Poems*: "Man's thoughts and loves and hates!/ Earth is my vineyard." Finally, where Tennyson was diffident about private convictions and careful to express them in as uncontroversial a way as possible, Browning, out of enthusiasm for his own highly individualistic beliefs, was unwilling to make concessions to the aptitudes and predilections of his readers.

Browning's most characteristic ideas are traceable to certain psychological assumptions adumbrated in the three substantial poems with which he inaugurated his career. These are: *Pauline* (1833), *Paracelsus* (1835), and *Sordello* (1840).* These works are in a sense variations on a single theme: the evolution of the creative impulse in artists beset by uncertainty as to the genuineness of their inspiration and the best uses that can be made of their talents. In *Pauline* these problems are formulated in terms of a conflict between reason and instinct. The poem introduces a youthful poet restive under the yoke of received opinion:

> How should this earth's life prove my only sphere?
> Can I so narrow sense but that in life
> Soul still exceeds it? In their elements
> My love outsoars my reason. . .

To the voice of common sense, recommending subordination of this idealizing tendency to the way of the world, the speaker protests:

> There's some vile juggle with my reason here;
> I feel I but explain to my own loss
> These impulses: they live no less the same.
> Liberty! What though I despair? my blood
> Rose never at a slave's name proud as now.
> O sympathies, obscured by sophistries!—
> Why else have I sought refuge in myself,
> But from the woes I saw and could not stay?

As a romantic assertion of the reality of the human emotions, in opposition to the delusory processes of ratiocination, *Pauline* establishes a point of view which dominates all Browning's subsequent thinking. It should be noted, furthermore, that the poet founds his faith in man's instinctual nature on private insights unsusceptible of demonstration by rational means. So, for example, he maintains that the appeal

---

* Although not published until three years after *Strafford*, *Sordello* was begun on the completion of *Pauline* in 1833.

of Christianity derives from the baffling challenge which Christ offers to philosophic inquiry:

> Is it not in my nature to adore,
> And e'en for all my reason do I not
> Feel him, and thank him, and pray to him—now?
> Can I forego the trust that he loves me?
> Do I not feel a love which only ONE . . .
> O thou pale form, so dimly seen, deep-eyed!
> I have denied thee calmly—do I not
> Pant when I read of thy consummate power,
> And burn to see thy calm pure truths out-flash
> The brightest gleams of earth's philosophy?

Pauline contains two additional passages in which the poet calls on his experience of the arts to prove the validity of intuitional experience. The first of these is the well-known evocation of a painting of Andromeda. The second, deriving from music, is still more explicit. The speaker addresses his imagined mistress as follows:

> Be still to me
> A help to music's mystery which mind fails
> To fathom, its solution, no mere clue!
> O reason's pedantry, life's rule prescribed!

The poet's decision, taken immediately hereafter, to shake off self-consciousness is dictated not so much by social awareness as by an intimation of nobler heights of imaginative being than he has yet attained:

> I'll look within no more,
> I have too trusted my own lawless wants,
> Too trusted my vain self, vague intuition—
> Draining soul's wine alone in the still night. . .

Once let the artist turn altruist, however, and the question then becomes how he can best exert influence on the minds of others. In his poem devoted to the pseudo-legendary figure of Paracelsus, Browning first attacks the problem of communication, while still insisting on the primacy of the intuitions over the rational intellect. *Paracelsus* is a study of intellectual pride and its humbling. The philosopher, conscious of his mission to arouse society with "new revealings," places entire confidence in his individual powers, and thereby repudiates both the guidance of tradition and the support of love, as personified by Festus and Michal. Festus repeatedly warns him of the danger of trying to do without human sympathy: "How can that course be safe which from the first/ Produces carelessness to human love?"; and again: "But do not cut yourself from human weal!" Paracelsus, however, sets off alone on his wanderings, strong in the conviction that he is sufficient unto himself and that ultimate truth has its seat in the depths of his inner consciousness.

Paracelsus is divided into five sections to suggest the stages in the hero's tragic progress. In the second part there begins for Paracelsus the betrayal by the intellect, although he continues to insist that this is the supreme faculty:

> God! Thou art mind! Unto the master-mind
> Mind should be precious. Spare my mind alone!
> All else I will endure. . .

The lyric poet Aprile now enters the scene to emphasize the protagonist's alienation. Aprile compensates for the weakness of his intellect by a capacity for love denied to Paracelsus. Lacking Festus' humble veneration for humanity, however, he loves unrealistically. For Aprile inhabits a Shelleyean world of make-believe where mankind is an idealized abstraction. In their isolation both Paracelsus and Aprile are self-infatuated, the one by the life of reason, the other by the life of the imagination. Paracelsus realizes that they are "halves of one dissevered world"; but although, having learned to love Aprile, he has begun to move towards recognition of the need for closer communion with his kind, he is not yet ready to renounce his chosen path. To the dying poet he says:

> We wake at length from weary dreams; but both
> Have slept in fairy-land: though dark and drear
> Appears the world before us, we no less

> Wake with our wrists and ankles jewelled still.
> I too have sought to KNOW as thou to LOVE—
> Excluding love as thou refusedst knowledge.
> Still thou hast beauty and I, power.

With the third section disillusionment sets in for Paracelsus. He has found that his teachings are unintelligible to the populace, and scorning the artifices of the demagogue, has taken refuge in aristocratic disdain for his audience. Aprile's example is for the moment lost on him. In his thinking of the dead poet merely as a devotee of art for art's sake, we can perhaps detect Browning's own rejection of that alluring doctrine:

> I cannot feed on beauty for the sake
> Of beauty only, nor can drink in balm
> From lovely objects for their loveliness;
> My nature cannot lose her first imprint;
> I still must hoard and heap and class all truths
> With one ulterior purpose: I must know!
>
> . . . For other men,
> Beauty is prodigally strewn around,
> And I were happy could I quench as they
> This mad and thriveless longing, and content me
> With beauty for itself alone. . .

Festus reappears to suggest that Paracelsus' difficulties are of his own making, the result of a deficiency in the loving wisdom of the heart; but the philosopher reasserts the supremacy of the individual:

> 'T is in the advance of individual minds
> That the slow crowd should ground their expectation
> Eventually to follow . . .

Yet he is not so sure of himself as once; and although without much humility, he is beginning to perceive that his failure may be attributable to pride of intellect:

> . . . were man all mind—he gains
> A station little enviable. From God

> Down to the lowest spirit ministrant,
> Intelligence exists which casts our mind
> Into immeasurable shade. No, no:
> Love, hope, fear, faith—these make humanity;
> These are its sign and note and character,
> And these I have lost!

Paracelsus next turns his mental powers to unscrupulous ends, and so betrays himself to the ways of the world. He condescends to magical practices in order to bedazzle his audience. Unwilling to bow to the authority of the magistrates at Basel, he is cast out as a charlatan. *Paracelsus* thus becomes the first of many compositions in which Browning was to show the enslavement of minds to ambition for material power. The coarsening of Paracelsus' fibre spreads out from the intellect through his whole nature and leads to sensual indulgence. He falls prey to morbid Satanism: "mind is nothing but disease,/ And natural health is ignorance." In a final despairing effort to hold onto some remnants of self-respect, he makes the gesture of arrogating to himself godlike infallibility:

> I am above them like a god, there's no
> Hiding the fact: what idle scruples, then,
> Were those that ever bade me soften it,
> Communicate it gently to the world,
> Instead of proving my supremacy,
> Taking my natural station o'er their head,
> Then owning all the glory was a man's!
> —And in my elevation man's would be.

It is only in his old age, a failure and on the point of death, that Paracelsus under Festus' ministrations finally attains to full recognition of his error. Man in his slow ascent of the evolutionary scale is to be pitied rather than disdained; his groping, but endlessly valiant struggle to rise is the very thing that makes him lovable. And the superior beings sent to guide the way must possess the faculty of love if they are to fulfill their function. Paracelsus retains to the end his confidence that he is one of those so elected; but the qualities on which he should have relied, as he now realizes, were his "inborn uninstructed impulses,"—not, that is to say, the reasoning mind, but

> perception unexpressed,
> Uncomprehended by our narrow thought,
> But somehow felt and known in every shift
> And change in the spirit,—nay, in every pore
> Of the body, even . . .

This God-given instinct he has perverted through the selfish desire for individual power; yet he cannot refrain from pointing out the temptation to deal with the world in its own terms:

> All quackery; all deceit; myself can laugh
> The first at it, if you desire; but still
> You know the obstacles which taught me tricks
> So foreign to my nature—envy and hate,
> Blind opposition, brutal prejudice,
> Bald ignorance—what wonder if I sunk
> To humor men the way they most approved?

And the poem leaves the reader with the ineradicable impression that in Browning's view the way of the original thinker must needs be a lonely one, since devotion to the best interests of humanity inevitably entails incomprehension and active hostility from all those whom one seeks to serve: "We have to live alone to set forth well/ God's praise."

In theme *Sordello* occupies a position midway between *Pauline* and *Paracelsus*. The first sections of *Sordello* trace the growth of a poet's mind, the later ones his career in the world. As had been the case with *Paracelsus*, *Sordello* represents an attempt on Browning's part to gain perspective on his own situation through imaginative treatment of an historical figure sufficiently obscure to allow considerable latitude of interpretation. The hero of the poem is obsessed by the problem of making himself heard. The theme of the artist's communicative function, emerging from a welter of imperfectly assimilated material, gives the work what little unity it possesses. Like the speaker in *Pauline*, Sordello is motivated in turn by two impulsions, one turning him inward towards self-contemplation, the other driving him outward to a life of action; and like Paracelsus, his career follows a pattern of alternating advance and retreat, as he assumes and is then dislodged from one position after another *vis-à-vis* society.

In total seclusion from worldly affairs Sordello passes his youth amidst the natural beauties of Goito. His imagination is peopled with ideal beings, and he dreams of emulating Apollo, the poet-god. But such isolation, with its inducements to egocentric complacency, is precarious at best; for we are told that

> this world of ours by tacit pact is pledged
> To laying such a spangled fabric low
> Whether by gradual brush or gallant blow.

Sordello's first departure from Goito into a larger sphere of activity comes about under auspicious circumstances. Inspired to spontaneous song, he vanquishes the reigning troubadour, Eglamor, at Palma's Court of Love. Eglamor is an interesting, though somewhat vague figure. He foreshadows the Pre-Raphaelite ideal of the artist wholly devoted to aesthetic discipline: "Then, how he loved that art!/ The calling making him a man apart/ From men." Like Aprile, however, his preference for fancy over fact is mitigated by a generous capacity for love; he dies acknowledging Sordello his master. Earlier in the poem Browning had specified two categories of poets. The first includes all those who feel

> A need to blend with each external charm,
> Bury themselves, the whole heart wide and warm,—
> In something not themselves; they would belong
> To what they worship. . .

Eglamor clearly belongs to the other category, described as follows:

> For there's a class that eagerly looks, too,
> On beauty, but, unlike the gentler crew,
> Proclaims each new revealment born a twin
> With a distinctest consciousness within,
> Referring still the quality, now first
> Revealed, to their own soul—its instinct nursed
> In silence, now remembered better, shown
> More thoroughly, but not the less their own. . .

Eglamor, at least, has the virtue of absorption in the technical demands of his craft. Sordello, on the other hand, vainglorious over his easy success, assumes that all he henceforth need do is give unbridled expression to his imagination: "So, range, free soul!—who, by self-consciousness,/ The last drop of all beauty dost express." At the furthest remove from Eglamor's perfectionism, his sole concern is for popular acclaim: " 't was the song's effect/ He cared for, scarce the song itself." In the outcome he falls between two stools. Lack of worldly experience, coupled with excessive self-confidence, causes him to go astray among abstractions which are meaningless to his audience. When he attempts to adopt more concrete modes of communication, notably the dramatic, he discovers his temperamental disaffinity to prevailing forms of thought. The man and the artist split apart:

> Weeks, months, years went by,
> And lo, Sordello vanished utterly,
> Sundered in twain; each spectral part at strife
> With each; one jarred against another life;
> The Poet thwarting hopelessly the Man,
> Who, fooled no longer, free in fancy ran
> Here, there,—let slip no opportunities
> As pitiful, forsooth, beside the prize
> To drop on him some no-time and acquit
> His constant faith (the Poet-half's to wit—
> That waiving any compromise between
> No joy and all joy kept the hunger keen
> Beyond most methods)—of incurring scoff
> From the Man-portion—not to be put off

With self-reflectings by the Poet's scheme,
Though ne'er so bright. Who sauntered forth in dream,
Dressed anyhow, nor waited mystic frames,
Immeasurable gifts, astounding claims,
But just his sorry self?—who yet might be
Sorrier for aught he in reality
Achieved, so pinioned Man's the Poet-part,
Fondling, in turn of fancy, verse; the Art
Developing his soul a thousand ways—
Potent, by its assistance, to amaze
The multitude with majesties, convince
Each sort of nature, that the nature's prince
Accosted it. Language, the makeshift, grew
Into a bravest of expedients, too;
Apollo, seemed it now, perverse had thrown
Quiver and bow away, the lyre alone
Sufficed. While, out of dream, his day's work went
To tune a crazy tenzon or sirvent—
So hampered him the Man-part, thrust to judge
Between the bard and the bard's audience, grudge
A minute's toil that missed its due reward!

There ensues a period of withdrawal to Goito and self-renewal at the font which symbolizes the inner sources of Sordello's creative being. As a result of the illumination received during this time, Sordello vows himself to a career of constructive endeavor in the cause of his countrymen suffering under the wars of the Guelphs and the Ghibellines. As happened to Paracelsus when he aspired the second time, however, Sordello is seduced by a thirst for power. Finding that Rome is not built in a day, he despairs once more and is ready to exchange his newly assumed mission for the consolations of the imagination. In vain his conscience reprimands him for failure to abide by the choice it dictates:

    Only bear in mind,
Ferrara's reached, Goito's left behind:
As you then were, as half yourself, desist!
—The warrior-part of you may, an it list,

> Finding real falchions difficult to poise,
> Fling them afar and taste the cream of joys
> By wielding such in fancy,—what is bard
> Of you may spurn the vehicle that marred
> Elys so much, and in free fancy glut
> His sense, yet write no verses—you have but
> To please yourself for law, and once could please
> What once appeared yourself, by dreaming these
> Rather than doing these, in days gone by.
> But all is changed the moment you descry
> Mankind as half yourself,—then, fancy's trade
> Ends once and always: how may half evade
> The other half? men are found half of you.
> Out of a thousand helps, just one or two
> Can be accomplished presently: but flinch
> From these (as from the falchion, raised an inch,
> Elys, described a couplet) and make proof
> Of fancy,—then, while one half lolls aloof
> I' the vines, completing Rome to the tip-top—
> See if, for that, your other half will stop
> A tear, begin a smile!

Not until after Salinguerra, the ruthlessly practical soldier who acts on instinct, has mocked his feeble vacillations does Sordello come to the recognition that it is the poet's true function to incite his auditors to noble actions:

> Thought is the soul of act, and, stage by stage,
> Soul is from body still to disengage
> As tending to a freedom which rejects
> Such help and incorporeally affects
> The world, producing deeds but not by deeds,
> Swaying, in others, frames itself exceeds,
> Assigning them the simpler tasks it used
> To patiently perform till Song produced
> Acts, by thoughts only, for the mind . . .

No sooner has Sordello found the direction in which he must henceforth move, however, than fresh temptations are placed in his way. With the twofold discovery that he is

Salinguerra's son and Palma's accepted lover, a career of boundless power opens up for him. In the ensuing conflict between altruism and the will to power, the former wins out, but the price of victory is extinction. Sordello stamps on Salinguerra's badge of authority and then, emotionally exhausted, dies. Into this somewhat ambiguous denouement Browning steps to confirm the reader's suspicion that Sordello's life is to be viewed as a tragic failure in its twin aspects—both the early immersion in fanciful dreams, the weakness of Pauline's lover, and the later surrender to selfish ambition, Paracelsus' flaw. Sordello's name is forgotten; his influence, ironically enough, survives to aftertimes in the sole unpremeditated and wholly instinctive utterance of his poetic being, the Elys lyric, as it is sung in fragmentary form by an Italian urchin.

II

"WITH THE WORLD AS STARTING POINT"

As we have seen, *Pauline*, *Paracelsus*, and *Sordello* are thematically interrelated by a like conflict; and each leads to the same conclusion: namely, that the artist can only achieve full self-realization through getting into productive communication with the external world. For Browning to embrace this theory, however, was one thing; to illustrate its operation through his own poetry was quite another. The choice presented to Pauline's lover, Paracelsus, and Sordello is clearly a projection of their creator's own dilemma in the erratic early years of his poetic career. John Stuart Mill's comment on *Pauline* is well-known: "With considerable poetic powers, the writer seems to me possessed with a more intense and morbid self-consciousness than I ever knew in any sane human being." This searching criticism made an enormous impression on the youthful Browning, and was perhaps as much as any other single influence instrumental in starting the poet on a succession of technical experiments expressly directed to the formation of a more objective manner.

The attempt to present Paracelsus' spiritual biography in dramatic form was a first step towards externalizing the author's inner perceptions. Fearful, however, that his audience would fail to understand what he was about, and perhaps somewhat suspicious as well of the perfect purity of his artistic motive, the poet took opportunity in the dedication to the original edition to explain the general purpose and method of the poem:

> I therefore anticipate his [the reader's] discovery, that it is an attempt, probably more novel than happy, to reverse the method usually adopted by writers whose aim it is to set forth any phenomena of the mind or the passions, by the operation of persons and events; and that, instead of having recourse to an external machinery of incidents to create and evolve the crisis I desire to produce, I have ventured to display somewhat minutely the mood itself in its rise and progress, and have suffered the agency by which it is influenced and determined, to be generally discernible in its effects alone, and subordinate throughout, if not altogether excluded: and this for a reason. I have endeavored to write a poem, not a drama. . . .

In *Sordello*, where the mode is narrative rather than dramatic, there is evident, beneath the incrustations of repeated revisions, the author's original intent to employ "an external machinery of incidents to create and evolve the crisis." Yet the principal difficulty which *Sordello* offers the reader is the labyrinthine complexity of the historical events which determine the hero's actions. In after years, with a better comprehension of where his true talent and interests lay, Browning tended to play down this element in *Sordello* on which he had originally lavished so much care. In dedicating the work to his friend Milsand in 1863, the poet wrote: "The historical decoration was purposely of no more importance than a background requires; and my stress lay on the incidents in the development of a soul: little else is worth study."

Browning met Macready in 1835, and two years later

Strafford inaugurated a decade's apprenticeship to the stage. Although Browning's plays were among his earliest productions, while Tennyson did not try his hand at writing for the theatre until the latter part of his life, both men may be said to have turned to dramatic writing out of a desire to reach a wider public. A distinction should be made, however, between the impulses which led Tennyson and Browning to the drama. The former, secure in his contemporary fame, was looking for new subject-matter of a dignity appropriate to the author of *Idylls of the King*. Browning, on the other hand, his head crammed with ideas but his reputation all to make, was seeking a manner which would put him into closer correspondence with his age. Even the most superficial consideration of Browning's relationship with Macready indicates how conscientiously the poet was bent on wooing public favor by means of his playwriting efforts. *A Blot in the 'Scutcheon* was announced to the great producer in the following hopeful way:

> "The luck of the third adventure" is proverbial. I have written a spick and span new Tragedy (a sort of compromise between my own notion and yours—as I understand it, at least) and will send it to you if you care to be bothered so far. There is *action* in it, drabbing, stabbing, et autres gentillesses,—who knows but the Gods may make me good even yet?

Despite this readiness to compromise, however, Browning was no dramatist for the stage, as anyone who has looked into his plays knows. Of interior or psychological action there is plenty and to spare; but the poet simply could not translate states of mind into the language of external conflict. From the first Macready sensed what was wrong. After rereading *Strafford*, he wrote in his diary: "I find more grounds for exception than I had anticipated. I had been too much carried away by the truth of character to observe the meanness of plot, and occasional obscurity." As if in tacit acknowledgment that this play invited such objections, Browning echoed his estimate of *Paracelsus* in the dedication to *Strafford*, where he described the drama as "one of Action in Character, rather than Character in Action."

In fact, one cannot escape the conclusion that, real as was his concern to gain an audience for his work, Browning quite early realized that he had no real talent for the theatre, and as a result inclined increasingly to use the dramatic form as a means for working out problems of artistic expression inherent in his own genius. In the choice and development of dramatic themes he exercised greater and greater originality out of seeming indifference to the conventions of theatrical representation; and after the completion of *Colombe's Birthday* in 1844, he sent a letter to Domett which announced, in effect, his decision no longer to write for production: "I feel myself so much stronger, if flattery not deceive, that I shall stop some things that were meant to follow, and begin again. I really seem to have something fresh to say." The later dramas, furthermore, are strongly characterized by the re-emergence of certain themes which were announced in *Pauline*, *Paracelsus*, and *Sordello*. It might even be argued that all of Browning's plays exploit a single situation. A choice confronts the protagonist between two lines of action, one dictated by innate idealism, the other by selfish calculation. The resulting internal conflict supplies the "dramatic" tension of the piece. Like Sordello, Anael, Djabal's lover in *The Return of the Druses*, and Mildred Tresham, the heroine of *A Blot in the 'Scutcheon*, both die of emotional exhaustion attributable to the clash between their material and spiritual interests. In *Colombe's Birthday*, *Luria*, and *A Soul's Tragedy*, external action has become almost non-existent, while the speeches of the characters, approximating dramatic monologues, expound with increasing definiteness that master concern in Browning's thinking—the conflict between the wisdom of the heart and the wisdom of the world.

It is too often forgotten that *Bells and Pomegranates* included, in addition to the five series devoted entirely to plays, three additional numbers containing dramatic experiments of a very different and much more original kind. These were: *Pippa Passes* (1841), *Dramatic Lyrics* (1842), and *Dra-*

matic *Romances and Lyrics* (1845). In explanation of the symbolic title, *Bells and Pomegranates*, the poet wrote: "I only meant by that title to indicate an endeavor towards something like an alternation, or mixture, of music with discoursing, sound with sense, poetry with thought." Towards this blending *Paracelsus* and *Sordello* contributed as much as the plays. The discipline of playwriting sharpened Browning's dramatic sense; but the kinds of dramatic struggle which excited his imagination, as we have seen, were those enacted within the minds of individual characters. In the dramatic lyric and its more sophisticated variation, the dramatic monologue, the poet discovered means for dressing his insights in a guise that would pass muster with a public which had been mystified by *Sordello* and bored by *Strafford*.

Although definitely transitional in character, *Pippa Passes* is the first poem which allows us clearly to identify the thematic motifs and technical methods which characterize Browning's mature manner. The lyric interludes of *Paracelsus* survive in Pippa's songs, but they are now keyed into the story in such a way as to influence its course at climactic moments. Likewise, while the poet still uses dialogue, dramatic effect is largely engendered through tensions antecedent to action. The subject-matter of the four episodes suggests a striving to fuse the subjective and objective strains in Browning's previous work. A wealth of incident is present by implication; yet the emphasis does not fall directly on the actions of the characters, but rather on the motives out of which action grows. The psychological analysis of motivation, furthermore, provides Browning with an opportunity for the kind of special pleading at which he was to become so adept. By this means he could endow the creatures of imagination with his own highly individualistic perceptions while seeming to present them as independent beings fully responsible for their own values.

Pippa's refrain, "God's in his heaven—/ All's right with the world!" is often cited as the *reductio ad absurdum* of Victorian optimism. This sentiment, however, is clearly meant to characterize the girl's naïveté and childlike faith, and not the milieu in which she lives. For Pippa's world is given over to the tyranny of church and state, to corrupt officialdom, to envy and malice and wanton cruelty, to adultery and blackmail and murder. The society which environs the girl from the silk mills of Asolo makes a mockery of lawful love, patriotism, the familial relationships, and art. As she wanders the streets on her annual holiday, she brushes shoulders with pimps, prostitutes, debauched students, informers, hired assassins, and parasites of every variety. Her immunity to worldly degradation lies in her very unworldliness. She is a child of nature, unlettered, inexperienced, guileless, endowed only with a happy disposition, innocence, and the wisdom of her intuitions. Like Aprile and Eglamor, with whom her kinship is evident, her only means of self-expression is lyric song. It is through the impact of these songs, so alien to the habits of mind of her auditors, that the theme of the poem comes out. They are heard by "Asolo's Four Happiest Ones" at critical moments in their lives; and they wholly alter the direction of the lives in question by forcing a choice on the hearers. Pippa's passing awakens the conscience of individuals hitherto enslaved by self-interest, and provokes conduct contrary to the courses of action mapped out by the conscious will. In each case the ultimate decision negates personal inclination and so discredits the materialistic values endorsed by society. Thus, Ottima and Sebald, having discovered a sense of guilt, will commit suicide; Jules and Phene will go away together without exacting revenge; Luigi will die in the cause of Italian liberation; and Monsignor will restore her rightful inheritance to Pippa.

Each of the four situations which Pippa influences by her celebration of intuitive feeling hinges on a conflict between individuals and some form of authority. Browning's poems, as we shall see, may be classified into three groups, conforming to the three aspects under which he saw the drama of solitary souls in their strife with the forces of organized society. One division poses the problem of intellectual assent to established institutions and involves a concept of power; a second poses the problem of emotional assent to conventional morality and involves a concept of love; and a third poses the problem of aesthetic assent to artistic traditions and involves a concept of the creative impulse. All three themes occur in *Pippa Passes*, which thus marks out the principal issues with which Browning was henceforth to be concerned.

In the two contrasting panels devoted to the pairs of lovers, Ottima and Sebald and Jules and Phene, Browning advances some of his most characteristic notions about sexual behavior, and in so doing raises issues little in accord with Victorian thinking about such matters. Confronted by a society which condones loveless marriages, we side with Ottima and Sebald in their splendidly reckless passion, and feel revulsion only after discovering that adultery has led to cold-blooded murder. Pippa's song awakens the lovers to their guilt; but the guilt, be it noted, is for the murder and not for the adultery. And the act of suicide which follows does not seem an additional crime, but rather a confirmation of love's intensity issued in repudiation of society and its usages. Jules is equally insubordinate to accepted norms of social conduct in his reaction to the cruel practical joke perpetrated by his fellow art students. To have cast off Phene and then avenged his legitimate grievance was obviously the course sanctioned by custom, and the one to which Jules inclined before Pippa's song educed a nobler impulse. In turning from hatred of the students to selfless love for Phene, who shares Pippa's natural innocence, Jules flies directly in the face of convention and thereby attains salvation. His escape to the Greek Isles is the traditional romantic comment on the corrupting ways of the world.

The two concluding episodes present individuals under the shadow of institutionalized authority, in the one case governmental repression represented by the Austrian rule in northern Italy, in the other religious formalism represented by the prestige of the Catholic Church. For Luigi, the champion of liberty, it would be easier to remain with his Chiara in Asolo. Pippa's song sends him on his mission to

Austria, and through averting immediate arrest, reserves him for a patriot's death. It is only on second thought that we realize that in order to establish his point the poet is countenancing political assassination. Monsignor in the last episode is a preliminary study for a whole family of cynical worldlings who choose the Church as the surest means of satisfying their thirst for power. In listening to Pippa's rhapsody rather than to the insidious arguments of the Intendant, Monsignor abandons the riches which would have smoothed his chosen career.

Finally, Jules' calling as a sculptor gives Browning an opportunity to introduce into *Pippa Passes* some of his theories about the rôle of the artist. Overly fastidious by temperament and fearful of exposure to the exacting touch of actuality, Jules has made an ivory tower for himself. Dreaming of ideal beauty, he has fallen into lifeless traditionalism. He describes for Phene a group of statuary on which he has been at work, the central figure of which reflects his concept of himself as the withdrawn and self-immersed votary of art for art's sake:

> Quite round, a cluster of mere hands and arms
> (Thrust in all senses, all ways, from all sides,
> Only consenting at the branch's end
> They strain toward) serves for frame to a sole face,
> The Praiser's in the center: who with eyes
> Sightless, so bend they back to light inside
> His brain where visionary forms throng up,
> Sings, minding not the palpitating arch
> Of hands and arms...

In Phene, however, Jules encounters the higher beauty of living reality which shows up his past work in its true light. The resulting break with the dead weight of inherited practice is exemplified in Jules' flight from his studio, and in his determination to find a new mode of artistic expression. We learn of the motives responsible for this decision through the letter which Monsignor quotes in the fourth episode:

> He never had a clearly conceived Ideal within his brain till to-day. Yet since his hand could manage a chisel, he has practised expressing other men's Ideals; and, in the very perfection he has attained to, he foresees an ultimate failure: his unconscious hand will pursue its prescribed course of old years, and will reproduce with a fatal expertness the ancient types, let the novel one appear never so palpably to his spirit. There is but one method of escape: confiding the virgin type to as chaste a hand, he will turn painter instead of sculptor, and paint, not carve, its characteristics . . .

Monsignor is sceptical of Jules' success in a career undertaken after so many years of discipleship to a false vision; but his remarks on the artist's change of heart reflect the value which Browning placed on originality, as over against a sterile traditionalism:

> He may—probably will—fail egregiously; but if there should arise a new painter, will it not be in some such way, by a poet now, or a musician (spirits who have conceived and perfected an Ideal through some other channel), transferring it to this, and escaping our conventional roads by pure ignorance of them. . .

From *Pippa Passes* to *Dramatic Lyrics* and *Dramatic Romances and Lyrics* is only a short step. In progressing from *Paracelsus* and *Sordello* to plays written expressly for the theatre, Browning had been following a blind alley. Now he had reversed his direction, and by so doing, had come in sight of his true destination, the dramatic monologue. In the dedication to *Strafford* he had correctly analyzed the bent of his genius; it was to treat "Action in Character, rather than Character in Action." But the murky and self-conscious involutions of *Pauline* had shown that the proper field for such action was not the artist's own character. Through his dramatic experiments Browning had learned to project his insights outward and to give them objective embodiment in imaginary characterizations. Henceforth he would drop the pretense of external action and confine his attention to the portrayal of individuals under the stress of such interior, psychological conflicts as characterized the play of his own complex and boldly original mind. Seemingly so remote from their creator in time and place and circumstance, these figures would thus become Browning's agents for delivering to his age the messages which he had failed to get across in other ways.

III

AUTHORITY AND THE REBELLIOUS HEART

Browning established his eminence among Victorian poets with four volumes published over a period of twenty years in mid-century. *Dramatic Lyrics* and *Dramatic Romances and Lyrics* were followed by two additional collections of short poems: *Men and Women* (1855) and *Dramatis Personae* (1864).* Whether the form be the lyric, the narrative, or the monologue, the poems in these volumes, as the titles indicate, exhibit a remarkable uniformity of conception in their concentration on the dynamics of behavior. Mindful of the reproof visited on his earlier writing because of its self-conscious quality, the poet rigorously externalized his perceptions under dramatic forms. The advertisement to the original *Dramatic Lyrics* in 1842 declares: "Such poems as the following come properly enough, I suppose, under the head of 'Dramatic Pieces;' being, though for the most part Lyric in expression, always Dramatic in principle, and so many utterances of so many imaginary persons, not mine." Henceforth Browning was to exploit all the devices of objectivity at his command in an effort to capture the attention of his age. When he was writing the poems to be gathered

* In the ensuing discussion no attempt is made to adhere to the chronological order of these four collections. The fact that for the edition of his poems in 1863 Browning retained the original titles of his first three volumes of short pieces, but completely redistributed their contents, is evidence enough that he did not attach any significance to dates of composition within this body of work.

in *Men and Women*, he informed Milsand: "I am writing—a first step towards popularity for me—lyrics with more music and painting than before, so as to get people to hear and see."

Yet, a review of the four key works, *Dramatic Lyrics*, *Dramatic Romances and Lyrics*, *Men and Women*, and *Dramatis Personae*, in the light of what has already been said about his previous work, and especially *Pippa Passes*, reveals that like Sordello's reliance on the font at Goito, Browning continued to depend for inspiration on the sources which had fed his imagination from the start. The dramatic technique, as he employed it, became simply a process of sublimation equivalent in stylistic terms to Tennyson's thematic use of dream, madness, vision, and the quest. By motivating the actors in his dramas with his own ideas and impulses, Browning could speak out with greater originality and boldness than would ever have been possible in his own person. One wonders how the Victorian middle class with its worship of conformity could have failed to take exception to the poet's outspoken flouting of social conventions. It can only be supposed that approving the apparent regard for morality in his teaching, contemporary readers did not bother to look below the surface to investigate the assumptions on which that morality was founded.

By his constant advocacy of intuitive over rational knowledge, Browning took over the anti-intellectualism of the Romantics and pushed it in the direction of pure primitivism. Along with Carlyle, although much more subtly, Browning endorsed the unconscious as the true wellspring of being. Pippa is only the first of a long line of innocents, including, to name only a few, the duke's last duchess, the maligned lady of *Count Gismond*, Brother Lawrance, the Pied Piper, and the resurrected Lazarus of *An Epistle of Karshish*. In Browning's world, the prophets and artists, the lovers and doers of great deeds are never primarily remarkable for intellectual power. Their supremacy is the result of a genius for experiencing life intuitively. They possess a phenomenal capacity for passionate emotion, combined with a childlike reliance on instinct. These qualities put them in conflict with conventionalized modes of social conduct. Whether it be Fra Lippo, or Rabbi Ben Ezra, or David in *Saul*, or the Grammarian, or Childe Roland, Browning's heroes are always the children of their intuitions.

In their capacity for instinctive action Browning's heroes are akin to Tennyson's visionaries. The moments of recognition come to both in the same mysterious and unpredictable ways. Thus, Childe Roland, reaching his journey's end, knows in a blinding flash what is expected of him. Abt Vogler and David improvise their rhapsodies in states of trance-like exaltation. More especially, true love is love at first sight. Such instantaneous perceptions of elective affinity occur, among other poems, in *Count Gismond, Cristina, The Statue and the Bust, Evelyn Hope*.

His belief that the intuitions operate through the instrumentality of the emotions rather than the intellect led Browning to a frank celebration of man's physical nature, very foreign to Victorian reticence in such matters. Remembering the Prior's pretty niece, Fra Lippo says: "If you get simple beauty and nought else,/ You get about the best thing God invents."* Such an admission is unthinkable in Tennyson, for whom the essential philosophic problem was to league mind and spirit into effective opposition against the bodily appetites. To Browning, on the other hand, flesh and the spirit seemed natural allies against the insidious distortions of the intellect. So Fra Lippo in his defense of the street-urchin's apprenticeship to life exclaims: "Why, soul and sense of him grow sharp alike." Browning's constant assertion of the soul's interrelationship with the body on an instinctual plane permits him to make claims for the latter which would not otherwise have been admissible. Indeed, two of the most forthright statements that fleshly and spiritual well-being are bound up together come from the mouths of holy men. The Apostle John in *A Death in the Desert* says:

* See Browning's defense of the nude in art in the Parleying *With Francis Furini*.

> But see the double way wherein we are led,
> How the soul learns diversely from the flesh!
> With flesh, that hath so little time to stay,
> And yields mere basement for the soul's emprise,
> Expect prompt teaching.

And in the words of Rabbi Ben Ezra:

> Let us not always say
> "Spite of this flesh to-day
> "I strove, made head, gained ground upon the whole!"
> As the bird wings and sings,
> Let us cry "All good things
> "Are ours, nor soul helps flesh more, now, than flesh helps soul!"

The vitalism inherent in Browning's emphasis on man's intuitive as opposed to his ratiocinative faculties further explains the poet's acceptance of the real and demonstrable, and, conversely, his distrust of make-believe. The characters in his poems whom we are asked to admire are all exceptionally clear-sighted in their confrontation of actuality. They see through the false shows at which society connives, preferring to meet life on its own terms rather than to indulge in fanciful self-delusion. Although Browning's lovers are usually unhappy, there is never any question of escape into a Tennysonian dream world. In his hopeless predicament the lover of *In a Gondola* three times falls to imagining ideal situations which would allow his mistress and himself to be together, and as often rejects the wish for the fact:

> Rescue me thou, the only real!
> And scare away this mad ideal
> That came, nor motions to depart!
> Thanks! Now, stay ever as thou art!

Finally, worldly criteria for success lose their validity in Browning's poetry. The poet's so-called philosophy of imperfection, with its lesson that "a man's reach should exceed his grasp," has anti-social implications. This belief holds that an individual's first and highest obligation is to fulfill his own being, regardless of consequences. A lifetime of devotion to settling "*Hoti's* business," properly basing *Oun*, and providing "us the doctrine of the enclitic *De*" entitles the grammarian to a final resting-place on the heights. The lover of *In a Gondola* makes a Romeo-like death in the fullness of his passion:

> The Three, I do not scorn
> To death, because they never lived: but I
> Have lived indeed, and so—(yet one more kiss)—can die!

And Childe Roland's ultimate intuition is that success in his quest means just to die bravely.

Once the intuitional psychology at the heart of Browning's thinking is fully understood, all the major thematic concerns in his poetry become meaningful as deriving therefrom. Among Victorian poets he is the great champion of individualism. If self-realization is the purpose of life, then it follows that any agency which thwarts that process is inimical to the best interests of human nature. And since formalized systems of thought operating through social institutions have always tended to repress freedom of belief and action, Browning's most characteristic poems have to do with the conflict between the individual and his environment. There is a wisdom of the mind and a wisdom of the heart; and the two are always at odds, since the one teaches compliance with the ways of the world while the other inculcates non-conformity. Thus, where his political and religious convictions or his beliefs about love and art are concerned, each man must make a choice between intellectual subservience to customary values and emancipation from all such restrictions.

In insisting on the integrity of the individual soul, Browning allies himself on one side with the Romantic poets, and on the other with the Pre-Raphaelites. He differs from both, however, in his concept of the artist's responsibilities. Whereas Byron delivered frontal assaults on contemporary manners and morals and Rossetti inclined to ignore his milieu, Browning adopted an oblique approach to his age. By dramatizing individual case histories, he stepped before his readers in such a variety of poetic guises that it was impossible to identify him with any single rôle. Furthermore, since he made his attacks piecemeal through anatomizing characters each of whom embodied but a single aspect of contemporary thought, he could be sure of enlisting on his side all those who did not share this particular foible, and so of forestalling unified opposition. It is only when the widely diversified types in Browning's catalogue are grouped according to family resemblance that one begins to comprehend the scope and consistency of the poet's opposition to existing values, and hence the extent of his alienation from Victorian society.

One such grouping, it has been suggested, would include all those characters whose ways of life are conditioned by some clearly defined set of conventions. Superficially dissimilar though they are, *My Last Duchess* and *Soliloquy of the Spanish Cloister* present versions of a single conflict. Just as the duke in the former is motivated in all he does by punctilious pride of rank, so the hypocritical friar who soliloquizes in the second poem appeals to the minutiae of religious observance. And just as the dead duchess in her childlike response to all innocent pleasures unknowingly made a mockery of her husband's ceremoniousness, so Brother Lawrence's every spontaneous action criticizes religious formalism. In both poems the central irony grows out of the fact that the speaker damns himself in endeavoring to cast discredit on his unsuspecting adversary.

So, in poem after poem representing every kind of career, the protagonist must make his decision between the practical inducements to worldly success and lonely integrity of spirit. The Lost Leader, who sold out "just for a handful of silver . . . just for a riband to stick in his coat," stands in telling contrast to the Italian in England who, even in exile, remains loyal to the patriot's dream. For the grammarian, gifted above his fellows, the search for knowledge means sacrifice of all that would otherwise have been his due:

> He knew the signal, and stepped on with pride
>   Over men's pity;

> Left play for work, and grappled with the world
> Bent on escaping...

Childe Roland's thoughts are saddened by memories of his lost companions, Cuthbert and Giles, who, presumably unable to sustain the rigors of the quest, fell away, seduced by the world's allurements. All the grotesque properties of this poem—the "hateful cripple," the "stiff blind horse, his every bone astare," the engine of torture, the "great black bird, Apollyon's bosom-friend"—are marshalled as if to epitomize the malice of society against the dedicated ones who step aside from the trodden path.

Browning's most forcible condemnations of rationalism, however, come in those poems which deal with the problems of religious belief. In *Christmas-Eve and Easter-Day*, published in the same year as *In Memoriam*, the poet had worked out the grounds of his own highly individualistic faith. It sprang from a purely intuitive conviction of the necessity for a loving God. *Saul* and *Rabbi Ben Ezra* give full expression to this religious optimism; but the modern reader may well take greater interest in those works which dramatize alternative positions and show the poet dealing with the sceptical tendencies in contemporary thought. Among the best things to be found in *Men and Women* and *Dramatis Personae* is a series of monologues surveying the principal intellectual traditions which have militated against the Christian revelation.

A uniform tone of nostalgia pervades *An Epistle, containing the Strange Medical Experience of Karshish, the Arab Physician; Cleon;* and *Caliban upon Setebos; or, Natural Theology in the Island*. The speaker in each poem, instinctively realizing the spiritual limitations of the system of thought to which he is committed, is driven against his will to postulate a Christian deity. Yet wistful longing never actualizes itself in terms of faith, because it is smothered under the weight of inherited prejudice. Karshish stands for the scientific mentality wholly at a loss to cope with the mystery of Lazarus' resurrection. Cleon, living in the end of the Hellenistic era, finds such meager consolation as he can in the synthesizing temper of a decadent culture. In the superficial view Caliban appears to belong among Browning's primitives; actually he is man materialized to the point where he can only construct God in his own capricious and spiteful image. The historical or literary guise under which these issues are presented suggests the devious operation of Browning's critical intent. The poet was not really interested in the historical process, as Carlyle or Ruskin tried to be; nor did he have Tennyson's genius for reanimating myth. Karshish, Cleon, and Caliban are representative Victorians in fancy dress. As time passed, Browning inclined more and more to put aside the cloak of historical remoteness and to address himself to the psychoanalysis of contemporary types. *Bishop Blougram's Apology* and *Mr. Sludge, "The Medium,"* for example, bring the charge of spiritual sterility directly home to Victorian society.

Bishop Blougram's Apology is an early example of the special pleading, the skillful conduct of casuistic argument, which bewildered so many of Browning's readers. The difficulty, of course, is that Blougram is a sort of devil's advocate who appropriates typical Browningesque doctrines and converts them to his own ends. In the words of his creator: "He said true things, but called them by wrong names." The whole tenor of the Bishop's plea points to the conclusion that worldly self-interest is identical with spiritual well-being. In demonstrating this line of reasoning, Blougram boldly enlists theories which have a diametrically opposed significance in Browning's own thinking. Thus, he says: "My business is not to remake myself,/ But to make the absolute best of what God made"; and again:

> Let us concede (gratuitously though)
> Next life relieves the soul of body, yields
> Pure spiritual enjoyment: well, my friend,
> Why lose this life i' the meantime, since its use
> May be to make the next life more intense?

Only gradually do we recognize the extent of the clever Bishop's compromise with the existing order. In making choice of a way of life, he has consulted only his physical comfort, out of regard for which he has become the servant of institutionalized religion. He has, in other words, allowed himself to be corrupted by the self-deluding operations of his own intellect. The key to Browning's meaning in the more abstruse dramatic monologues may nearly always be discovered in the culminating action. In this case Gigadibs instinctively revolts against Blougram's intellectual gymnastics, and turning his back on England, takes up a Carlylean life of unthinking action as a colonist.

Mr. Sludge, "The Medium" follows a similar pattern. Browning, of course, had no use for mediums, seeing in their vogue clear evidence of the frivolous sensation-seeking of a society that had lost its spiritual bearings. Nevertheless, until the last extraordinary diatribe which reveals Sludge as the unregenerate charlatan he is, the poet allows his protagonist to make out the best possible case for himself. Ironically, despite the fact that Sludge has been caught redhanded at his sham practices, he has relied on trickery for so long that he is partially self-duped:

> I tell you, sir, in one sense, I believe
> Nothing at all,—that everybody can,
> Will, and does cheat: but in another sense
> I'm ready to believe my very self—
> That every cheat's inspired, and every lie
> Quick with a germ of truth.

More damaging, however, as a concealed expression of Browning's own sense of the price which society pays for trifling with its genuine spiritual impulses, is Sludge's mocking vindication of himself. In a world where the prizes go to those who live by their wits, Sludgehood is a normal phenomenon:

> Or, finally,
> Why should I set so fine a gloss on things?
> What need I care? I cheat in self-defence,
> And there's my answer to a world of cheats!
> Cheat? To be sure, sir! What's the world worth else?

Browning's intuitionism announces itself most ardently when he writes about love, this being a subject which he handles with greater candor and penetration than any other poet of the early and mid-Victorian periods. It is not hard to understand why he should have thought the experience of love so important. Through the emotions which it releases man reaches heights of intensity, both physical and spiritual, such as are achievable in no other way. Romantic love, however, is little subject to discipline; and the Victorians in their regard for social stability endeavored to safeguard themselves against its disruptive power behind an elaborate system of conventions. A double standard of conduct was in force for the sexes, and the family stood as the central support of the entire social fabric. To the authority of these ideals Tennyson's poetry bears constant testimony. Browning, on the other hand, challenges the sexual morality of the Victorians at nearly every point. His interest is in the fulfillment of passion, rather than in the preservation of domestic proprieties. In no way are his convictions less conformable to accepted theories than in his refusal to recognize any basis for social inequality between men and women. His adoration of Elizabeth Barrett no doubt explains a good deal in this connection; but while Browning yielded to no other Victorian in his idealization of womanhood, his thinking had very little in common with the contemporary concept of the womanly woman. Only Meredith's heroines challenge Browning's in the qualities of fortitude, loyalty, idealism, intelligence, and insight. The Euripides of *The Last Adventure of Balaustion* is speaking for his creator when he says: "Mere puppets once, I now make womankind,/ For thinking, saying, doing, match the male." Browning, like Meredith, finds that the woman is usually right. With a few exceptions, his love lyrics fall into two classes. In the first the speaker is a man who has been rejected and who humbly accepts responsibility for failure, attributing it to some inadequacy in his own nature. In the second it is the woman who has been cast off. She too is humble; but we are made to feel that she suffers not because of any innate unworthiness, but rather because of some flaw in her lover.

The central problem in Browning's love poetry is invariably one of communication between the sexes. The intangible influences which encourage or destroy intimacy between men and women elicit all his skill in psychological analysis; for love exists in and through human intuitions. Reference has already been made to the poet's belief that destined lovers recognize each other on first sight. But these moments of full and perfect communion are precarious; and, save for the most exceptional cases, the initial harmony does not survive social pressures or the importunities of individual temperament. It is rare in Browning's work to find such a poem as *By the Fire-Side*, in which the lovers have so come to exist in each other that one of them can say:

> When, if I think but deep enough,
>   You are wont to answer, prompt as rhyme;
> And you, too, find without rebuff
>   Response your soul seeks many a time
> Piercing its fine flesh-stuff.

More commonly the good moment passes, as in *Two in the Campagna*, where we watch it slip away despite the lovers' longing to prolong their felicity; or *The Last Ride Together*, in which the speaker strives desperately to eternalize his fleeting togetherness with the woman he loves.

Ideal love is for Browning the consummation of an intuitive process by which the lovers transcend the barriers of their separate individualities and achieve spiritual union. Whenever this happens, there results the most exquisite and productive form of communication possible between human beings. The very possibility of a love like this excites the heroine of *The Flight of the Duchess* to say:

> If any two creatures grew into one,
> They would do more than the world has done:
> Though each apart were never so weak,
> Ye vainly through the world should seek

For the knowledge and the might
Which in such union grew their right...

Browning's men and women, then, are always seeking to pierce the barrier which, in his favorite metaphor, separates two isolated souls reaching towards each other. The lover of *In a Gondola* pleads with his mistress:

> Do, break down the partition-wall
> 'Twixt us, the daylight world beholds
> Curtained in dusk and splendid folds!
> What's left but—all of me to take?

And in *By the Fire-Side* Browning, speaking for once in his own person, describes the loss of personal identity under love's mysterious spell:

> If two lives join, there is oft a scar,
>   They are one and one, with a shadowy third;
> One near one is too far.
>
> A moment after, and hands unseen
>   Were hanging night around us fast;
> But we knew that a bar was broken between
>   Life and life: we were mixed at last
> In spite of the mortal screen.

As one would expect from what has already been said, Browning holds that undue reliance on the intellect with its ulterior motivations makes for failure in affairs of the heart. The feminine nature is wiser than the masculine in its instinctive response to emotional impulse. In a number of poems love is destroyed through the man's determination to establish his mental superiority over the woman. This is the theme of *Mesmerism*, for example, as well as of *A Woman's Last Word* in which the woman soliloquizes:

> What so false as truth is,
>   False to thee?
> Where the serpent's tooth is
>   Shun the tree—

Since in the poet's thinking the intellectual faculties are self-corrupting and prone to infection by the uses of the world, another group of poems, written from the female point of view, lays blame for the man's infidelity on the temptations held out by society. Examples in this vein are *Any Wife to Any Husband*, and the group of highly sophisticated lyrics, *James Lee's Wife*. The comparatively early *Cristina* departs from the usual pattern of Browning's love poems after he had come to know Elizabeth Barrett. For here it is the woman who is found wanting to the moment of recognition when "mine and her souls rushed together":

> Oh, observe! Of course, next moment,
>   The world's honours, in derision,
> Trampled out the light for ever:
>   Never fear but there's provision
> Of the devil's to quench knowledge
>   Lest we walk the earth in rapture!
> —Making those who catch God's secret
>   Just so much more prize their capture!

Browning's conviction that the passionate intensity of romantic love is incompatible with conventionalized social morality leads him to glorify the one at the expense of the other. That perennial theme, the world well lost for love, is so appealing that Victorian readers in their sentimentality were apparently willing to overlook its frequent anti-social corollary in Browning's poetry, where the decision to give all for love more often than not involves some course of action at variance with established codes of conduct. Too extreme, perhaps, is the example of *Porphyria's Lover* where the demented narrator has committed murder and in this way made the final choice for a mistress

> Too weak, for all her heart's endeavour,
> To set its struggling passion free
>   From pride, and vainer ties dissever,
>   And give herself to me for ever.

In *The Flight of the Duchess*, however, we are compelled to sympathize with the duchess in her flight from the staidly formalistic home of her husband to join the gypsies; and the prevaricating speaker in *Too Late* seems most manly when he reconstructs the lost opportunity to take his beloved away from her husband, by force if necessary. *In a Gondola* presents a more fatal but equally persuasive picture of adultery as the solution to loveless marriage. And the inescapable implication of *Respectability* is that the illicit affair there described has gained its intensity and seriousness from being carried on outside the pale of social conventions:

> Dear, had the world in its caprice
>   Deigned to proclaim "I know you both,
>   "Have recognized your plighted troth,
> "Am sponsor for you: live in peace!"—
> How many precious months and years
>   Of youth had passed, that speed so fast,
>   Before we found it out at last,
> The world, and what it fears?
>
> How much of priceless life were spent
>   With men that every virtue decks,
>   And women models of their sex,
> Society's true ornament,—
> Ere we dared wander, nights like this,
>   Thro' wind and rain, and watch the Seine,
>   And feel the Boulevard break again
> To warmth and light and bliss?
>
> I know! the world proscribes not love;
>   Allows my finger to caress
>   Your lips' contour and downiness,
> Provided it supply a glove.
> The world's good word!—

In a Balcony and *The Glove* present in unequivocal terms the conflict between the wisdom of the intuitions and the usages of society. The theme of *In a Balcony* is conveyed in Norbert's reference to the "instincts of the heart that teach the head." The Queen, a marble figure of authority, comes, through passion for her minister of state, to recognize the hollowness of worldly power. Of the reality of love, on the contrary, she learns:

> 'T is as different from dreams,
> From the mind's cold calm estimate of bliss,
> As these stone statues from the flesh and blood.

Meanwhile, Constance, the Queen's protegée, who resembles the speaker in *Respectability* in her fear of the world's callous incomprehension, would prefer that her liaison with Norbert remain clandestine. In effect, she is matching wits against society out of a desire to secure her lover to herself. When Norbert wants to make an open declaration of their attachment, she replies:

> A year of this compression's ecstasy
> All goes for nothing! You would give this up
> For the old way, the open way, the world's,
> His way who beats, and his who sells his wife!
> What tempts you?—their notorious happiness
> Makes you ashamed of ours?

In the end Constance prevails on Norbert to make his request in a manner so ambiguous that the Queen misunderstands his intention and believes that her own love is returned. Only when Constance's subterfuges have ruined her hopes does she learn the error of playing the world's game in the world's way. Then finally she lets her heart speak out without restraint. She is willing to sacrifice her happiness to Norbert's career, but at the same time she will stop treating love as though it were a marketable commodity:

> I know the thriftier way
> Of giving—haply, 't is the wiser way.
> Meaning to give a treasure, I might dole
> Coin after coin out (each, as that were all,
> With a new largess still at each despair)
> And force you keep in sight the deed, preserve

> Exhaustless till the end my part and yours,
> My giving and your taking; both our joys
> Dying together. Is it the wiser way?
> I choose the simpler; I give all at once.
> Know what you have to trust to, trade upon!
> Use it, abuse it,—anything but think
> Hereafter, "Had I known she loved me so,
> And what my means, I might have thriven with it."
> This is your means. I give you all myself.

The social satire in *The Glove* results from a seeming paradox in the lady's behavior. Her motive for casting the glove into the lion-pit seems purely capricious; and the reader's first inclination is to side with King Francis' court in its condemnation of the lady and approval of De Lorge when he flings the glove back in her face after its retrieval. On reconsideration, however, we perceive that our initial judgment was conditioned by a code of etiquette, rather than by any real concern for the heroine's situation. By trifling with convention in an apparently irresponsible way, she has shown up the ingrained conventionality of her admirer whose bravery, like his subsequent rudeness, was displayed not for the lady's sake, but solely to win popular approval. The dénouement reveals the poet's meaning. The lady, followed by the youth who alone comprehends her action, departs from the artificial life of the court, while De Lorge remains to marry a lady-in-waiting and to see her become the king's mistress, while he is relegated to the position of glove-bearer.

If, for Browning, true love necessitates total disregard of the ways of the world, then it follows that self-interest is love's greatest enemy. A long succession of poems, concerned with individuals for whom the voice of society drowns out that of passion, dramatizes, on the negative side, the poet's sense that no worldly gain is ever achieved without spiritual loss. The disillusioned lover of *Dîs Aliter Visum; or, Le Byron de nos Jours* recalls in bitterness of heart how he let opportunity slip through his fingers from cynical disbelief that the good moment could be prolonged:

> She might take me as I take her.
>   Perfect the hour would pass, alas!
> Climb high, love high, what matter? Still,
>   Feet, feelings, must descend the hill:
> An hour's perfection can't recur.

So, instead, he has elected the tamer consolation of a career:

> What? All I am, was, and might be,
>   All, books taught, art brought, life's whole strife,
> Painful results since precious, just
>   Were fitly exchanged, in wise disgust,
> For two cheeks freshened by youth and sea?

But the moment, once gone past, does not return; and in the resolution we learn that each has made a wretched marriage, he with a young ballet-dancer, she with a too-old whist-player. Artistic ambition is the force which keeps the lovers of *Youth and Art* apart; but through their failure to perceive the all-important connection between art and life, the former has betrayed them to triviality. The girl, who would surpass Grisi, is now queen at *bals-paré*; and the sculptor, aspiring to replace Gibson, has had to be content with the dubious distinction of membership in the Royal Academy.

Browning's most provocative examination of failure in love as the penalty of faint-hearted conformity to social conventions occurs in *The Statue and the Bust*. The duke first beheld the lady on the day of her wedding to another man, and at once their souls "rushed together." Neither is restrained by moral scruples; yet they postpone the consummation of their love. Each is content with the daily encounter when the duke rides under the window where his beloved sits like another Lady of Shalott, but more remote from reality in her too-patient waiting. So the passing of time and the inconsequential demands of everyday existence imperceptibly dull the edge of resolve, although the lovers continue to delude themselves with the belief that such steadfastness as theirs must eventually be rewarded. Meanwhile, it is better not to provoke a scandal:

> And still, as love's brief morning wore,
> With a gentle start, half smile, half sigh,
> They found love not as it seemed before.
>
> They thought it would work infallibly,
> But not in despite of heaven and earth:
> The rose would blow when the storm passed by.
>
> Meantime they could profit in winter's dearth
> By store of fruits that supplant the rose:
> The world and its ways have a certain worth:
>
> And to press a point while these oppose
> Were a simple policy; better wait:
> We lose no friends and we gain no foes.

When it is too late, they awaken to the realization that they have wasted their lives in make-believe:

> And both perceived they had dreamed a dream;
>
> Which hovered as dreams do, still above:
> But who can take a dream for a truth?
> Oh, hide our eyes from the next remove!

In the end the lovers call in art to eternalize their devotion; but the statue and the bust mock rather than glorify the impulse which brings them into being. Fixed in their apartness, they are as futile and as static as the couple they commemorate. Art has been made a substitute for, not a confirmation of life. That there might be no mistaking his meaning, Browning attached a coda to the poem. In Hamlet's phrase, "The readiness is all." Virtue is not in the goal, but in the passionate intensity of striving:

> Do your best, whether winning or losing it,
>
> If you choose to play!—is my principle.
> Let a man contend to the uttermost
> For his life's set prize, be it what it will!
>
> The counter our lovers staked was lost
> As surely as if it were lawful coin:
> And the sin I impute to each frustrate ghost

Is—the unlit lamp and the ungirt loin,
Though the end in sight was a vice, I say.

If we turn now to Browning's aesthetics, it is immediately apparent from such poems as *Youth and Art* and *The Statue and the Bust* that for this poet art could never supplant life. No position is more consistently maintained throughout his writing than the one deriving from the assumption that all enduring artistic expression is incidental to the experience which inspires it. Poems otherwise so different as *The Last Ride Together, In a Balcony, Cleon, Old Pictures in Florence, "Transcendentalism: A Poem in Twelve Books," James Lee's Wife*, and *One Word More* reiterate the author's vitalism. Art exists simply as one form of creative endeavor to educe life's meaning. The test of an artist's genius lies in his ability to move his audience to action. The Pied Piper, Fra Lippo Lippi, and the David of *Saul* have this faculty in common. The rats and children of Hamelin Town jubilantly follow wherever the piper's music leads. Fra Lippo is going to have to repaint his fresco of St. Laurence at Prato since the faithful are obliterating its details in their devout rage. The mounting ecstasy of David's songs lifts from Saul's spirit the gloom which has incapacitated him.

On first glance, Browning's artistic theories seem to accord fully with his age in its endorsement of the Ruskinian arguments that the highest art results from the perception of moral truth and promotes virtuous conduct. The poet's application of these propositions, however, is again suggestive of a double awareness. Just as the religious or political man must take a stand with regard to institutionalism and the lover with regard to conventional morality, so the artist is threatened by the tyranny of tradition. As it impinges on the life of the imagination, traditionalism has a dual authority. Its influence may be largely intellectual, regimenting instinct to a lifeless formalism. This way leads to art for art's sake. Or, in its more popular aspect, tradition may inform the artist's desire to communicate and so make of him a virtuoso. Whether he inhabit an ivory tower or the market place, the artist who subordinates his native talent to traditional modes has, in Browning's opinion, betrayed his birthright.

The nameless painter of *Pictor Ignotus*, like Aprile and Eglamor, has sought refuge from the harsh importunities of the world in the recesses of his inner being. As one naturally

> inquisitive, to scan
> The licence and the limit, space and bound,
> Allowed to truth made visible in man,

he is all too conscious of the loss in vitality to his painting consequent on denial of the sensory world. He looks outward and sadly asks: "O human faces, hath it spilt, my cup?" Self-withdrawal, we learn, has not taken place out of temperamental inability to respond to external stimuli, but rather because the painter shrinks from the callously imperceptive way that would-be connoisseurs deal with artists and their work. Yet within the privacy of his individual consciousness he discovers no impulse towards original creation, but only the pale inspiration of inherited tradition. The sole consolation left him after producing unending variations on stock religious themes is that he has at least dictated the terms of his defeat:

> If at whiles
> My heart sinks, as monotonous I paint
> These endless cloisters and eternal aisles
> With the same series, Virgin, Babe and Saint,
> With the same cold calm beautiful regard,—
> At least no merchant traffics in my heart;
> The sanctuary's gloom at least shall ward
> Vain tongues from where my pictures stand apart:
> Only prayer breaks the silence of the shrine
> While, blackening in the daily candle-smoke,
> They moulder on the damp wall's travertine,
> 'Mid echoes the light footstep never woke.
> So, die my pictures! surely, gently die!
> O youth, men praise so,—holds their praise its worth?

Blown harshly, keeps the trump its golden cry?
Tastes sweet the water with such specks of earth?

The reasons for the failure of Andrea del Sarto are at once more complex and more symptomatic of the iconoclastic bias which carries over into Browning's aesthetic thinking. Where the speaker in *Pictor Ignotus* is frightened of the world's rough handling, Andrea has shamelessly courted popularity. The unknown painter's talent is exercised for purely private ends; Andrea paints to make money, allowing his choice of subjects to be determined by the market. He panders to the type of material-minded collector that Browning describes in *My Last Duchess* and *The Bishop Orders his Tomb at St. Praxed's Church*. The Pictor Ignotus follows in the tradition of the Primitives who stressed soul at the expense of body; Andrea is no less slave to a realistic tradition which ignores spiritual overtones in its care for anatomic fidelity. Reluctant to acknowledge where he has gone wrong, Andrea, like the unknown painter, hypocritically pretends to exist in the realm of his imaginings:

I, painting from myself to myself,
Know what I do, am unmoved by men's blame
Or their praise either.

Later on he declares: "Beside, incentives come from the soul's self;/ The rest avail not." But the hypocrisy of this statement, when applied to his own work, is evident even to Andrea. The error lies not in his hand with its matchless skill, but in the soul which directs that hand. Preferring any compromise to the loss of his worthless wife, the painter has silenced the admonitions of his spiritual nature. Thinking of the gigantic, though flawed genius of Michelangelo and Leonardo and Raphael, he ejaculates: "The sudden blood of these men!" The recognition that he can put over against their achievements only a certain cold proficiency wrings from him the lament: "But all the play, the insight and the stretch—/ Out of me, out of me!" No sooner does he undertake to correct a clumsy line in a drawing by Raphael than the chalk falls from his fingers: "Ay! but the soul! he's

Rafael! rub it out!" Andrea's virtuosity, we see, is simply a skill acquired through patient mastery of others' techniques, handed down in the schools and now corrupted for venal ends. It is his unforgivable fault to be faultless: "Well, less is more, Lucrezia: I am judged."

In "An Essay on Shelley," written in 1852 to preface a spurious collection of that poet's letters, Browning distinguished between two kinds of objective poet or "fashioner." Concerning the creative impulse of the first kind, the question to be asked is: "Did a soul's delight in its own extended sphere of vision set it, for the gratification of an insuppressible power, on labor, as other men are set on rest?" For the second class, the question is rephrased as follows: "Or did a sense of duty or of love lead it to communicate its own sensations to mankind? Did an irresistible sympathy with men compel it to bring down and suit its own provision of knowledge and beauty to their narrow scope?" *Pictor Ignotus* and *Andrea del Sarto* seem to exemplify the corrupt extremes of these two types. The unknown painter has become the morbidly self-conscious victim of his "soul's delight in its own extended sphere of vision," while Andrea in his desire to communicate has sacrificed originality and compelled his talent "to bring down and suit its own provision of knowledge and beauty" to the "narrow scope" of a vulgar audience. "An Essay on Shelley," however, goes on to propose another kind of poet whose response to experience is primarily subjective. This is the seer, described by Browning as follows:

> He, gifted like the objective poet with the fuller perception of nature and man, is impelled to embody the thing he perceives not so much with reference to the many below as to the one above him, the supreme Intelligence which apprehends all things in their absolute truth,—an ultimate view ever aspired to, if but partially attained, by the poet's own soul. . . . Not with the combination of humanity in action, but with the primal elements of humanity, he has to do; and he digs where he stands,—preferring to seek them in his own soul as the nearest reflex of the absolute Mind, according to the in-

tuitions of which he desires to perceive and speak. . . . He is rather a seer, accordingly, than a fashioner, and what he produces will be less a work than an effluence.

Although in his Shelley essay Browning declined to favor either the objective or the subject artist at the expense of the other, the general tone of his remarks strongly suggests that in his concept of the seer he was proposing a higher orientation for the poetic impulse than would result from conforming to the demands either of the individual ego or of society at large. And certainly in Browning's own poetry devoted to the arts and their practice it is the seer who emerges as the supreme type of artist, embodying in transmuted form the two aspects of the fashioner and merging them under the authority of a transcendent vision adequate to the opposing impulses which inhere in a double awareness.

Although *Christmas-Eve and Easter-Day* is largely a defense of Browning's particular brand of Christianity, the philosophic implications of religion and art were so closely allied in his thinking that the poem is also a declaration of his aesthetic creed. *Christmas-Eve* considers among other things the discrepancy between the ideal and the actual in this life—all that is signified by Abt Vogler's statement: "On earth the broken arcs; in heaven, a perfect round." The ideal, as it exists in God, is unattainable on earth; but this knowledge does not exonerate humanity from attempting the impossible; for in the effort lies the hope of spiritual salvation. Hence Andrea del Sarto's saddened perception: "Ah, but a man's reach should exceed his grasp,/ Or what's a heaven for?" The artist, endowed with special intuitions, is better equipped than other men to apprehend the spirit world. His senses are more keenly responsive to beauty and his mind probes deeper into the laws of cause and effect; but the faculty on which before all others he relies is imaginative insight. Possession of this attribute to an unequalled degree made Shakespeare a poet apart. But, as Browning proceeds to expound in *Easter-Day*, the artist's unique gifts impose on him the highest possible responsibility. Perceiving the divine plan, he must place his genius at God's disposal. Thus, although the creative impulse has its source within the individual consciousness, its operation must not be expended on self-expression, but rather on elucidation of the heavenly will. It is on these grounds that Browning takes issue with art for art's sake. Whereas the deluded devotee of this doctrine endeavors to meet self-imposed standards of perfection, the true artist hears a more imperious voice speaking through his intuitions. While humbly aware that the human imagination is at best a distorting medium, he nevertheless tries, as much as possible, to keep his message uncontaminated by the vanity of artifice. So the apocalyptic presence in *Easter-Day* admonishes the desperate poet who places reliance in his own earth-bound powers:

> "And so much worse thy latter quest,"
> (Added the voice,) "that even on earth—
> Whenever, in man's soul, had birth
> Those intuitions, grasps of guess,
> Which pull the more into the less,
> Making the finite comprehend
> Infinity,—the bard would spend
> Such praise alone, upon his craft,
> As, when wind-lyres obey the waft,
> Goes to the craftsman who arranged
> The seven strings, changed them and rechanged—
> Knowing it was the South that harped.
> He felt his song, in singing, warped;
> Distinguished his and God's part: whence
> A world of spirit as of sense
> Was plain to him, yet not too plain,
> Which he could traverse, not remain
> A guest in:—else were permanent
> Heaven on earth its gleams were meant
> To sting with hunger for full light,—
> Made visible in verse, despite
> The veiling weakness,—truth by means
> Of fable, showing while it screens,—
> Since highest truth, man e'er supplied,
> Was ever fable on outside.

Such gleams made bright the earth an age;
Now the whole sun 's his heritage!
Take up thy world, it is allowed,
Thou who hast entered in the cloud!"

Browning's belief that the creative instinct can only function at its highest potential under divine inspiration is the counterpart of Tennyson's reliance on vision. It follows, then, that the poet-seer must acknowledge the sanction under which he fulfills his mission, and that, in Browning's own words, he will be "impelled to embody the thing he perceives not so much with reference to the many below, as to the one above him, the supreme Intelligence which apprehends all things in their absolute truth." *How It Strikes a Contemporary* exemplifies this concept of the artist in his capacity as God's "recording chief-inquisitor." The protagonist of the poem is a solitary figure, alert to every incident in the life around him, yet mysteriously alien to his environment, his whole loyalty absorbed by the "King" to whom he writes his nightly missive. Of the poet-seer Browning also says that his writing will "be less a work than an effluence." *Saul* and *Abt Vogler* illustrate the true nature of artistic inspiration. David in the former poem, at the approach of the final ecstatic vision of Christ, flings away the harp which has formalized his earlier utterances: "Then truth came upon me. No harp more—no song more!" And in contrast to the musician who labors over the mannered fugues of Hugues of Saxe-Gotha, Abt Vogler is a master of extemporization. Vogler, furthermore, is playing in an empty church solely for his own pleasure when the inspiration descends. His mystic communion with God is thus achieved as a private revelation. And although his improvisations can never be recaptured on earth, he is consoled by the knowledge that they have reached the One to whom they were addressed:

All we have willed or hoped or dreamed of good shall exist;
  Not its semblance, but itself; no beauty, nor good, nor power
Whose voice has gone forth, but each survives for the melodist
  When eternity affirms the conception of an hour.

The high that proved too high, the heroic for earth too hard,
　The passion that left the ground to lose itself in the sky,
Are music sent up to God by the lover and the bard;
　Enough that he heard it once: we shall hear it by-and-by.

But Abt Vogler remains something of an exception in Browning's gallery of artists. Even the seer's field of activity is this world and the life which he shares with other men. God is manifest through his handiwork, and all that mortals can know of his being comes in rightly interpretating the phenomena which condition earthly existence. It is on these phenomena that the imagination must exercise itself, avoiding all willful delusions prompted by the intellect. Any work of the imagination which fails to take cognizance of the facts of human experience is necessarily for Browning either false or imperfect. Thus, in *Old Pictures in Florence* he chooses Christian in preference to Greek art because of the classic artist's unrealistic refusal to "paint man man." Similarly, the speaker in the eighth lyric of *James Lee's Wife* has learned from Leonardo that there is more true beauty in the work-worn hand of a peasant than in any academic dream of perfection that "lived long ago or was never born." And in "*Transcendentalism: A Poem in Twelve Books*" the youthful poet gets severely scolded for letting his vision of actuality become obscured by metaphysical theories: "So come, the harp back to your heart again!/ You are a poem, though your poem's naught."

The greatest artists are those whose senses and intuitions work together in harmonious unison. The great enemy of man's intuitional nature, as we have seen, is the intellect; and in artistic enterprises the intellect's weapon of attack against the freshness and immediacy of sensory impressions is tradition. Therefore, the artists whom Browning holds up for admiration are, like his lovers and men of action, non-comformists, rebels, and individualists on instinct. The fullest expression of the poet's aesthetic philosophy is to be found in *Fra Lippo Lippi*. The circumstances under which we encounter Fra Lippo are significant in themselves; for he has just been apprehended as a potential law-breaker. We learn that he has fled the confinement of his patron's house because it is carnival time and he is unable to resist the lure of the streets. The irrepressible gaiety of life is implicit in the jigging refrain that keeps running through the painter's mind:

> *Flower o' the broom,*
> *Take away love, and our earth is a tomb!*

With this preparation, it is not surprising to find that Fra Lippo has rejected the institutional repression of the Church, and especially that he has thrown over traditional forms of ecclesiastical art as exemplified in the work of such artists as Fra Angelico and Lorenzo Monaco. Fra Lippo is one of Browning's incorruptible innocents. He paints by instinct; and what he paints is the world of his perceptions, not an intellectualized abstraction of it: "The world and life's too big to pass for a dream." But underlying the intensity of his response to human experience is the innate perception of a higher reality made manifest, if at all, through the appearances of this world. The artist cannot do better than reproduce with as great fidelity as possible his individual sense of the observed fact; in so doing he records his own gratitude for the privilege of living, and in the process opens the eyes of others to the meaning of life:

> However, you're my man, you've seen the world
> —The beauty and the wonder and the power,
> The shapes of things, their colours, lights and shades,
> Changes, surprises,—and God made it all!
> —For what? Do you feel thankful, ay or no,
> For this fair town's face, yonder river's line,
> The mountain round it and the sky above,
> Much more the figures of man, woman, child,
> These are the frame to? What's it all about?
> To be passed over, despised? or dwelt upon,
> Wondered at? oh, this last of course!—you say.
> But why not do as well as say,—paint these

Just as they are, careless what comes of it?
God's works—paint any one, and count it crime
To let a truth slip. Don't object, "His works
"Are here already; nature is complete:
"Suppose you reproduce her—(which you can't)
"There's no advantage! you must beat her, then."
For, don't you mark? we're made so that we love
First when we see them painted, things we have passed
Perhaps a hundred times nor cared to see;
And so they are better, painted—better to us,
Which is the same thing. Art was given for that;
God uses us to help each other so,
Lending our minds out. Have you noticed, now,
Your cullion's hanging face? A bit of chalk,
And trust me but you should, though! How much more,
If I drew higher things with the same truth!
That were to take the Prior's pulpit-place,
Interpret God to all of you! Oh, oh,
It makes me mad to see what men shall do
And we in our graves! This world's no blot for us,
Nor blank; it means intensely, and means good:
To find its meaning is my meat and drink.

In the appeal which his paintings make to the emotions of an unsophisticated populace Fra Lippo finds the ultimate vindication of his artistic theories. But while Browning believed that great art would always communicate so long as the sensibilities of its audience had not been deadened by tradition or materialized by social pressures, the half-hearted reception of his own early work inclined him to emphasize the creator's individual integrity rather than his influence. After *Sordello*, worldly prestige is never invoked as a consideration relevant to artistic success. Almost invariably, the artists in his poetry are somewhat alien figures, either neglected or misprized by the society in which they live. Even Fra Lippo shows a defensive attitude in challenging the tradition-ridden prejudices of his age. In *A Toccata of Galuppi's* the composer plays his premonitory compositions to an unheeding audience. *Memorabilia* and *Popularity* have a like theme in the disheartening failure of Shelley and Keats to make an impression on their generation. And in *One Word More* Browning, speaking out of his own experience, refers to the intolerable burden of misunderstanding to which the modern poet is subject when once he has assumed the prophet's rôle:

> Wherefore? Heaven's gift takes earth's abatement!
> He who smites the rock and spreads the water,
> Bidding drink and live a crowd beneath him,
> Even he, the minute makes immortal,
> Proves, perchance, but mortal in the minute,
> Desecrates, belike, the deed in doing.
> While he smites, how can he but remember,
> So he smote before, in such a peril,
> When they stood and mocked—"Shall smiting help us?"
> When they drank and sneered—"A stroke is easy!"
> When they wiped their mouths and went their journey,
> Throwing him for thanks—"But drought was pleasant."
> Thus old memories mar the actual triumph;
> Thus the doing savours of disrelish;
> Thus achievement lacks a gracious somewhat;
> O'er-importuned brows becloud the mandate,
> Carelessness or consciousness, the gesture.
> For he bears an ancient wrong about him,
> Sees and knows again those phalanxed faces,
> Hears, yet one time more, the 'customed prelude—
> "How shouldst thou, of all men, smite and save us?"
> Guesses what is like to prove the sequel—
> "Egypt's flesh-pots—nay, the drought was better."
>
> Oh, the crowd must have emphatic warrant!
> Theirs, the Sinai-forehead's cloven brilliance,
> Right-arm's rod-sweep, tongue's imperial fiat.
> Never dares the man put off the prophet.

Browning's masterwork, *The Ring and the Book*, like Tennyson's *Idylls of the King*, draws together the principal strands in its author's thinking and integrates them within a single grand design. Where Tennyson turned to legend, Browning characteristically found his theme in the court records of an old criminal trial. The case history of Count Guido Franceschini's murder of his wife, Pompilia, not only raised psychological problems which challenged the author's analytic habits of mind, but also offered a type of situation which could be counted on to hold the attention of an audience schooled to melodrama. The details of the affair were certainly sensational. Yet for all its violence and sordid malignancy, the case invited moralistic interpretation, since it involved within a religious framework all the familial relationships—filial piety, connubial faith, mother-love. And, indeed, *The Ring and the Book* has continued to be cited as the final summation of those strenuous qualities of optimism and moral fervor which, according to the received notion, made Browning a representative Victorian.

If *The Ring and the Book* is reexamined in the light of what has been said in the foregoing pages, however, it may appear that this treatment of the conflict between good and evil in terms of domestic tragedy dramatizes certain concepts not altogether congenial to the age in which it was written. As is also true of *Idylls of the King*, *The Ring and the Book* needs to be approached on more than one level if its theme is to become fully evident. The reader who bothers to look below surface meanings finds opening up unexpected perspectives into the author's mind. For *The Ring and the Book* not only presents a full-scale vindication of Browning's intuitional psychology, it also embodies the author's moral and aesthetic philosophy.

Pompilia is the central figure among Browning's heroines. In common with Pippa she possesses the wisdom of the heart in its purest form. She is illiterate, and by heredity and environment the victim of every mischance. Her only defense against the world is the primitive faith which finds expression in natural goodness and a boundless capacity for love; but these qualities stand by her through all her fearful trials. Browning would persuade us that a corrupt social order is solely responsible for Pompilia's misfortunes. The initial injustice is traced back to the circumstances of her birth as the by-product of a prostitute's struggle for survival. At successive periods she is victimized by Violante's snobbery, by Guido's greed, and by the rigid authoritarianism of church and state. She submits to the tyranny of each, because in her naïveté she has accepted the world's assurance that parents, husbands, and social institutions have a care for the best interests of the individuals placed in their charge. In so doing she goes against her intuitions which tell her that she is at the mercy of hostile forces; and her ultimate revolt, when it comes, is an instinctive one motivated by a frantic determination to give her son the freedom she has never enjoyed.

Perhaps the most skillful stroke in Browning's portrayal of Pompilia is the way he suggests her intuitive reaction against the falsity of the social conventions under which she suffers. The girl's imagination operates through symbols, the significance of which is never explicit to her, although she feels and acts under their emotional drive. No other character in the poem has anything like her insights. Thus, for example, the memory of the church where she was married brings to her mind the marble lion in the street outside: "With half his body rushing from the wall,/ Eating the figure of a prostrate man." As a child she had always borne her offering to

> the poor Virgin that I used to know
> At our street-corner in a lonely niche,—
> The babe, that sat upon her knees, broke of...

Thoughts of Caponsacchi and St. George go hand in hand because she had once seen the saint's exploit depicted in a tapestry. Her decision to flee from Guido's bondage, taken in the first blinding apprehension of pregnancy, is dramatized through a passage in which Pompilia unknowingly recreates the scene of the Annunciation as she must have known it from a hundred Renaissance paintings.

Pompilia is the only character in *The Ring and the Book*

whose actions are never (save for her escape from Arezzo) calculated in advance. Even the Pope and Caponsacchi pause to estimate the probable consequences of their conduct. Guido, of course, is all materialized body, as Pompilia is all etherealized spirit. He is the darkness to her light,* the hate to her love, the craft to her guilelessness. But all possible variants of their difference may be subsumed under the one enormous antithesis between conscious intellect and unconscious intuition. As we shall see, the evil in Guido does not derive from mere conformity with the ways of the world; its power is deeper and more enigmatic. Like Iago, Guido deliberately exploits social usages which have no real meaning for him. He is the completely rational man; and by showing the lengths to which rationality, undirected by any altruistic motive, can go, Browning immeasurably strengthens his case against over-intellectualism. For Guido is incapable of any decisive action which has not first gone sour through delay. The campaign of spite incidental to getting rid of Pietro and Violante, the slow, relentless persecution of Pompilia, the involved maneuvers to entrap Caponsacchi in the plot are all characteristic of a man who has never been able to bring any undertaking to a conclusive issue, who has mismanaged his patrimony, trifled with religious orders, frittered away years of sycophantic time-serving in Rome. No court, Browning hints, would have convicted him had he murdered Pompilia and Caponsacchi in hot blood when he caught up with them at Castelnuovo. The stupid oversight as a result of which the assassins are apprehended before they can make good their escape is, we feel, a fittingly ironic commentary on Guido's want of imagination.

Pompilia, Caponsacchi, and the Pope share a lonely eminence, environed on every side by the outraged forces of social prejudice. Of the ten books which bear directly on the poem's action, four (*Giuseppe Caponsacchi, Pompilia, The Pope*, and

---

* An interesting and important study might be made of light effects in Browning's work. The poet constantly calls on the painter's eye in composing his scenes. See the chapter on Gerard de Lairesse in W. C. DeVane's *Browning's Parleyings; The Autobiography of a Mind*.

Guido) are most helpful in illuminating the truth as Browning perceived it. The other books call in for purposes of contrast a variety of conventionalized views of the affair. Since the persons who give their versions are, in fact, types representative of standard societal attitudes, the crime is made to take on far-reaching implications. Ultimately the problem expands to include the nature of the individual's responsibilities to the institutions on which any social order is based.

The three introductory monologues present the gossip about Guido's crime current in Roman society. The speaker in *Half-Rome* is a jealous husband who has reason to suspect a rival. He naturally takes Guido's side, and in so doing distorts the facts to reflect his own spiritual meanness. *The Other Half-Rome* comes to Pompilia's defense in a no less biased way. Here the narrator is a sentimentalist of the kind to be titillated by a *crime passionel*. Taking for granted an adulterous passion between Pompilia and Caponsacchi, he endows their intrigue with all the elements of cloak-and-dagger romance played by stock characters. *Tertium Quid* adds cynical commentary from the mouth of a total worldling. The speaker is wholly detached, interested only in displaying his wit to a fashionable audience. He refuses to commit himself to any moral judgment, but rather makes a malicious game of sorting over all conceivable motives for the murder. The civilized man, he would have us understand, is a relativist who knows that right and wrong are never absolute, since they depend on the particular circumstances of a given situation. In these three books Browning is showing, in effect, that society is too much dominated by its own selfish interests ever to be able to adjudicate the actions of its individual members.

The books devoted to the arguments of the lawyers broaden Browning's social satire to include the institution of law which pretends to hold the scales of justice. Here the anti-social implications are still more prominent, for the two attorneys make a travesty of legal procedure. Hyacinthus resolves in his defense of Guido to uphold his client's conduct on the score of wounded honor. The trial, offering at best an opportunity to exercise his talent for casuistry, seems rather a joke to him. While he prepares his brief, the concerns really uppermost in his mind are his small son, the purity of his Latin, malice against his rival, and the joys of the table. His celebration of natural man's reliance on instinct, although applied to Guido, is in actuality a vindication of Pompilia and Caponsacchi. In his self-admiring speech, Bottinius, the state prosecutor, juggles with logic and parades all the tricks of the rhetorician. His repeated insinuations of Pompilia's wantonness would be more appropriate in Guido's support. We are not surprised to learn in the last book that Bottinius has made a *volte-face* and is now getting ready to defame the girl's reputation, partly as a means of depriving her son of his inheritance, but more to assert the law's authority in an unjust cause. In these two books, then, it is Browning's intent to show that the machinery of social justice is as prejudiced as public opinion, and no more capable of distinguishing between right and wrong.

At the summit of the social hierarchy stand church and state; and in *The Ring and the Book* Browning's severest strictures are reserved for these ultimate seats of authority. The governor of Arezzo, concerned only to guarantee property and rank, delivers Pompilia back into her husband's hands when she throws herself on his mercy. And the central government in Florence condemns Pompilia *in absentia* and would unhesitatingly have exonerated Guido and his companions had they succeeded in escaping from papal territory. Even darker is Browning's portrayal of ecclesiastical administration in its abandonment to material self-interest. The archbishop to whom Pompilia despairingly appeals is the religious counterpart of the governor, and equally ready to sacrifice the individual to the system. Of him Pompilia says: "My heart died out at the Archbishop's smile;/ —It seemed so stale and worn a way o' the world." Even the Augustinian friar, although moved to pity by Pompilia's plight, is afraid to jeopardize his career by any overt action in her behalf. Caponsacchi's scornful comment on him is significant: "He fears God, why then needs he fear the world?"

It is through the characters of Guido and the Pope, however, that Browning most fully develops the anti-social implications of his theme in *The Ring and the Book*. Although poles apart in other respects, the two are alike in three ways: both are thinkers rather than doers; both seek a rational basis for intuitive perceptions; and both are intellectually emancipated from social conventions. In his first monologue Guido cleverly exploits every vulgar prejudice that has found voice in the three preceding books. The inference is inescapable: if Guido's actions are to be judged by worldly standards, then he is innocent. Notice, for example, how shrewdly he translates the marital relationship into terms calculated to discomfit his inquisitors:

> Am I to teach my lords what marriage means,
> What God ordains thereby and man fulfils
> Who, docile to the dictate, treads the house?
> My lords have chosen the happier part with Paul
> And neither marry nor burn,—yet priestliness
> Can find a parallel to the marriage-bond
> In its own blessed special ordinance
> Whereof indeed was marriage made the type:
> The Church may show her insubordinate,
> As marriage her refractory. How of the Monk
> Who finds the claustral regimen too sharp
> After the first month's essay? What's the mode
> With the Deacon who supports indifferently
> The rod o' the Bishop when he tastes its smart
> Full four weeks? Do you straightway slacken hold
> Of the innocents, the all-unwary ones
> Who, eager to profess, mistook their mind?—
> Remit a fast-day's rigor to the Monk
> Who fancied Francis' manna meant roast quails,—
> Concede the Deacon sweet society,
> He never thought the Levite-rule renounced,—
> Or rather prescribe short chain and sharp scourge
> Corrective of such peccant humors? This—
> I take to be the Church's mode, and mine.

It is only in his second monologue that Guido, now shorn of hope, declares himself in his true colors and lets it be seen that he is in his way as little conformable to traditional codes of behavior as Pompilia. Perhaps part of the fascination which Browning found in the workings of the criminal mentality was their very oppugnancy to the hollow formalities of social intercourse. In any event, Guido in his farewell appearance arouses moral indignation of a kind hardly to be satisfied by the edict of any earthly tribunal. The reader is appalled to realize that this world should after all provide so fair a field for the exercise of man's infernal potentialities.

Just as, on the one side, Guido for all his intelligence possesses only the most rudimentary kind of social conscience, so, on the other, the Pope in his spirituality has passed through and beyond the limitations of convention. Thus, while the two characters stand apart from society, they look on it from opposite extremes. Guido makes capital of institutions; the Pope, deriving his authority from the greatest of all institutions, seeks the living reality within the outer shell. Guido treats the world as his friend, in order further to corrupt it to his own ends; the Pope repudiates the world, fearing its powers of corruption over himself.

The Pope voices Browning's conviction that men are to be judged not by their actions, but by the motives which generate those actions:

> For I am 'ware it is the seed of act,
> God holds appraising in his hollow palm,
> Not act grown great thence on the world below,
> Leafage and branchage, vulgar eyes admire.

The world, of course, values only appearances. Therefore, it is vain to try to make of society an agency for the moral discipline of its members: "What does the world, told truth, but lie the more?" Still, the world has its use as a spiritual point of reference; the degree of opposition or submission to its dictates is the measure of the soul's state of grace. Thus, the Pope, fully sensible of human fallibility, does not at first trust his intuitions in apportioning guilt to those who have had a hand in Pompilia's death, but brings their conduct to the bar of Christian justice. When viewed in this light, Guido and his associates are seen to have misused their worldly privileges and thereby to have strengthened the existing powers of evil. Thanks to Guido's example, intrinsically noble ideals of conduct have been further degraded:

> Honor and faith,—a lie and a disguise,
> Probably for all livers in this world,
> Certainly for himself!

As the Pope passes in review the characters who have persecuted Pompilia, he finds each guilty of a vice indicative of its possessor's rejection of spiritual salvation for material ends. Guido is perhaps the exception here, since his inborn capacity for hatred would have put him outside the pale of humanity under any circumstances. But all of the others bear the world's stigma in some characteristic form: ambition for Paul, lust for Girolamo, greed for the hired assassins, power for the archbishop. Social institutions, the Pope sorrowfully concludes, simply consolidate the selfish interests of the individuals on whom they depend:

> Since all flesh is weak,
> Bind weaknesses together, we get strength:
> The individual weighed, found wanting, try
> Some institution, honest artifice
> Whereby the units grow compact and firm!
> Each props the other, and so stand is made
> For our embodied cowards that grow brave.

It is small wonder, then, that the Pope, now in his extreme old age and worn out in the search for truth, yearns for a better world where knowledge will be simply a matter of intuitive perception:

> We men, in our degree, may know
> There, simply, instantaneously, as here
> After long time and amid many lies,
> Whatever we dare think we know indeed...

At the end of his life the Pope's sympathy goes out to those in whom instinct and act are as one. For in unhesitating response to emotional impulse, as over against the devious processes of the intellect, he recognizes the token of God's immanence in human affairs. Caponsacchi is exonerated in the Pope's eyes because he acted "at an instinct of the natural man," and so revealed himself a true exemplar of "the chivalry/ That dares the right and disregards alike/ The yea and nay o' the world." It is Pompilia, however, who fully confirms the Pope's faith. In the naked simplicity of her feelings, in her yielding to the promptings of primitive instinct, he perceives the operation of a moral sense about which civilized society knows nothing. Her decision to fly from Guido bore witness to a higher fidelity than is due to conventional canons of behavior:

>   But, brave,
> Thou at first prompting of what I call God,
> And fools call Nature, didst hear, comprehend,
> Accept the obligation laid on thee,
> Mother elect, to save the unborn child. . .

Under the shadow of death the Pope pins his faith to a loving God, as revealed not through the intellectual traditions of the Church, but through the intuitions of an innocent victim of the Church's authority:

>   First of the first,
> Such I pronounce Pompilia, then as now
> Perfect in whiteness: stoop thou down, my child,
> Give one good moment to the poor old Pope
> Heart-sick at having all his world to blame—
> Let me look at thee in the flesh as erst,
> Let me enjoy the old clean linen garb,
> Not the new splendid vesture! Armed and crowned,
> Would Michael, yonder, be, nor crowned nor armed,
> The less pre-eminent angel? Everywhere
> I see in the world the intellect of man,
> That sword, the energy his subtle spear,
> The knowledge which defends him like a shield—

> Everywhere; but they make not up, I think,
> The marvel of a soul like thine, earth's flower
> She holds up to the softened gaze of God!
> It was not given Pompilia to know much,
> Speak much, to write a book, to move mankind,
> Be memorized by who records my time.
> Yet if in purity and patience, if
> In faith held fast despite the plucking fiend,
> Safe like the signet-stone with the new name
> That saints are known by,—if in right returned
> For wrong, most pardon for worst injury,
> If there be any virtue, and praise,—
> Then will this woman-child have proved—who knows?—
> Just the one prize vouchsafed unworthy me,
> Seven years a gardener of the untoward ground
> I till,—this earth, my sweat and blood manure
> All the long day that barrenly grows dusk:
> At least one blossom makes me proud at eve
> Born 'mid the briers of my enclosure!

Interest in the Pope's monologue as a lofty exposition of Browning's own philosophic optimism has tended to obscure the dramatic relevance of the grounds on which the old man finally judges Guido. After he has reached the end of his metaphysical speculations, a new voice is heard, advocating mercy. This is "the spirit of culture," ironically described as

> a new tribunal now
> Higher than God's—the educated man's!
> Nice sense of honor in the human breast
> Supersedes here the old coarse oracle...

Disguised in the Mephistophelean guise of cool and lucid reasonableness, worldly interest summons all its inducements in a final endeavor to undermine the Pope's confidence in the validity of his position. The assault comes from every side, and the logical inconsistency of many of the arguments is concealed by the cogency of their appeal to human weakness. Since Guido has taken minor orders, his acquittal is essential to preservation of the Church's prestige. To condemn him would look like an attempt to cover up Caponsacchi's guilt, a blunder calculated to play straight into the hands of the Molinists. In tune with the absolutist drift of the times, intervention in Guido's behalf offers a fitting opportunity for the arbitrary assertion of papal power. The death of the criminals would jeopardize the very compacts which knit society together: the wife's obedience to her husband, the servant's fealty to his master. And so on. "Mercy is safe and graceful," says the voice of the world. And because the safe thing and the graceful thing spell damnation, the Pope in a final gesture of repudiation seizes pen and signs Guido's death-warrant:

> Enough, for I may die this very night:
> And how should I dare die, this man let live?

Pompilia completes the Pope as a speculative man, and in the same way she completes Caponsacchi as a man of action. In both cases she accomplishes this by releasing their intuitive being from the shackles of tradition and convention. On the evidence, there can be no doubt that Pompilia and Caponsacchi in Browning's conception loved each other. Their moment of recognition demonstrates the poet's doctrine of elective affinity. Guido's forged correspondence had prepared each to take the cheapest view of the other; but at the first meeting of their eyes and without the need for a spoken word, the two penetrate the deception. A flash of insight tells Caponsacchi that Pompilia could not possibly have written those *billets-doux*:

> . . . oh! I gave a passing glance
> To a certain ugly cloud-shape, goblin-shred
> Of hell-smoke hurrying past the splendid moon
> Out now to tolerate no darkness more,
> And saw right through the thing that tried to pass
> For truth and solid, not an empty lie. . .

And Pompilia with equal certainty has taken measure of the priest:

> But now, that you stand and I see your face,
> Though you have never uttered word yet,—well, I know,
> Here too has been dream-work, delusion too,
> And that at no time, you with the eyes here,
> Ever intended to do wrong by me. . .

After this, the confederacy of Pompilia and Caponsacchi against the world is a foregone conclusion. In her time of need Caponsacchi without a moment's hesitation brushes aside the proprieties, unmindful that his conduct in arranging Pompilia's escape is on the face of it a betrayal of his priestly function and of her wifely duties. At Castelnuovo it is not only Guido but all society with its outraged prejudices which comes between them. Thinking of Caponsacchi's rustication at Civita, Pompilia cries: "do I once doubt/ The world again is holding us apart?" But although separated, each finds through the other courage to face his solitary fate. Henceforth the priest will go about his duties sustained by dreams of what might have been:

> I do but play with an imagined life
> Of who, unfettered by a vow, unblessed
> By the higher call,—since you will have it so,—
> Leads it companioned by the woman there.

And the dying Pompilia finds solace in the hope of meeting Caponsacchi in heaven, there to be joined with him in everlasting union.

The anti-social bias that is inseparable from Browning's ideal of romantic love emerges through the evolution of Caponsacchi's character after he has come under Pompilia's influence. Before this his career in the Church had promised well on the basis of accomplishments anything but spiritual. "The young frank personable priest" had declared himself "earth's clear-accepted servitor." The Church had need for such sparkling young aristocrats in its fashionable forefront; and as long as he wore his vestments with dash and elegance, his superiors were ready to overlook the peccadilloes incidental to the rôle. When Caponsacchi exchanges play-acting for the real thing, however, when the mistress becomes the runaway wife of a nobleman in minor orders, when the hand accustomed to twanging a lute and inditing a sonnet grips a sword, the situation takes on a very different complexion. To Pompilia's eyes Caponsacchi may seem the reembodiment of St. George, but the Renaissance Church found saintliness an inconvenient concept.

When called on by his examiners to explain his motive in befriending Pompilia, Caponsacchi champions the superiority of intuition over reason in as forthright a manner as the Pope:

"Thought?" nay, Sirs, what shall follow was not thought:
I have thought sometimes, and thought long and hard.
I have stood before, gone round a serious thing,
Tasked my whole mind to touch and clasp it close,
As I stretch forth my arm to touch this bar.
God and man, and what duty I owe both,—
I dare to say I have confronted these
In thought: but no such faculty helped here.
I put forth no thought,—powerless, all that night
I paced the city: it was the first Spring.
By the invasion I lay passive to,
In rushed new things, the old were rapt away;
Alike abolished—the imprisonment
Of the outside air, the inside weight o' the world
That pulled me down. Death meant, to spurn the ground,
Soar to the sky,—die well and you do that.
The very immolation made the bliss;
Death was the heart of life, and all the harm
My folly had crouched to avoid, now proved a veil
Hiding all gain my wisdom strove to grasp:
As if the intense centre of the flame
Should turn a heaven to that devoted fly
Which hitherto, sophist alike and sage,
Saint Thomas with his sober gray goose-quill,
And sinner Plato by Cephisian reed,
Would fain, pretending just the insect's good,

> Whisk off, drive back, consign to shade again.
> Into another state, under new rule
> I knew myself was passing swift and sure...

The "new rule" which the priest has accepted is, of course, that of man's instinctual nature. From Pompilia he has learned the heart's wisdom; and Browning wants us to realize that, having experienced the compulsion of love, he is at last qualified to do God's work. "Priests," says Caponsacchi, "should study passion; how else cure mankind,/ Who come for help in passionate extremes?" Whatever future awaits him in the way of ecclesiastical preferment, we may be sure that, awakened by Pompilia, he will never again subscribe to the comfortable forms of worldly religion. He conducts his defense in a spirit of fierce and belligerent individualism. The responsibility for Pompilia's tragic death he attributes directly to the organized forces of justice, which in their regard for the word rather than the spirit have disastrously bungled their God-given function. His furious indictment of officialdom for its blindness to truth evokes by inference Browning's own antipathy to social institutions:

> But you were law and gospel,—would one please
> Stand back, allow your faculty elbow-room?
> You blind guides who must needs lead eyes that see!
> Fools, alike ignorant of man and God!

The first and last books of *The Ring and the Book* discuss the circumstances under which the poem came to be written and the manner of its writing. Here Browning reveals with unusual explicitness his aesthetic theories. There is first the belief that the artist carries on his work under the express sanction of God. Thus, we are told "a Hand,/ Always above my shoulder" one day pointed out amid the bric-à-brac of a Florentine street-mart the Old Yellow Book in which the poet found his subject. The literal accuracy of the "ring" metaphor has been questioned, but the meaning which Browning meant to convey through its use is clear enough. The truth about Guido's murder of Pompilia reposed in the legal documents containing the details of the case, but was only to be deduced through interpretation of the material by a mind endowed with imaginative insight. Describing how he ultimately penetrated the raw facts to the heart of their significance, the poet says:

> I fused my live soul and that inert stuff,
> Before attempting smithcraft,

with the result that "the life in me abolished the death of things." The inference here is unmistakable. The artist's attitude towards his subject-matter is highly subjective, depending on the private vision which the imagination sheds on the facts with which it works. Browning makes lofty claims for the inner urge from which the creative act originates:

> Yet by a special gift, an art of arts,
> More insight and more outsight and much more
> Will to use both of these than boast my mates,
> I can detach from me, commission forth
> Half of my soul. . .

At the same time he scrupulously traces the artist's special insights, not to any center of self-sufficiency in the individual being, but rather to the Creator of all being. Man is, properly speaking, incapable of creation; at best, he seeks to imitate the creative process as it occurs in God's mind. In so doing, he fulfills the supreme law of life—the aspiration to comprehend, however imperfectly, the divine purpose:

> I find first
> Writ down for very A B C of fact,
> "In the beginning God made heaven and earth;"
> From which, no matter with what lisp, I spell
> And speak you out a consequence—that man,
> Man,—as befits the made, the inferior thing,—
> Purposed, since made, to grow, not make in turn,
> Yet forced to try and make, else fail to grow,—
> Formed to rise, reach at, if not grasp and gain
> The good beyond him,—which attempt is growth,—
> Repeats God's process in man's due degree,
> Attaining man's proportionate result,—

Creates, no, but resuscitates, perhaps.
Inalienable, the arch-prerogative
Which turns thought, act—conceives, expresses too!

Thus it is that Browning can call his poem his "due to God," since the artist's primary responsibility must be to the source of his inspiration.

As interpreter of God's will to humanity, however, the artist has a secondary responsibility to society. Near the end of the first book Browning addresses his Victorian readers as follows:

> Such, British Public, ye who like me not,
> (God love you!)—whom I yet have labored for,
> Perchance more careful whoso runs may read
> Than erst when all, it seemed, could read who ran,—
> Perchance more careless whoso reads may praise
> Than late when he who praised and read and wrote
> Was apt to find himself the selfsame me,—
> Such labor had such issue, so I wrought
> This arc, by furtherance of such alloy,
> And so, by one spirt, take away its trace
> Till, justifiably golden, rounds my ring.

This is an important confession of the change that had taken place in the poet's concept of his relationship to his audience. He admits the importance to the artist of the communicative faculty. Having in his early work misestimated the capabilities of his readers, he has subsequently made a sincere attempt to capture their attention through writing more intelligibly. On the other hand, he categorically denies that he has courted a wider circle of readers out of any desire for popularity. He is willing to adapt his manner to the world's capacity, but his matter is in higher keeping.

With the body of the poem behind, Browning goes on in the concluding lines to develop the theory which he had previously sketched in *Fra Lippo Lippi*. First he suggests that the true theme of *The Ring and the Book* is

> This lesson, that our human speech is naught,
> Our human testimony false, our fame
> And human estimation words and wind.

But since it ought to be obvious that ultimate truth is only apprehensible by intuitive means, "Why," he continues, "take the artistic way to prove so much?" The answer follows at once:

> Because, it is the glory and the good of Art,
> That Art remains the one way possible
> Of speaking truth, to mouths like mine at least.

The elaboration of the meaning contained in these lines leads the poet to acknowledge the double awareness as a condition of artistic expression. The creative impulse, originating as imaginative insight in the individual consciousness, imposes on the artist the obligation to find suitable forms for its embodiment, since the process of arousing men's deeper responses begins in an appeal to their superficial sympathies. The artist mediates between God and humanity; and his art, if truly inspired, in giving pleasure becomes at the same time a means of grace:

> But Art,—where man nowise speaks to men,
> Only to mankind,—Art may tell a truth
> Obliquely, do the thing shall breed the thought,
> Nor wrong the thought, missing the mediate word.
> So may you paint your picture, twice show truth,
> Beyond mere imagery on the wall,—
> So, note by note, bring music from your mind,
> Deeper than ever e'en Beethoven dived,—
> So write a book shall mean beyond the facts,
> Suffice the eye and save the soul beside.

IV

"MY HUNGER BOTH TO BE AND KNOW THE THING I AM"

The different points of view exemplified in the series of dramatic monologues which makes up *The Ring and the Book* gave Browning an opportunity to synthesize all the dominant tendencies in his thinking. His later work introduces no new themes, although the reader who is principally interested in the poet's ideas will here find them reaffirmed with increasing conviction and specificity. Thus, *La Saiziaz*, "A Pillar at Sebzevar" from *Ferishtah's Fancies*, and the Parleying *With Bernard de Mandeville* extend the intuitional foundations of the poet's religious faith; and the Parleying *With Charles Avison* is his strongest statement of the supremacy of instinct over intellect in the creative act. The loss of individual integrity through submission to the tyranny of institutions continues to elicit his anti-social bias. *Prince Hohenstiel-Schwangau, Saviour of Society* and the Parleying *With George Bubb Dodington* are mordant studies of political temporizers, while Léonce Miranda, the protagonist of *Red Cotton Night-Cap Country; or Turf and Towers*, is destroyed by religious superstition. Browning's unorthodox theories about love and the relations between the sexes are set forth in such poems as *Fifine at the Fair, The Inn Album, A Forgiveness*, and the Parleying *With Daniel Bartoli*. And a very large number of poems touch on one or another aspect of his aesthetic theories. The interpenetration of reality by imaginative insight informs the important critical pronouncements in the two works constructed around translations of Euripidean tragedies, and in the Parleyings *With Francis Furini* and *With Gerard de Lairesse*. The concept of the poet-seer, directly inspired by and owing primary allegiance to God, accounts for the treatment of René Gentilhomme in *The Two Poets of Croisic* and also for the Parleying *With Christopher Smart*.

If, however, Browning was content in his later poetry to reformulate themes which we have already sufficiently explored in his better-known work, he continued to the end of his career to invent new forms for the projection of those themes. This constant technical experimentation is the most interesting and suggestive critical problem relating to his final literary period. Tennyson's last poems reflect a divided intent; part are transparently popular in tone, while others have the quality of private utterance. Browning, on the other hand, continued to try to resolve the artistic dilemma posed by a double awareness, through his search for poetic forms responsive to both conditions of sensibility.

In the dramatic monologue, as practised in his period of greatest achievement, the poet might be supposed to have found his rightful manner; and the wonder is that after *The Ring and the Book* his writing in this vein shows such a falling off. The explanation lies in a failure in dramatic sense, disastrous for a poet who saw all life as conflict. Just as Browning's dramas are deficient in external action, so the later monologues lack internal action of the kind produced by emotional intensity. Ironically enough in one who so distrusted the theorizing faculty, intellect comes to preponderate over feeling. What these poems offer is not the throb of passion, but the psychoanalytic investigation of motives behind impulses which never themselves get actualized. Having previously dispensed with incident, Browning now tends at one further remove to refuse emotional involvement in the situations he evokes. And, correspondingly, the reader finds it more and more difficult to care very greatly why a character acts in a given way when the act itself, anticipated or retrospective, has not been made to seem interesting or significant.

Fifine at the Fair is a case in point. After reading it (and the other long and intricate monologues of the period), one cannot help thinking that had Browning seen fit to take up the writing of novels he might have foreshadowed the accomplishments of Meredith, Conrad, and James. But for all the fascination of its protagonist, a latter-day Don Juan, and the subtle relevance of his arguments to modern habits of mind, the dialectics of *Fifine at the Fair* are too diffuse and centrifugal to answer the demands of poetic form. The emotional conflict created in the hero by the rival attractions of the spiritual Elvire and the fleshly Fifine is a valid one; but long before the final choice is made, the initial tension has become slack, weighted down under an excessive burden of intellectual speculation. Browning has perfected his skill in special pleading to the point of over-sophistication, and the reader finds himself wondering whether the Don's ambiguous nature may not after all reflect his creator's own inability to make up his mind. Browning clearly sympathizes with the libertine's restiveness under a system of individually repressive social conventions, for he puts into his character's mouth many of his own opinions about love and society and art. Like Bishop Blougram, the Don has a faculty for calling true things by false names; only in *Fifine at the Fair* Browning overreaches himself and so loses control over his argument. For such appeal as the poem makes rests in the very skill with which the protagonist rationalizes his selfish desires and thereby reduces morality to conform to private convenience. Deprived of any ethical sanction, the emotions become the plaything of intellectual casuistry; and this too often seems to be the case in those later monologues where the dramatic conflict enacts itself on a level of abstract ideas.

The obscurity in which Browning's sophistries too often involved him in such poems as *Fifine at the Fair* was in the nature of a return to the manner of *Pauline* and *Sordello*; and his reputation suffered accordingly. It was clearly in an effort to free himself from this subjective vein that the poet turned to straight narrative in the two series of *Dramatic Idyls*. As the use of the term Idyls indicates, Browning was here following Tennyson's lead, although with the intention of showing up the laureate's timid avoidance of actuality. The handling of realistic details in these poems does not, however, compensate for the author's technical inferiority to Tennyson as a story-teller. If the springs of motivation in *Fifine at the Fair* and *Red Cotton Night-Cap Country* are unduly complex, many of the *Dramatic Idyls* suffer from the opposite failing of inadequate motivation. The climactic events of *Iván Ivánovitch*, *Clive*, and *Muléykeh*, for example, seem arbitrary to the point of improbability. Whereas the resolution of a poem like *The Glove* arouses the reader to self-recognition, the Browning of the later monologues often seems content with the short-lived shock produced by a surprise ending.

Other groups of poems show that Browning was continuing his search for ways of enlivening recondite material. *Ferishtah's Fancies* is a variation on the formula of *Pippa Passes*. Indeed, as early as *Paracelsus* he had inserted lyric interludes into other types of poetry as a kind of emotional leitmotiv. The use of lyrics to comment on philosophic discourse in *Ferishtah's Fancies*, however, is a good deal less effective than the handling of this device in the more dramatic circumstances of *Paracelsus* and *Pippa Passes*. In *Parleyings with Certain People of Importance in Their Day*, Browning had recourse to another early method for the projection of his ideas: namely, the study of historical individuals in the context of cultural movements. As W. C. DeVane has conclusively demonstrated, the Parleyings are of unparalleled value in analyzing the origin and development of Browning's characteristic theories; but their appeal is limited to those whose interest is in the man rather than the artist.

The peevish and spiteful treatment of his critics in *Pacchiarotto, with Other Poems* evidences the poet's anxiety about his erratic hold on the reading public. In defense of his later work he constantly makes two assertions which have the appearance of special pleading in his own behalf. If his poetry seems difficult, that is because his audience, expecting cowslip-wine, gets nettle-broth instead. To express this concept he employs the further metaphors of the nut in *Jochanan Hakkadosh* and of the ortolan in the Prologue to *Ferishtah's Fancies*. The external appearance of neither is inviting; he who would savor their true flavor must bite through a resistant covering. Browning offers a more elevated version of his artistic intent at this time in the Epilogue to the second series of *Dramatic Idyls*, in which the lyric poet of the first stanza harks back to Aprile and Eglamor:

"Touch him ne'er so lightly, into song he broke:
Soil so quick-receptive—not one feather-seed,
Not one flower-dust fell but straight its fall awoke
Vitalizing virtue: song would song succeed
Sudden as spontaneous—prove a poet-soul!"

          Indeed?

Rock's the song-soil rather, surface hard and bare:
Sun and dew their mildness, storm and frost their rage
Vainly both expend,—few flowers awaken there:
Quiet in its cleft broods—what the after-age
Knows and names a pine, a nation's heritage.

Concurrently, the poet makes much of the fact that his writing is founded in actuality. Its life-principle is the "sap of prose experience"; his "fancy wells up through corrective fact." So, in his later poems, such as the Prologue to *Asolando*, the author constantly affirms the all-importance of seeing things as they are:

  Friend, did you need an optic glass,
    Which were your choice? A lens to drape
  In ruby, emerald, chrysopras,
    Each object—or reveal its shape
  Clear outlined, past escape,

  The naked very thing?—so clear
    That, when you had the chance to gaze,
  You found its inmost self appear
    Through outer seeming—truth ablaze,
  Not falsehood's fancy-haze?

And here once again the concept of a double awareness enters in. With Browning's emphasis on fact the Victorian age could take no issue; however, it might well do so with his undisguised *sense* of fact. In *Pacchiarotto, with Other Poems* the poet had insisted on the rigorous objectivity of his attitude; but coupled with an admission of the difficulties offered by his work, this defense stands self-convicted of disingenuousness. Fact may be, indeed usually is, Browning's starting-point; but when submitted to analysis by his inquiring and subtle mind and interpreted in the light of this process, the original fact acquires highly subjective meanings and becomes principally significant as an index to the poet's individual consciousness.

It is all very well for Don Juan to say in *Fifine at the Fair*:

And—consequent upon the learning how from strife
Grew peace—from evil, good—came knowledge that, to get
Acquaintance with the way o' the world, we must not fret
Nor fume, on altitudes of self-sufficiency,
But bid a frank farewell to what—we think—should be,
And, with as good a grace, welcome what is—we find.

But how is this statement to be squared with the Don's earlier confession of intense self-consciousness: "My hunger both to be and know the thing I am," a statement which might stand as the epigraph to the history of Browning's mind? For the poet, while professing dependence on the outer world, could never accept its evidences until they had first passed through the filter of his imagination. Thus, he addresses Gerard de Lairesse as follows:

. . . for sense, my De Lairesse,
Cannot content itself with outward things,
Mere beauty: soul must needs know whence there springs—
How, when and why—what sense but loves, nor lists
To know at all.

And again, further elaborating the necessity for the artist to probe beneath the surface of outward seeming, the poet has the protagonist of *Red Cotton Night-Cap Country* say:

Along with every act—and speech is act—
There go, a multitude impalpable
To ordinary human faculty,
The thoughts which give the act significance.
Who is a poet needs must apprehend
Alike both speech and thoughts which prompt to speak.
Part these, and thought withdraws to poetry:
Speech is reported in the newspaper.

Browning, as we have seen, asserted that intuition is the ultimate means of knowledge, and that the faculty which enables the artist to approach truth is imaginative insight. In his own case these faculties operated most successfully through a form of dramatic perception in which the fact and its ulterior meaning become fused into unity by a single act of apprehension. But with the decline of dramatic sensibility in his later work, fact and meaning draw apart, so that he depends increasingly on the rationalizing intellect to set up correspondence between them. Whether the successes of his middle period are attributable to the glow of emotional maturity, or to the perfecting of a suitable form, or to both, it is only in the poems of these years (and perhaps occasionally in the Indian summer of *Asolando*) that we find the inner and outer consciousness held in equipoise. In the later poetry as in the early efforts, the split in awareness is manifest. Into the character of Euripides, as conceived in *Balaustion's Adventure* and *The Last Adventure of Balaustion*, Browning incorporated his reading of the dilemma which tormented the Victorian artist. The evidence is contained not only in the partisan words of Balaustion, but also, with surprising impartiality, in Aristophanes' criticism of his rival. Euripides, coming in the wake of Sophocles, is made to say: "I, his successor, . . ./ Incline to poetize philosophy,/ Extend it rather than restrain." And Aristophanes then proceeds to describe Euripides' introspective habit of mind in terms that clearly echo Browning's own rueful recognition of the unpredictable and alienating ways of his imagination:

> His task is to refine, refine,
> Divide, distinguish, subtilize away
> Whatever seemed a solid planting-place
> For footfall,—not in that phantasmal sphere
> Proper to poet, but on vulgar earth
> Where people used to tread with confidence.
> There's left no longer one plain positive
> Enunciation incontestable
> Of what is good, right, decent here on earth.

Arnold

And lie thou there,
My laurel bough!
Scornful Apollo's ensign, lie thou there!
Though thou hast been my shade in the world's heat—
Though I have loved thee, lived in honouring thee—
Yet lie thou there,
My laurel bough!

I am weary of thee.
I am weary of the solitude
Where he who bears thee must abide—
Of the rocks of Parnassus,
Of the gorge of Delphi,
Of the moonlit peaks, and the caves.
Thou guardest them, Apollo!
Over the grave of the slain Pytho,
Though young, intolerably severe!
Thou keepest aloof the profane,
But the solitude oppresses thy votary!
The jars of men reach him not in thy valley—
But can life reach him?
Thou fencest him from the multitude—
Who will fence him from himself?
He hears nothing but the cry of the torrents,
And the beating of his own heart.
The air is thin, the veins swell,
The temples tighten and throb there—
Air! Air!

Take thy bough, set me free from my solitude;
I have been enough alone!

    EMPEDOCLES ON ETNA

ARNOLD

I
"THE DIALOGUE OF THE MIND WITH ITSELF"

With Matthew Arnold the dilemma of the modern artist in society becomes fully explicit. For Arnold's critical habit of mind led him to attempt to analyze and define in objective terms that sense of alienation which we have most often encountered in the work of Tennyson and Browning under the guise of a vaguely realized malaise. In directly confronting the motives for his antipathy to the Victorian age, Arnold was concerned not only to clarify his own relationship to that age, but also to reaffirm the traditional sovereignty of poetry as a civilizing agent. Thus, whereas Tennyson and Browning ultimately relied on private revelation derived from mystical or instinctual, and in either case irrational, sources, Arnold looked for inspiration to the great humanistic idea which asserts that man is the measure of all possibilities.

This is not, of course, to imply that Arnold found it any easier than Tennyson or Browning to come to terms with the age. If the Victorians distrusted the visions of the seer and the instincts of the primitive, they were hardly more sympathetic to Arnold's advocacy of culture as enlisting the whole nature of man in opposition to the Zeitgeist. To a much greater extent than holds true for either Tennyson or Browning, the poetry of Arnold bears testimony to its author's refusal to compromise with the spirit of his era. The protagonists of his poems are invariably lonely and isolated figures, alien to their environment. Mycerinus, the Forsaken Merman, the Scholar-Gipsy, Empedocles, the author of 'Obermann' display an unmistakable family likeness, since all are, in fact, projections of their creator's own essential homelessness in the Victorian world.

To a Gipsy Child by the Sea-Shore may serve to illustrate Arnold's fondness for themes traceable to an obsession with the problem of estrangement. The gipsies reappear in both *Resignation* and *The Scholar-Gipsy*, where also their deracinated condition epitomizes spiritual exile. The gipsy boy and his mother are described as reluctant to acknowledge even the most elementary of ties: "half averse/ From thine own mother's breast, that knows not thee." Between the poet and the child, on the other hand, a passing glance creates a bond of sympathy. Searching for an analogy to the impression of sadness thus conveyed, Arnold surmises whether the other's mood is not like

> Some exile's, mindful how the past was glad?
> Some angel's, in an alien planet born?

More remarkable than the young gipsy's mournfulness, however, is the stoicism with which it is borne, a stoicism suggestive of clear-eyed and unflinching disillusionment:

> Is the calm thine of stoic souls, who weigh
> Life well, and find it wanting, nor deplore;
> But in disdainful silence turn away,
> Stand mute, self-centred, stern, and dream no more?

In truth, the secret of the gipsy's dignity is in his aloofness to the circumstances of earthly existence; his is the satanic sorrow of the infernal visitant who cannot forget lost felicity:

> Ah! not the nectarous poppy lovers use,
> Not daily labour's dull, Lethæan spring,
> Oblivion in lost angels can infuse
> Of the soil'd glory, and the trailing wing.

The vicissitudes of worldly being may dull the edge of grief;

but a mood so noble in its origin, the poet suggests, can never be wholly displaced. Rather, there is tragic grandeur in so accepting an alien fate.

The grounds for Arnold's antagonism to his age emerge in a large number of poems originally published in the volumes of 1849 and 1852. From these it is apparent that the author was in closer touch with the society about him than either Tennyson or Browning, so that his criticism of contemporary manners and morals has an authority and immediacy lacking in either of his brother-poets. Put quite simply, Arnold felt that the temper of Victorian society was destructive of individual integrity and wholeness of being. Any serious-minded person, who in all sincerity desired to cultivate his own garden, was obliged at every turn to resist intrusive pressures hostile to the philosophic mind. The threat to self-possession embodied in the superficial values of modern life is repeatedly formulated in such poems as *The World's Triumphs*, *A Question*, *The World and the Quietist*, and *Horatian Echo*. This conflict receives what is perhaps its classic expression in *The Buried Life*, which appeals to the innermost recesses of being as the ultimate refuge against the frivolous solicitations of the external world. Because he lacks the courage of his own innate convictions, the average man looks around him and invites: "Of all the thousand nothings of the hour/ Their stupefying power." In a manner prophetic of much twentieth-century writing Arnold equates the social whirl where "light flows our war of mocking words" with a flight from self-consciousness. We are reminded

> How frivolous a baby man would be—
> By what distractions he would be possess'd,
> How he would pour himself in every strife,
> And well-nigh change his own identity—

But whether the social mask be worn instinctively to hide an inner vacuity or whether it be deliberately assumed to shield a central core of sensitivity, the penalty is the same: disintegration of individuality, estrangement not only from one's kind, but from oneself as well:

> I knew the mass of men conceal'd
> Their thoughts, for fear that if reveal'd
> They would by other men be met
> With blank indifference, or with blame reproved;
> I knew they lived and moved
> Trick'd in disguises, alien to the rest
> Of men, and alien to themselves. . .

In a social order built on pretense and subterfuge, lasting attachments are formed with difficulty. The group of poems inspired by Arnold's early failure in love involves most of the factors in modern life which the author found most disruptive of inner harmony. Marguerite, viewed in artistic perspective, appears less a real woman than a symbolic presentment of romantic love in all its distracting appeal. From the earliest stages of the affair Arnold was evidently fearful lest submission to her spell would deprive him of the power of self-direction and lead him astray amidst the dizzying cross-currents of the senses. The Yale Manuscript carries an entry for the year 1849 indicative of Arnold's intention to write a poem on the refusal of limitation by the sentiment of love. But do not all the lyrics devoted to Marguerite embroider on this theme? As finally arranged, furthermore, they show a definite progression through which the poet moves towards a clearer and clearer understanding of the motives underlying his reluctance to submerge his identity in a one-sided relationship. At first, in *Parting*, there is merely the unhappy awareness of temperamental variance: "And what heart knows another?" This realization then supplies in *Isolation. To Marguerite* the motive for self-withdrawal. Since "the heart can bind itself alone," the poet abandons all hope of fulfillment through shared experience:

> Farewell!—and thou, thou lonely heart,
> Which never yet without remorse
> Even for a moment didst depart

> From thy remote and spheréd course
> To haunt the place where passions reign—
> Back to thy solitude again!

And finally in the lyric entitled *To Marguerite—Continued* the poet's estrangement from his mistress undergoes a further expansion to include the concept that in the modern world there no longer exists any channel for communication between one individual and another on the level of the deeper sensibilities. The impossibility of true love is thus emblematic of a general breakdown in human intercourse. Every man has, in truth, become an island.

> Yes! in the sea of life enisled,
> With echoing straits between us thrown,
> Dotting the shoreless watery wild,
> We mortal millions live *alone*.
> The islands feel the enclasping flow,
> And then their endless bounds they know.
>
> But when the moon their hollows lights,
> And they are swept by balms of spring,
> And in their glens, on starry nights,
> The nightingales divinely sing;
> And lovely notes, from shore to shore,
> Across the sounds and channels pour—
>
> Oh! then a longing like despair
> Is to their farthest caverns sent;
> For surely once, they feel, we were
> Parts of a single continent!
> Now round us spreads the watery plain—
> Oh might our marges meet again!
>
> Who order'd, that their longing's fire
> Should be, as soon as kindled, cool'd?
> Who renders vain their deep desire?—
> A God, a God their severance ruled!
> And bade betwixt their shores to be
> The unplumb'd, salt, estranging sea.

Exacerbated in his outward contacts with the age, the youthful Arnold followed the way of escape endorsed by the preceding generation of romantic poets; he accepted his alienation and sought to make a virtue of it. The life of the imagination, however, cannot be wholly self-sustaining. The thinking of both Tennyson and Browning, as we have seen, operated within a transcendental frame of reference. Arnold lacked any such resources of imaginative being. Incapable either of Tennyson's mystical double-vision or of Browning's primitive vitalism, he tried to rationalize his impulses. Proof though he might be against worldly delusions, he yet feared the worse delusion of creating an inner world in his own image. As a result, much of the poetry in the volumes of 1849 and 1852, as well as later, is the record of the author's search for a principle of authority conformable alike to his subjective consciousness and to some mode of belief sanctioned by tradition.

Orthodox Christianity was intellectually inadmissible to Arnold. Very little of his early poetry exhibits any serious preoccupation with the Christian revelation. Perhaps the nostalgic undertone of *Dover Beach* is as close as the poet comes to an admission of the consolations offered by religion. But with the "melancholy, long, withdrawing roar" of the Sea of Faith sounding in his ears, he faces a world bereft of any spiritual motive, a world which offers: "Nor certitude, nor peace, nor help for pain." And in exemplification of the failure of religion as an informing principle in modern life, there is nothing to match the culminating figure of *Dover Beach*:

> And we are here as on a darkling plain
> Swept with confused alarms of struggle and flight,
> Where ignorant armies clash by night.

Out of his profound veneration for Goethe and Wordsworth, Arnold courted nature in the hope of receiving under its benign patronage spiritual intimations more responsive to his individual needs. Yet, while such a poem as *Parting* seems to suggest the possibility of correspondence between man and the natural order, the poet generally regards any such idea as a deliberate fiction of the poetic imagination. Arnold's nature poetry clearly reveals a dualistic habit of mind. *The Youth of Nature* develops the argument that natural laws function according to their own logic, totally oblivious of human participation. The theory that nature has a separate existence recurs in *Self-Dependence* and in *A Wish*, where the writer speaks of

> The world which was ere I was born,
> The world which lasts when I am dead;
>
> Which never was the friend of *one*,
> Nor promised love it could not give,
> But lit for all its generous sun,
> And lived itself, and made us live.

Man has his assigned rôle. To solicit nature's intervention in the performance of this rôle is to confuse two distinct planes of being. Hence the warning of *In Harmony with Nature*: "Man must begin, know this, where Nature ends;/ Nature and man can never be fast friends." At best, Nature provides an example from which humanity may learn valuable lessons in achieving its own goals. One such lesson is the union of industriousness and serenity, as set forth in the sonnet *Quiet Work* and in *Lines Written in Kensington Gardens*. In *The Youth of Man* nature is invoked to teach self-reliance: "Rally the good in the depths of thyself!" But more frequently Arnold tends to equate the tranquilizing effect of natural phenomena with his ideal of intellectual freedom based on largeness and clarity of mind. It is in this exalted context that he apostrophizes nature in the concluding lines of *A Summer Night*:

> But I will rather say that you remain
> A world above man's head, to let him see
> How boundless might his soul's horizons be,
> How vast, yet of what clear transparency!
> How it were good to abide there, and breathe free. . .

Although he was unable to compensate for his sense of isolation by appealing to orthodox religious beliefs or to a form of natural supernaturalism, Arnold refused to grant that man is an accidental phenomenon. Throughout all his earlier poetry there persists a curiously classic fatalism. Some mysterious force presides over the human situation. This force is never very clearly defined; it goes variously under the names of necessity or fate or destiny, all of which terms, one is tempted to say, are merely so many metaphorical disguises for Arnold's obsession with the Zeitgeist. Sometimes the agent is endowed with godlike attributes, though hardly those of the Christian deity. In *To Marguerite—Continued*, for example, the poet ascribes the distances between individuals to the fact that: "A God, a God their severance ruled!"

Necessity for Arnold is whatever negates freedom of will. The speaker in *Stanzas in Memory of the Author of 'Obermann'* says:

> We, in some unknown Power's employ,
> Move on a rigorous line;
> Can neither, when we will, enjoy,
> Nor, when we will, resign.

The individual finds that he has to postulate some mysterious and superhuman power in order to account for the limitations of his faculties, especially as a social being. The three lyrics which introduce the Marguerite series, *Meeting*, *Parting*, and *A Farewell*, all assume that the relationship is predestined to failure:

> . . . we wear out life, alas!
> Distracted as a homeless wind,
> In beating where we must not pass,
> In seeking what we shall not find . . .

Occasionally the poet implies that man's isolation is assumed out of selfish regard for his own interests. This is the case in the second of the two political sonnets, *To a Republican Friend*, where the poet, musing "on what life is," reaches the conclusion that

> ... this vale, this earth, whereon we dream,
> Is on all sides o'ershadow'd by the high
> Uno'erleap'd Mountains of Necessity,
> Sparing us narrower margin than we deem.
>
> Nor will that day dawn at a human nod,
> When, bursting through the network superposed
> By selfish occupation—plot and plan,
>
> Lust, avarice, envy—liberated man,
> All difference with his fellow-mortal closed,
> Shall be left standing face to face with God.

More often, however, man's confinement to the lonely prison of selfhood is not of his own choosing, but has been somehow imposed by circumstances beyond his control. Thus, in *The Buried Life* we are told:

> Ah! well for us, if even we,
> Even for a moment, can get free
> Our heart, and have our lips unchain'd;
> For that which seals them hath been deep-ordain'd!

That the individual should be condemned to live unto himself Arnold was reluctantly prepared to accept as a condition of modern life, but that he should on top of that lack the incentive of a distinctly perceived private goal seemed too harsh a decree. *Self-Deception* records the mood of bewildered despair in which the poet cast about for an explanation of why he had been granted inborn potentialities, and yet denied the opportunity to make any constructive use of them:

> Then, as now, this tremulous, eager being
> Strain'd and long'd and grasp'd each gift it saw;
> Then, as now, a Power beyond our seeing
> Staved us back, and gave our choice the law.
>
> Ah, whose hand that day through Heaven guided
> Man's new spirit, since it was not we?
> Ah, who sway'd our choice, and who decided
> What our gifts, and what our wants should be?

For, alas! he left us each retaining
Shreds of gifts which he refused in full.
Still these waste us with their hopeless straining,
Still the attempt to use them proves them null.

And on earth we wander, groping, reeling;
Powers stir in us, stir and disappear.
Ah! and he, who placed our master-feeling,
Fail'd to place that master-feeling clear.

We but dream we have our wish'd-for powers,
Ends we seek we never shall attain.
Ah! *some* power exists there, which is ours?
Some end is there, we indeed may gain?

The state of mind here described was fraught with tragic implications for Arnold. Among his first efforts to objectify his own situation in narrative and dramatic forms occur two poems on the theme of individual talent frustrated by an alien environment. The good ruler Mycerinus, forestalled by the "stern sentence of the Powers of Destiny," withdraws from the world to take such solace as may be found in purely self-regarding pastimes. The King in Bokhara likewise learns that even the most humane governors are subject "unto a rule more strong than theirs"; and while he submits to the letter of the law, he does so in bitterness and desolation of heart.

Although they react very differently to the inscrutable dictates imposed on them, Mycerinus and the King in Bokhara exhibit a like fatalism. Their lonely stoicism, akin to that of the gipsy child, reflects Arnold's own attitude. Betrayed by all else, the individual may yet consult the laws of his own essential nature. "Man cannot, though he would, live chance's fool," declares the poet of *Human Life*. From which we are to understand that even though we have fallen on a barren time and lost touch with our fellows and with the universe, we still have the possibility of salvation within ourselves. Poem after poem in the volumes of 1849 and 1852 invokes, through such phrases as "man's one nature," the "soul well-knit," and "my nature's law," the classical concept of equanimity as the highest achievement of individual self-integration.

The essential conflict which Arnold was to develop through so many variations is present as early as the sonnet, *Written in Butler's Sermons*. On the one hand, the world with its manifold claims exerts a centrifugal pressure on man's nature. This tendency towards fragmentation is counteracted, however, by a nucleus of individuality, the buried life which makes for unity, stability, and equilibrium:

> Affections, Instincts, Principles, and Powers,
> Impulse and Reason, Freedom and Control—
> So Men, unravelling God's harmonious whole,
> Rend in a thousand shreds this life of ours.
>
> Vain labour! Deep and broad, where none may see,
> Spring the foundations of that shadowy throne
> Where man's one nature, queen-like, sits alone,
> Centred in a majestic unity...

The same idea appears in *Religious Isolation, Human Life, The Second Best*, and *The Youth of Man*. It also provides the solution to Mycerinus' dilemma. The king abdicates and goes into self-imposed exile, where, we are told,

> he, within,
> Took measure of his soul, and knew its strength,
> And by that silent knowledge, day by day,
> Was calm'd, ennobled, comforted, sustain'd.

The normal circumstances of life, however, do not often provide opportunity for an act of renunciation so decisive as that initiated by Mycerinus. More commonly, the disassociation exists as a state of mind, but the individual is not the less committed to his choice if he hopes to avoid the vitiating influences of the Time Spirit. Among the entries in the Yale Manuscript occurs the following: "Our remotest self must abide in its remoteness awful & unchanged, presiding at the tumult of the rest [?] of our being, changing thoughts contending desires &c as the moon over the agitations of the

Sea." And many years afterwards this random jotting attained final expression in the dominant metaphor of *Palladium*. The mind, it seems, is divided between a double awareness. One part, controlling the active will, inclines the possessor to engage in worldly affairs. The other part, passively centered in contemplation, is circumscribed by the inner consciousness. It is this second part which bears the burden of alienation, and must do so, if the individual's outer awareness is to remain uncorrupted by exposure to the ways of the world, is to have a point of reference other than the debased values current in society:

> Set where the upper streams of Simois flow
> Was the Palladium, high 'mid rock and wood;
> And Hector was in Ilium, far below,
> And fought, and saw it not—but there it stood!
>
> It stood, and sun and moonshine rain'd their light
> On the pure columns of its glen-built hall.
> Backward and forward roll'd the waves of fight
> Round Troy—but while this stood, Troy could not fall.
>
> So, in its lovely moonlight, lives the soul.
> Mountains surround it, and sweet virgin air;
> Cold plashing, past it, crystal waters roll;
> We visit it by moments, ah, too rare!
>
> We shall renew the battle in the plain
> To-morrow;—red with blood will Xanthus be;
> Hector and Ajax will be there again,
> Helen will come upon the wall to see.
>
> Then we shall rust in shade, or shine in strife,
> And fluctuate 'twixt blind hopes and blind despairs,
> And fancy that we put forth all our life,
> And never know how with the soul it fares.
>
> Still doth the soul, from its lone fastness high,
> Upon our life a ruling effluence send.
> And when it fails, fight as we will, we die;
> And while it lasts, we cannot wholly end.

It is thus apparent that Arnold looked to the life of the imagination as a place of refuge from the spirit of the age. But if the poet could not endure the conditions of contemporary life, he found it equally difficult to live exclusively for and to himself. Unsustained by any real religious or philosophic faith, he fell back, as had been suggested, on a form of stoicism based on the assumption that each individual must rely on the laws of his own nature. Bleak enough at the best times, this creed would become intolerably so when the individual, for whatsoever reason, doubted his powers of endurance. And Arnold was recurrently prone to misgivings that made a mockery of any pretense of self-possession.

Fear of the Zeitgeist, on one hand, and distrust of his own innate perceptions, on the other, imposed on Arnold's poetry a reciprocal stress that accounts for its characteristic tone of indecision. In *Stagirius* the writer asks release "from doubt, where all is double." The first stanza of this poem, which dates from as early as 1844, makes a typical plea against "the world's temptations." But by a reversal of responsibility the second stanza asks release from the spiritual pride which, repudiating the world, falls into self-infatuation and hence error of a worse kind:

> When the soul, growing clearer,
>   Sees God no nearer;
> When the soul, mounting higher,
>   To God comes no nigher;
> But the arch-fiend Pride
> Mounts at her side,
> Foiling her high emprise,
> Sealing her eagle eyes,
> And, when she fain would soar,
> Makes idols to adore,
> Changing the pure emotion
> Of her high devotion,
> To a skin-deep sense
> Of her own eloquence;
> Strong to deceive, strong to enslave—
>   Save, oh! save.

In Utrumque Paratus presents a more philosophic account of the difficulties into which the poet was led by his dualistic tendency of mind. Once grant a Prime Mover behind the universe, and the individual's willful severance from his kind becomes justifiable as a holy quest, conducting in "lonely pureness to the all-pure fount" of ultimate truth. But if everything happens by chance (the opinion to which Arnold seems to incline, in this poem at least), then self-immersion denotes a rejection of life itself:

> Oh when most self-exalted, most alone,
>   Chief dreamer, own thy dream!
> Thy brother-world stirs at thy feet unknown,
> Who hath a monarch's hath no brother's part;
> —Oh, what a spasm shakes the dreamer's heart!
> '*I, too, but seem.*'*

The Marguerite lyrics, as a confession of failure to get outside the limitations of self through love, are Arnold's most subjective statement of his sense of apartness. Yet even here the yearning for union with another is present as a constant undertone and goes far towards cancelling the overt theme. *Isolation. To Marguerite* concludes with the following wistful reference to the experience

> Of happier men—for they, at least,
> Have *dream'd* two human hearts might blend
> In one, and were through faith released
> From isolation without end
> Prolong'd; nor knew, although not less
> Alone than thou, their loneliness.

---

* Twenty years later in the collected *Poems* of 1869 Arnold replaced this stanza with one which shows a significant change in emphasis:

> Thy native world stirs at thy feet unknown,
>   Yet there thy secret lies!
> Out of this stuff, these forces, thou art grown,
> And proud self-severance from them were disease.
> O scan thy native world with pious eyes!
> High as thy life be risen, 'tis from these;
>   And these, too, rise.

A similar nostalgia informs *To Marguerite—Continued*, and enters still more explicitly into *The Forsaken Merman*. It is impossible not to perceive in the latter poem a metaphorical presentation of the poet's hapless passion for the shadowy Marguerite. The incongruous mating of the merman and the earth-born woman symbolizes a deeper spiritual incompatibility to which the bereft lover is reluctant to reconcile himself.

Other poems, less personal in their implications, show Arnold fully aware that self-withdrawal cannot be accomplished without a grievous sacrifice of social sympathies. Most revealing in this connection are the passages which have survived from two early attempts to handle Greek tragedy. The chorus in the *Fragment of an 'Antigone'* commends the man who puts familial duties above selfish regard for his own well-being:

> Him then I praise, who dares
> To self-selected good
> Prefer obedience to the primal law,
> Which consecrates the ties of blood; for these, indeed,
> Are to the Gods a care;
> That touches but himself.

The *Fragment of Chorus of a 'Dejaneira,'* presumably written at about the same time, comments as follows on the victims of *hybris*:

> Little in your prosperity
> Do you seek counsel of the Gods.
> Proud, ignorant, self-adored, you live alone.

It is vain for such individuals to consult the oracles:

> For you will not put on
> New hearts with the enquirer's holy robe,
> And purged, considerate minds.

Stoical submission to an alien destiny can never quell the individual's instinctive desire for shared experience. Of this fact the King in Bokhara, among others, becomes tragically aware. That Arnold felt increasingly the loneliness of exclusive self-preoccupation is evident from the prevalence in the 1852 volume of poems which lament the conditions attendant on this state of being. *Human Life, Euphrosyne,* and *Too Late* are all concerned with man's inherent human craving for affection. And for a poet who had known the bitter disillusionment of unequal love, *The Buried Life* and *Dover Beach* evidence a most strange and unexpected reversal of the sentiments displayed in the Marguerite lyrics.* For the buried life, we are told, is most likely to declare itself under the impress of strong emotion, such as occurs in moments of perfect togetherness "when a belovéd hand is laid in ours," while in *Dover Beach* the lover relies, in the absence of all other consolations, on communion with his mistress:

> Ah, love, let us be true
> To one another! for the world, which seems
> To lie before us like a land of dreams,
> So various, so beautiful, so new,
> Hath really neither joy, nor love, nor light,
> Nor certitude, nor peace, nor help for pain. . .

Arnold's early poetry, therefore, is prevailingly ambivalent, alternating between emotional involvement in the life of his times and aloofness therefrom. And sooner or later it was to his art that the poet always appealed to mediate a conflict that he had failed to resolve by other means. In Arnold's thinking the relationship of the individual to society is inseparable from the dilemma of the modern artist. As a result, the volumes of 1849 and 1852 include a number of poems which develop the aesthetic aspect of alienation. Furthermore, the intimate discussion of artistic problems contained in Arnold's correspondence with Clough during this period makes it possible to analyze with considerable precision the successive stages through which the author passed in trying to formulate a concept of the poetic function, answerable both to his own inclinations and to the needs of the age.

* It might be argued, of course, that by this time Arnold had met and fallen in love with his future wife.

Arnold's letters to Clough, written in the late months of 1847 and during 1848, persistently maintain that the spirit of the times is inimical to disinterested creative endeavor. Indeed, the second letter in the published series discusses the pitfalls lying in wait for the artist who achieves any measure of popular success:

> But never without a Pang do I hear of the growing Popularity of a strong minded writer. Then I know... the strong minded writer will lose his self-knowledge, and talk of his usefulness and imagine himself a Reformer, instead of an Exhibition.... we, my love, lovers of one another and fellow worshippers of Isis, while we believe in the Universality of Passion as Passion, will keep our Aesthetics by remembering its onesidedness as doctrine.

As the concluding sentence clearly suggests, Arnold is at this time disposed to treat poetry as a cloistral rite. Clough's earnest didacticism too often seemed a criticism of his own disinclination to get involved in issues of contemporary moment. At one time he chastises his friend for his attempts "to *solve* the Universe"; on another occasion he calls him "a mere d---d depth hunter in poetry." Again, sensing Clough's kind of poetry as an implied reproach to his own, he falls back on the classic apology of the devotee of art for art's sake: "A growing sense of the deficiency of the *beautiful* in your poems, and of this alone being properly *poetical* as distinguished from rhetorical, devotional or metaphysical, made me speak as I did." Unable to condone "Tennyson's dawdling with [the] painted shell" of the universe, Arnold yet finds such poets as Keats or Browning even more reprovable for having allowed themselves "to be prevailed over by the world's multitudinousness." The times have corrupted literary taste along with everything else. Of friends who admire Clough's *Bothie* he scornfully writes that they have been "sucked... into the Time Stream in which they... plunge and bellow." By way of contrast, Arnold boasts to Clough of his own immunity to coercion, of his stubborn refusal to let the age impose on him its definition of the artist's rôle: "I . . . took up Obermann, and refuged myself with him in his forest against your Zeit Geist."

The dangers of contemporaneity which had upset Clough's equilibrium and threatened his own, Arnold embodied in the temptations to which the speaker in *The New Sirens* is exposed. The gloss which Arnold provided for Clough makes the poem's meaning unmistakable. Siren voices have lured the protagonist, himself a poet, down from the lonely heights. In responding to their call, he has betrayed the austere purity and freedom of the life of the imagination:

> From the dragon-warder'd fountains
> Where the springs of knowledge are,
> From the watchers on the mountains,
> And the bright and morning star;
> We are exiles, we are falling,
> We have lost them at your call—
> O ye false ones, at your calling
> Seeking ceiled chambers and a palace-hall!

Since the sirens, as we are informed, symbolize romantic love, their conception may well have been inspired by Marguerite; but as Marguerite herself came in retrospect to stand for many things, so the sirens epitomize not only undisciplined passion, but also the nervous instability of modern society. The poet, it will be noted, is mocked for preferring the wisdom of the intellect to that of the heart:

> 'Come,' you say, 'the brain is seeking,
> While the sovran heart is dead;
> Yet this glean'd, when Gods were speaking,
> Rarer secrets than the toiling head.'

Even though partially seduced and to this extent disabled in his creative faculty, the poet has not fully succumbed to the blandishments of the sirens. Before it was too late, he heard "the north wind blowing," and shocked into wakefulness, saw the revellers in their true light as "unsphered, discrowned creatures." The prose exegesis of *The New Sirens* indicates that Arnold was thinking of himself when he cast his poet for the part of disenchanted onlooker. Thus, he asks of the distraught maidens: "do your thoughts revert to that life of the spirit to which, like me, you were once attracted, but which, finding it hard and solitary, you soon abandoned for the vehement emotional life of passion as 'the new Sirens?'" And again in his paraphrase of the poem's dénouement, Arnold incontestably identifies himself with the protagonist who is made to say: "I, remaining in the dark and cold under my cedar, and seeing the blaze of your revel in the distance, do not share your illusions: and ask myself whether this *alternation* of ennui and excitement is worth much? whether it is in truth a very desirable life?"

Arnold's final estimate of *The New Sirens*, which few would dispute, was: "it is exactly a mumble." If art is to be a barricade against the Time Spirit, then it must be created with all the skill at the artist's command. In *Horatian Echo* the poet cautions his "ambitious friend" not to let popular versifiers challenge him on the grounds of formal excellence:

> Only, that with no finer art
> They cloak the troubles of the heart
> With pleasant smile, let us take care. . .

During 1849 a significant shift of emphasis takes place in Arnold's letters to Clough. The poet no longer makes so much of artistic intransigeance. Instead of justifying his work as a gesture of protest against the age, he now takes the position that great art is its own justification. For the moment he follows a line which, if prolonged, would have led to the doctrine of art for art's sake. Especially revealing are the views contained in a letter written in early February 1849. The poetic quality most to be cultivated is "naturalness," by which we are to understand "an absolute propriety—of form." This is "the sole *necessary* of Poetry as such: whereas the greatest wealth and depth of matter is merely a superfluity in the Poet *as such*." Arnold then weighs the relative merits of content and form:

> I often think that even a slight gift of poetical expression

which in a common person might have developed itself easily and naturally, is overlaid and crushed in a profound thinker so as to be of no use to him to help him to express himself.—The trying to go into and to the bottom of an object instead of grouping *objects* is as fatal to the sensuousness of poetry as the mere painting, (for, *in Poetry*, this is not *grouping*) is to its airy and rapidly moving life.

In conclusion he focuses his argument on Clough's poetry. The judgment passed on his friend's failure has now a firmer basis in aesthetic theory:

—You succeed best you see, in fact, in the hymn, where man, his deepest personal feelings being in play, finds poetical expression as *man* only, not as artist:—but consider whether you attain the *beautiful*, and whether your product gives PLEASURE, not excites curiosity and reflection. . . . Reflect too, as I cannot but do here more and more, in spite of all the nonsense some people talk, how deeply *unpoetical* the age and all one's surroundings are. Not unprofound, not ungrand, not unmoving:—but *unpoetical*.

Through dedication to his art Arnold was reaching after a greater degree of detachment, not only from the age, but also from that part of his nature which was akin to the age. He refers to an acquaintance who "urges me to speak more from myself: which I less and less have the inclination to do." Self-sufficiency remains an ideal, but now rather as an essential condition of creativity than as conducive to peace of mind. Later in 1849 he refers to himself as an artist "whose one natural craving is not for profound thoughts, mighty spiritual workings etc. etc. but a distinct seeing of my way as far as my own nature is concerned." In revulsion against the romantic attitude towards art, he writes to his sister: "More and more I feel bent against the modern English habit (too much encouraged by Wordsworth) of using poetry as a channel for thinking aloud, instead of making anything." Such poems as *Mycerinus*, *The Sick King in Bokhara*, and

The Forsaken Merman, in which the narrative or dramatic modes are employed to mask the immediacy of the themes to the author's personal situation, show Arnold moving in the direction of greater objectivity. But this tendency is more clearly traceable in poems dealing more or less directly with aesthetics.

The Strayed Reveller, which supplied the title for the 1849 volume, bears a specious resemblance to *The New Sirens* in several ways, but actually reaches a conclusion very different from that endorsed in the earlier poem. Like the poet in *The New Sirens*, the reveller has descended from his native sphere on the heights; but now Arnold no longer identifies himself with his protagonist—quite the contrary, in fact. The first poet manages to free himself from the spell of the sirens. The strayed reveller, on the other hand, is a willing loiterer in Circe's palace. He can sing only when intoxicated by the magic wine which induces in him a frenzy as debasing to the creative impulse, one may suppose, as is bestiality to man's physical nature. Ulysses symbolizes heroic action, totally unlike the passion-vexed gyrations of the sirens, whose song, according to tradition, he likewise heard, but without turning aside. Of the exploits of such heroes the reveller knows nothing, save what he has learned from Silenus. Yet the true poets are those who have participated most intensely in the ardors of earthly existence:

> . . . such a price
> The Gods exact for a song:
> To become what we sing.

The reveller is the prisoner of his own self-infatuated imagination. His visions are meaningful to him alone, because he has never connected them with the general sum of human experience. In an interval of clear-sightedness, before plunging back into drunken frenzy, he confesses to Ulysses the desolating isolation of the artist who from his remote point of vantage looks down on the activities of the world "without pain, without labour."

The argument of *The Strayed Reveller*, however, is referable only to ideal ages, filled with the rumor of epic themes. And increasingly Arnold was aware of the very unideal character of his own age. Sometimes the tone of his letters verges on despair:

> My dearest Clough these are damned times—everything is against one—the height to which knowledge is come, the spread of luxury, our physical enervation, the absence of great *natures*, the unavoidable contact with millions of small ones, newspapers, cities, light profligate friends, moral desperadoes like Carlyle, our own selves, and the sickening consciousness of our difficulties; but for God's sake let us neither be fanatics nor yet chalf blown by the wind. . . .

One unfailing source of consolation was the literature of the past. Insecure and sensing the exiguity of his poetic resources, Arnold looked to other writers for guidance in his effort to determine his own proper attitude. This attitude would lie somewhere between the positions described in *The New Sirens* and *The Strayed Reveller*. It would provide for the aloofness which the poets of the two poems have in common; but for the rancor of the first it would substitute equanimity, and in place of the self-indulgent delusions of the other, it would provide an objective grasp on reality. Such were the qualities which Arnold recognized and venerated in Sophocles "who saw life steadily, and saw it whole," and in Shakespeare, "self-school'd, self-scann'd, self-honour'd, self-secure." For much the same reasons he especially singled out, among artists closer to his time, Goethe and Wordsworth, praising the "wide and luminous view" of the one, and the "sweet calm" of the other.

The same motive which induced Arnold the man to try to relate his sense of spiritual isolation to some system of religious or philosophic thought made Arnold the artist seek an objective basis for his aesthetic alienation. The poem entitled *Resignation* grows directly out of meditations over the quality of serene detachment in the poets whom he most admired. But as these artists had not thought of poetry as primarily a means of escape from the world, so Arnold now tries to rationalize the essentially introspective impulse within his own work by assigning it an altruistic motive.

The speaker in *Resignation*, who is, of course, Arnold, has stationed himself on a lofty outlook. Much has been made of the poet's use of running water to symbolize human existence under its temporal aspect, but his preoccupation with high places is equally remarkable. Mountains and, indeed, eminences of every kind are the natural habitat for Arnold's characters, such settings being used to dramatize the isolation of superior souls. We have already noted in *The New Sirens* and *The Strayed Reveller* how the descent of the two poets from their upland fastnesses to the peopled valleys is made a metaphor for their worldly contamination. The philosophic mind, it seems, needs some such point of vantage as a means of reducing the banal affairs of everyday life to proper scale. So Alaric, the "lonely conqueror" of the Rugby prize poem, strikes a romantic pose atop the Capitoline Hill from which to brood over the civilization he has brought low. So the scholar-gipsy looks over Oxford from the Cumnor Hills. So also Heine gazes out from Brocken-tower, Odin scans Midgard from Valhalla, and the shepherd in *Sohrab and Rustum*

> . . . from his mountain-lodge descries
> A far, bright city, smitten by the sun,
> Through many rolling clouds. . .

Remoteness of perspective, however, need not necessarily emphasize individual apartness; it may also lead to a perception of "our true affinities of soul." This is the experience of the poet in *Resignation*:

> From some high station he looks down,
> At sunset, on a populous town;
> Surveys each happy group, which fleets,
> Toil ended, through the shining streets,
> Each with some errand of its own—
> And does not say: *I am alone.*

Although the gipsies in *Resignation* help to bring into relief the poet's isolation from society, their attitude of fatalistic hopelessness does not suffice for him. Nor is he willing to rest in self-contemplation:

> The poet, to whose mighty heart
> Heaven doth a quicker pulse impart,
> Subdues that energy to scan
> Not his own course, but that of man.

He feels impelled to submerge his individuality in the whole world of animate being: "That general life, which does not cease." The artist, he discovers, has a natural aptitude for sharing in this "general life," which is

> The life he craves—if not in vain
> Fate gave, what chance shall not control,
> His sad lucidity of soul.

In this poem the writer's sister, the Fausta of the subtitle, has the task of defending the position which Arnold himself had adopted in previous poems. According to her argument, the poet is a man apart. By virtue of his capacity for intense feeling, he can at will escape into the life of the imagination:

> In the day's life, whose iron round
> Hems us all in, he is not bound;
> He leaves his kind, o'erleaps their pen,
> And flees the common life of men.
> He escapes thence, but we abide—
> Not deep the poet sees, but wide.

For Fausta the last line of this passage signifies the artist's lack of involvement in the human drama; but Arnold reinterprets its meaning to support his own very different assumptions. If the poet enjoys a kind of "rapt security," this is not because his sensibilities are different from those of other men, but rather because his "natural insight" enables him intuitively to "discern/ What through experience others learn." The poet stands aside so that he may by

> winning room to see and hear,
> And to men's business not too near,
> Through clouds of individual strife
> Draw homeward to the general life.

The account of the poet's function set forth in *Resignation* was to remain, however, an ideal which Arnold never fully realized in his own poetry. Elsewhere he had advocated stoical self-possession, a quiet and a fearless mind, as the best antidote against "the something that infects the world"—yet without being able, as we have seen, to surmount the philosophic difficulties attendant on such a position. In the same way, a concept of the aesthetic impulse, whereby "sad lucidity of soul" guarantees "the poet's rapt security," proposes a kind of imaginative vision which Arnold could admire in others, but which lay outside his own scope. It is all very well for the Goethe of *Memorial Verses* to say: "The end is everywhere,/ Art still has truth, take refuge there!" But with his confidence a good deal shaken by the cool reception of the 1849 poems, Arnold inclines more readily to the view expressed in *Stanzas in Memory of the Author of 'Obermann'*:

> Some secrets may the poet tell,
> For the world loves new ways;
> To tell too deep ones is not well—
> It knows not what he says.

In fact, the first Obermann poem presents a literary variant of Arnold's relationship to the social life of his times. An age given over to superficiality could not but be antagonistic to the ways of the imagination:

> Too fast we live, too much are tried,
> Too harass'd, to attain
> Wordsworth's sweet calm, or Goethe's wide
> And luminous view to gain.

Too nervously distracted to perceive and hence "draw homeward to the general life," and yet too fastidious to mingle with the world on its own terms, the poet has no choice but to follow such writers as Senancour into the wilderness of self-exile. Arnold's temperamental sympathy with Senancour led him to fancy a close parallel in their situations, and so to make of the author of *Obermann* a symbol of the alienation imposed on the modern artist: "The world is with him in his solitude far less than it is with them [other writers of the sentimental school]; of all writers he is the most perfectly isolated and the least attitudinising." Yet in everything that he has to say about Senancour as a companion spirit, there is present a tone of hesitancy. However strong a case might be made for the French writer's aloofness, there was no denying that this attitude, as symptomatic of the "unstrung will" and the "broken heart," had been fatally disabling to creative endeavor. When he despairs of success in his own writing, Arnold is capable of moving to this extreme; but a deep conviction of the poet's traditional responsibility to his culture will not allow him even at such times completely to disassociate himself from the world about him. His efforts to clarify his concept of the function of the artist invariably lead back in the end to that duality of awareness which is present in all his thinking. There are two worlds in conflict, an inner and private one of the individual consciousness, and an outer and public one of shared experience. The artist like the man eddies in between, caught by alternating currents of attraction and repulsion:

> Ah! two desires toss about
> The poet's feverish blood.
> One drives him to the world without,
> And one to solitude.

All tne various elements of this conflict are orchestrated in *Empedocles on Etna*, the dramatic narrative which supplied the title for the 1852 volume. Fifteen years later the poet was emphatically to deny that he had used "Empedocles and Obermann as mouthpieces through which to vent my own opinions." But this *ex post facto* declaration was certainly disingenuous. Even without the testimony of the poem itself, the prose exegesis of *Empedocles on Etna* in the Yale Papers presents too many parallels with Arnold's acknowledged view of his situation at this period to leave much room for doubt that the poet was writing with his own dilemma in mind. The combination of the narrative and dramatic modes, with which he had experimented in such works as *The Sick King in Bokhara*, was no doubt chosen in the interests of objectivity. Yet "the dialogue of the mind with itself" makes up the true substance of the poem. Pausanias and Callicles serve to personify aspects of Empedocles' nature which he has outgrown and left behind. They represent the extremes between which his past life had vacillated, Pausanias being an embodiment of the *homme moyen sensuel* and Callicles standing for the lonely artist dedicated to the life of the imagination.

Empedocles on Etna is divided into two acts, corresponding to the two worlds which divide the protagonist's being. In the first part, where he has Pausanias for auditor, the Sicilian philosopher gives rein to his rancor against contemporary society. He has outlived his time, and now in old age has chosen exile in preference to the frivolous ways of a later generation. The mirror metaphor, here introduced, brilliantly evokes the fragmentation of values which occurs once the traditional centers of conviction within a society have lost their magnetism. The sophists with their sneering materialism and the hypocritical saints with their "pious wail" are in rival ascendancy over humanity. The individual who would retain his identity has no choice but to sink into himself:

> And we feel, day and night,
> The burden of ourselves—
> Well, then, the wiser wight
> In his own bosom delves,
And asks what ails him so, and gets what cure he can.

But self-knowledge brings with it bitter recognition of the cosmic extent of man's alienation: "No, we are strangers here; the world is from of old." Empedocles states Arnold's own matured belief that in their even-handed operations natural laws are careless of human destiny:

> Nature, with equal mind,
> Sees all her sons at play;
> Sees man control the wind,
> The wind sweep man away;
> Allows the proudly-riding and the foundering bark.

Religious systems are an ineffectual expedient, whereby mankind endeavors to pass off the responsibility for his unhappy lot on the "harsh Gods and hostile Fates." The wise individual is he who realistically accepts the limitations of earthly existence and makes the best of them. Empedocles' long diatribe to Pausanias is introduced by Callicles' first song which recounts how the aged centaur, Chiron, played mentor to the young Achilles, opening his eyes to the beneficence of nature. The advice given by Empedocles to Pausanias thus constitutes a bitter travesty of the situation described in this lyric. When the philosopher has concluded his lesson, Callicles is again heard, this time singing of the contentment which Cadmus and Harmonia found in their divinely decreed exile. As if aware of the implied irony with reference to his own forlorn and outcast state, Empedocles ends by sending Pausanias back to the world of men.

The second part of the poem takes up after Empedocles has ascended almost to the summit of Etna. It is evening now; and the setting, described as a "charr'd, blacken'd, melancholy waste," is symbolic of the sage's extreme dejection. Having repudiated Pausanias' offer of sympathy, Empedocles confronts his isolation, only to find its burden as intolerable as the alternative of fellowship with his kind:

> And being lonely thou art miserable,
> For something has impair'd thy spirit's strength,
> And dried its self-sufficing fount of joy.
> Thou canst not live with men nor with thyself—

Once again the voice of Callicles rises in contrapuntal response to the philosopher's tortured thoughts. By now it has become apparent that Callicles' lyrics subserve a twofold purpose. Each calls up a myth which is apposite to Empedocles' state of mind at the moment, but which, by virtue of being a myth, has the effect of objectifying and extending the implications of the protagonist's introspective struggle. Each also suggests a philosophic solution to this struggle, which Empedocles in his intense self-absorption either ignores or willfully perverts. Thus, Callicles' third song tells of Typho's rebellion against Zeus the lawgiver, and of the punishment visited on his senselessly prolonged resistance. But Empedocles is blind to the admonishment concealed in his disciple's graceful narrative. Emotionally overwrought, he instinctively sides with Typho in his futile rage.

Then Callicles sings of the transcendent power of poetry, as betokened by Apollo's triumph over Marsyas. And again Empedocles, totally involved on his own predicament, adopts a private reading, and launches into a resentful outburst against the tyranny to which the god of poetry subjects his votaries. Of all conditions of loneliness none is so intolerable as that which the artist experiences when he enters the service of the imagination:

> And lie thou there,
> My laurel bough!
> Scornful Apollo's ensign, lie thou there!
> Though thou hast been my shade in the world's heat—
> Though I have loved thee, lived in honouring thee—
> Yet lie thou there,
> My laurel bough!
>
> I am weary of thee.
> I am weary of the solitude
> Where he who bears thee must abide—
> Of the rocks of Parnassus,
> Of the gorge of Delphi,
> Of the moonlit peaks, and the caves.
> Thou guardest them, Apollo!
> Over the grave of the slain Pytho,
> Though young, intolerably severe!

Thou keepest aloof the profane,
But the solitude oppresses thy votary!
The jars of men reach him not in thy valley—
But can life reach him?
Thou fencest him from the multitude—
Who will fence him from himself?
He hears nothing but the cry of the torrents,
And the beating of his own heart.
The air is thin, the veins swell,
The temples tighten and throb there—
Air! Air!

Take thy bough, set me free from my solitude;
I have been enough alone!

Recoiling from the consciousness of spiritual vacuity, Empedocles reverts in thought to the society of human beings, who at first

> gladly welcome him once more,
> And help him to unbend his too tense thought,
> And rid him of the presence of himself,
> And keep their friendly chatter at his ear,
> And haunt him, till the absence from himself,
> That other torment, grow unbearable;
> And he will fly to solitude again,
> And he will find its air too keen for him,
> And so change back; and many thousand times
> Be miserably bandied to and fro . . .

And so he continues to vacillate under ever-tightening tension between the outer world where he is homeless and the inner world of sterile speculation, without ever achieving quietude and a sense of unity with the universal harmony. In the process he has lost all capacity for emotional response, until now he finds himself: "Nothing but a devouring flame of thought—/ But a naked, eternally restless mind!" Empedocles' tragedy, then, is the tragedy of the uncommitted intellect, neither profound enough long to support a life of contemplation, nor strong enough to persevere in a life of action. And it is towards an agonized recognition of this central dislocation that Empedocles' frenzied thoughts spiral down in the most splendidly sustained passage that Arnold ever wrote:

> But mind, but thought—
> If these have been the master part of us—
> Where will *they* find their parent element?
> What will receive *them*, who will call *them* home?
> But we shall still be in them, and they in us,
> And we shall be the strangers of the world,
> And they will be our lords, as they are now;
> And keep us prisoners of our consciousness,
> And never let us clasp and feel the All
> But through their forms, and modes, and stifling veils.
> And we shall be unsatisfied as now;
> And we shall feel the agony of thirst,
> The ineffable longing for the life of life
> Baffled for ever; and still thought and mind
> Will hurry us with them on their homeless march,
> Over the unallied unopening earth,
> Over the unrecognizing sea; while air
> Will blow us fiercely back to sea and earth,
> And fire repel us from its living waves.
> And then we shall unwillingly return
> Back to this meadow of calamity,
> This uncongenial place, this human life;
> And in our individual human state
> Go through the sad probation all again,
> To see if we will poise our life at last,
> To see if we will now at last be true
> To our own only true, deep-buried selves,
> Being one with which we are one with the whole world;
> Or whether we will once more fall away
> Into some bondage of the flesh or mind,
> Some slough of sense, or some fantastic maze
> Forged by the imperious lonely thinking-power.
> And each succeeding age in which we are born

Will have more peril for us than the last;
Will goad our senses with a sharper spur,
Will fret our minds to an intenser play,
Will make ourselves harder to be discern'd.
And we shall struggle awhile, gasp and rebel—
And we shall fly for refuge to past times,
Their soul of unworn youth, their breath of greatness;
And the reality will pluck us back,
Knead us in its hot hand, and change our nature
And we shall feel our powers of effort flag,
And rally them for one last fight—and fail;
And we shall sink in the impossible strife,
And be astray for ever.

Finally, as if in answer to the philosopher's desperate yearning for spiritual clarity and certitude, he is vouchsafed a revelation of emancipation from self through oneness with the general life. Before the exaltation of this moment can pass, he plunges into the crater. Callicles has the final word in his hymn to Apollo, which voices a serene and joyous acceptance of things as they are. Although Callicles has previously sung that "the lyre's voice is lovely everywhere," he now concludes that the scene of Empedocles' suicide is wanting in poetic inspiration.

II

POETRY AS MAGISTER VITAE

If it seems that a disproportionate amount of space has been devoted to the volumes of 1849 and 1852, it should be remembered how comparatively short Arnold's poetic career was to be and how much of the work for which he is now valued was written before he was thirty years of age. More immediately important considerations, however, center attention on this body of poetry. For Arnold's genius, maturing earlier than that of either Tennyson or Browning, was at the same time more subjective in its expression. Perceptions which occur in the youthful poetry of Tennyson and Browning as vaguely sensed states of mind achieve full self-awareness and a high degree of articulation in Arnold. The critic is already foreshadowed in the poet's tendency to analyze and to make discriminatory judgments even with himself as subject.

All the more significant, then, is the *volte-face* in aesthetic intent which took place during the year intervening between the publication of the *Empedocles* volume and the collected *Poems* of 1853. There can be no doubt that the change is in large part attributable to Arnold's dissatisfaction at the critical reception of his previous work. Try as he might to feign indifference over the unenthusiastic notices accorded to his maiden efforts, he was no more impervious than Tennyson or Browning to claims which the age made on its artists. In fact, the very inconclusiveness of Arnold's effort to locate some individual principle of integration must ultimately have been a decisive factor in turning him outward for relief from a suffocating sense of inner disharmony. With *Empedocles on Etna* he had pressed self-scrutiny to its farthest imaginable lengths, and come up against blank despair. As if appalled by the process of introspection, the poet drew back, never again to probe so deeply into the dark recesses of self.

During 1850 and 1851 Arnold and Clough were much together in London, and there was a resulting hiatus in their interchange of letters. When resumed in 1852, this correspondence at once indicated the road which Arnold had been travelling in the interim. He finds the world increasingly "uncomfortable for those of any natural gift or distinction"; but now he has decided that part of the blame for this state of affairs belongs to the gifted artists who have "not trained or inspired or in any real way changed" society, so that "the world might do worse than to dismiss too high pretensions, and settle down on what it can see and handle and appreciate." After likening himself to "a gifted Roman falling on the uninvigorating atmosphere of the decline of the Empire," the poet concludes on the following note: "Still nothing can absolve us from the duty of doing all we can to keep alive our courage."

Four months later, in October, comes a statement of poetic principle which amounts to a radical revision of the position so vigorously supported throughout the letters written during 1848 and 1849. Arnold has to a large extent abandoned the criterion of form in judging the merits of an artistic composition. Great art endures by reason of its thematic content. Especially is this true for modern poetry. Whereas the Elizabethan poets exhibit an "exuberance of expression" appropriate to "a youthful age of the world," the poets of more mature times should concentrate on meaning rather than manner. The romantic poets failed through taking the Elizabethans for models; and critics by bestowing praise in the wrong places have perpetuated the error:

> They still think that the object of poetry is to produce exquisite bits and images . . . whereas modern poetry can only subsist by its *contents*: by becoming a complete magister vitae as the poetry of the ancients did: by including, as theirs did, religion with poetry, instead of existing as poetry only, and leaving the religious wants to be supplied by the Christian religion, as a power existing independent of the poetical power. But the language, style, and general proceedings of a poetry which has such an immense task to perform, must be very plain direct and severe: and it must not lose itself in parts and episodes and ornamental work, but must press forwards to the whole.

On further consideration, Arnold reaches the conclusion that significance of theme is unavailing unless its treatment arouses in the reader a pleasurable reaction. "As for my poems," he writes at the end of 1852, "they have weight, I think, but little or no charm." He goes on to take his work to task for precisely the same reasons which had earlier formed the basis for his disapproval of Clough's writing. Consistent with these reformed views, he is ready to disown the *Empedocles* volume. It is only excusable, if at all, on the half-hearted plea that the author had therein endeavored to portray with fidelity the alien circumstances under which the modern artist works:

> *You* in your heart are saying *mollis et exspes* over again. But woe was upon me if I analysed not my situation: and Werter[,] Réné[,] and such like[,] none of them analyse the modern situation in its true *blankness* and *barrenness* and *unpoetrylessness*.

Having decided that his poetry has so far been inconsequential in content, Arnold next brings the process of reappraisal to bear on the stylistic qualities of his compositions. And here too he finds no cause for complacency. The initial failure in conception carries over into the performance; an inchoate condition of inner consciousness is reflected in disunity and incongruity of outer form. In answer to his sister's expressions of bewilderment over the tenor of *Empedocles on Etna, and Other Poems*, Arnold writes:

> Fret not yourself to make my poems square in all their parts, but like what you can my darling. The true reason why parts suit you while others do not is that my poems are fragments—*i.e.*, that I am fragments, while you are whole; the whole effect of my poems is quite vague & indeterminate—this is their weakness; a person therefore who endeavored to make them accord would only lose his labor. . . .

For a full and orderly declaration of the changes which had taken place in Arnold's aesthetic theories, however, one must turn to the Preface which he affixed to the *Poems* of 1853. This was the poet's first venture into the field of formal criticism; and although ostensibly written to vindicate his poetic practice in the accompanying volume, it lays down many of the principles which were to characterize his future critical pronouncements. By implication at least, this essay is a recantation of everything that no longer satisfied him in the content and form of his earlier poetry. The Preface opens with an explanation of why *Empedocles on Etna* is omitted from the collection. Arnold allows that the poem is a truthful presentment of the temper of modern life. "The calm, the cheerfulness, the disinterested objectivity" so typical of Greek genius in its prime, Empedocles has lost, to fall victim to morbid self-consciousness:

> ... the dialogue of the mind with itself has commenced; modern problems have presented themselves; we hear already the doubts, we witness the discouragement, of Hamlet and of Faust.

But an artistic representation is not justifiable on the score of its relevance to the reader's experience, however strong the contemporary appeal. For, the argument continues, if the representation is to be truly poetical: "It is demanded, not only that it shall interest, but also that it shall inspirit and rejoice the reader: that it shall convey a charm, and infuse delight." Because *Empedocles on Etna* seems calculated to depress rather than to exhilarate the feelings of the reader, Arnold finds it unsuitable for inclusion among the poems by which he wishes to be known. "What then," he asks, "are the situations, from the representation of which, though accurate, no poetical enjoyment can be derived?" With his treatment of Empedocles in mind, he makes the following answer:

> They are those in which the suffering finds no vent in action; in which a continuous state of mental distress is prolonged, unrelieved by incident, hope, or resistance; in which there is everything to be endured, nothing to be done.

Having accounted for the suppression of *Empedocles on Etna*, Arnold turns to a discussion of the principles which should govern the modern poet in the practice of his art. The first consideration, we learn, is the selection of the kinds of actions which have been "the eternal objects of Poetry, among all nations and at all times." Excellent actions are defined as: "Those, certainly, which most powerfully appeal to the great primary human affections: to those elementary feelings which subsist permanently in the race, and which are independent of time." As indicating a fundamental shift in Arnold's aesthetic position, two implications emerge from the foregoing statement. In the first place, the principal emphasis is now placed on content, rather than on form. Secondly, theme must be connected with the primal human sympathies in such a way as to awaken a general emotional response. Arnold borrows the term *pragmatic* to describe the kind of poetry which he has in mind. This is to say that the artist's controlling intent must be communicative on a level of impersonal apprehension; his purpose is the objective one of providing grounds for imaginative activity in which the largest possible audience can participate. Judged by such standards, poems of the type to which *Empedocles on Etna* belongs can hardly be regarded otherwise than as the self-infatuated lucubrations of a hopelessly private and introspective individual. In the zeal of his reformed beliefs Arnold harshly condemns a contemporary critic's advocacy of false aims in stating that: "A true allegory of the state of one's own mind in a representative history is perhaps the highest thing that one can attempt in the way of poetry." The words are attributed to another, but one can hardly avoid the suspicion that Arnold introduced the quotation with his own previous work in mind.

Excellent actions, however, are not enough in themselves; they "are to be communicated in an interesting manner by the art of the Poet." In order to convey the precise function of artistic form, Arnold takes over from Goethe the concept of *Architectonicè*, by which we are to understand "that power of execution, which creates, forms, and constitutes: not the profoundness of single thoughts, not the richness of imagery, not the abundance of illustration." In other words, form rightly conceived is the means whereby the imagination externalizes its operations. The form of a work of art is important only as an unobtrusive construct, imparting coherence and lucidity to theme. It must never call attention to itself; it is rather to be sensed as the shaping faculty making for unity of impression. On these grounds Arnold takes issue with such imitators of Shakespeare as Keats, who, endowed with verbal felicity, overlay and so obscure or falsify their meaning out of undue attention to surface effects. In their work the sum of the parts is greater than the whole; and manner, superseding matter, leads to the worst excesses of art for art's sake. Preciosity is the technical counterpart of the dialogue of the mind with itself; the one is as harmful to perfection of artistic performance as the other is to nobility of artistic conception. The ancients are "the best models of instruction for the individual writer," Arnold says, because they above all others exemplify "three things which it is vitally important for him to know:—the all-importance of the choice of a subject; the necessity of accurate construction; and the subordinate character of expression."

No final evaluation can be placed on the poetic theories defined in the Preface without taking into account the artistic goal which Arnold contemplated as attainable through their application. Poetry of the highest order, he says, always aims at instilling a "moral impression." To the creation of this effect both content and form contribute. Thus, "a great action treated as a whole" results in "unity and profoundness of moral impression." These sentiments bespeak Arnold's theoretical mastery over those elements in his artistic consciousness which had previously made for alienation. Henceforth he would address himself directly to his age, seeking to combat its "spiritual discomfort" by writing poetry of "moral grandeur," such as springs from "great actions, calculated powerfully and delightfully to affect what is permanent in the human soul."

Insofar as the 1853 Preface is a disavowal of the life of the imagination lived in isolation from the outer world, it reflects an evolution in the author's aesthetic philosophy similar to that which we have already followed in Tennyson and Browning. Arnold's attempt to deal with the dilemma of the artist in Victorian society, however, is more systematic and thoroughgoing than the similar efforts made by his fellow poets. Whereas Tennyson and Browning were principally concerned to remedy those personal eccentricities which the critics had stressed as militating against their popular acceptance, Arnold, no less eager to gain for himself an audience, dreamed likewise of recapturing for poetry its former prestige as a cultural agent. Tennyson's early poetry had seemed thematically insignificant; Arnold, indeed, must have had some such notion in mind when he wrote of this poet's "dawdling with [the] painted shell" of the universe. Then with the English Idyls Tennyson began to treat realistic subjects deliberately chosen for their relevance to the life of the period. The youthful Browning, on the other hand, had suffered opprobrium for his obscurity; and here again Arnold was acutely voicing the prevailing view when he remarked that in failing to clarify his ideas, Browning had allowed himself "to be prevailed over by the world's multitudinousness." Browning's experiments with the dramatic mode and eventual development of the monologue came about, as we have seen, under the impulse to find a manner more conformable to the aptitudes of contemporary readers.

In his Preface Arnold proposed for himself an all-inclusive reform in poetic practice which would affect both form and content in their communicative aspects. Like Tennyson, he had come to accept the poet's obligation to concern himself only with themes of general moral import. Like Browning, he was now prepared to sacrifice the subtleties of private intuition to meaningful structure. But unlike either Tennyson or Browning, his concessions imply no disposition to allow the age to influence his actual performance, such as is too often recognizable in the work of the two others. Contemporaneity cannot guarantee thematic significance any more than liveliness of expression can pass as a substitute for the grand style. By taking the writers of Greece as his models, Arnold had nothing less in mind than to restore to Victorian England the literary magnificence of classic times. The Empedoclean dialogue of the mind with itself was to be replaced by an outward communion between the artist and his public conducted on a no less elevated plane.

III

MYTH AND THE TIME SPIRIT

The 1853 Preface constitutes a sort of poetic manifesto, defining the ideals which Arnold proposed henceforth to keep before him. And, indeed, all of his poetry subsequent to 1852 should be read with the Preface in mind. At first the poet seems to have been persuaded that theory and performance are synonymous, and that he had hit on his rightful manner—a manner as native to his talents as it was to be salutary for the age. In the first glow of enthusiasm over *Sohrab and Rustum* he confesses to Clough in May 1853 a sense of regret for time wasted hitherto: "I feel immensely —more and more clearly—what I *want*—and what I have (I believe) lost and choked by my treatment of myself and the studies to which I have addicted myself." Yet by the end of this year during which he had also written his crowning work, *The Scholar-Gipsy*, misgivings have again set in. Convinced that he had correctly prescribed for his times that kind of poetry which was needed, he still despairs of his ability to provide it. If he persists at all, it is solely because creative endeavor fortifies his spirits:

> A thousand things make one compose or not compose: composition seems to keep alive in me a *cheerfulness*— a sort of Tuchtigkeit, or natural soundness and valiancy, which I think the present age is fast losing—that is why I like it.
>
> I am glad that you like the Gipsy Scholar—but what does it *do* for you? Homer *animates*—Shakespeare *animates*—in its poor way I think Sohrab and Rustum *animates*—the Gipsy Scholar at best awakens a pleasing melancholy. But this is not what we want.
>
> > The complaining millions of men
> > Darken in labour and pain—
>
> what they want is something to *animate* and *ennoble* them—not merely to add zest to their melancholy or grace

to their dreams.—I believe a feeling of this kind is the basis of my nature—and of my poetics.

From the foregoing quotation it is evident that Arnold held fast by the principles laid down in the Preface. Once announced, they henceforth formed the core of his artistic creed. An unusual capacity for self-criticism, however, harassed him into acknowledging his failure to live up to the standards which he had imposed on himself. As a result, there inhere in Arnold's work, as in that of Tennyson and Browning, evidences of a divided aim, a double awareness. Like Tennyson and Browning, Arnold sought to make his inner vision subserve ends dictated from outside; but to the extent that his temperamental alienation was more self-conscious, he lacked the saving faculty for compromise, for disguising his true intent under apparent meanings of a more ingratiating kind. In the 1853 Preface Arnold had set an impossible goal both for himself and for his readers; had he demanded less from either, his poetic career might have been prolonged.

With the ostensible purpose of calling a halt to the dialogue of the mind with itself, Arnold took up the most objective of all poetic forms: the narrative and dramatic. These modes, together with the elegiac, account for virtually all of the important poems which he wrote after 1852. If the elegy was to become his distinctive type of utterance, he did not revert exclusively to it until after he had first attempted to restore to poetic narrative and drama something of the dignity and elevation which they had enjoyed in ancient times. Yet *Tristram and Iseult, Sohrab and Rustum, Balder Dead*, and *Merope* retain their interest not because of what they pretend to be, but rather because they throw so much light on the limitations of the Victorian literary sensibility. Endeavoring to rise above himself, the poet succeeded only in etching his own lineaments more ineffaceably on his work. Of the Tennyson of *Idylls of the King* and of the Browning of *The Ring and the Book*, it can be said that they were fully equal to their themes as they conceived them. For all Arnold's scrupulosity to keep himself out of his more ambitious poems, there remains a discrepancy between intent and achievement which reveals the artist's failure ever to sublimate the life of the imagination through the creation of objective equivalents for internal states of mind.

Arnold, like Tennyson, turns to myth and legend for inspiration. Indeed, Arnold's first long work in the heroic manner, *Tristram and Iseult*, employs material which Tennyson was later to use in two books of *Idylls of the King*. *Tristram and Iseult* was first published in 1852 along with *Empedocles on Etna*; but it reappeared in 1853 in a version so altered as to indicate that the author must have been putting the poem in final form at the same time that the Preface was occupying his thoughts. Arnold's treatment of the legend is in no sense traditional. Despite the blending of narrative and dramatic techniques, the sections devoted to the ill-fated passion of the lovers remain curiously lifeless. The poet's sympathies are reserved for Iseult of Brittany whose story is presented in an elegiac vein wholly at variance with the tragic intensity which seems to be aimed at elsewhere. The total effect is not unlike that made by certain of Tennyson's domestic Idyls. Since the heroine is confined to the rôle of passive onlooker, her situation can hardly be said to provide opportunity for the display of "an excellent action." It may be asked, indeed, whether her dilemma is not rather like that of Empedocles, one of those "in which there is everything to be endured, nothing to be done."

And what, we ask, is the real theme of Arnold's *Tristram and Iseult*? Does it come to anything more than a condemnation of that romantic love which had obsessed the poet as a personal problem in the Marguerite lyrics and *The New Sirens*? Can it not be said, in other words, that legend is here invoked simply as a means of dignifying and imparting an appearance of objective validity to an experience largely subjective in its implications? And even so, the mask of impersonality imposed too severe restrictions on the wearer. Not content to allow his narrative to carry its own implicit meaning, the poet must near the end step forward in person to comment on what has happened. There are, the reader learns, two classes of individuals who waste their lives. The first is made up of the worldlings whose capacity for generous emotion has been blasted by "the gradual furnace of the world." The second category includes those self-corrupted beings who have become enslaved by their passions.* Here belongs Tristram as the prototype of emotional instability. Having just completed his portrayal of Iseult of Brittany's noble stoicism, Arnold is unable to restrain his indignation against the heedless agent of her suffering. The dénouement brings on a spontaneous outburst of annoyance calculated to destroy any illusion of detachment built up in the foregoing sections. "And yet," says Arnold, "I swear, it angers me to see/ How this fool passion gulls men potently."

If the content of *Tristram and Iseult* fails to accord with the theories about subject-matter set forth in the 1853 Preface, the structure of the poem is equally at variance with the concept of form therein developed. Just as Iseult of Brittany takes no integral part in the action on which her fate depends, so the reader is kept a spectator, conscious at all times of barriers which discourage too great involvement in the tragic plight of the actors. In seeking ways to objectify his drama, Arnold forfeited that direct appeal to the human sympathies which, according to the Preface, is the test of an artist's mastery over his material. For example, in the concluding episode of section two, as rewritten for the 1853 volume, the huntsman in the tapestry is brought to life so that he can speculate about the meaning of the scene which confronts him. Clearly the poet intended in this way to heighten the tragic fact that Tristram and Iseult have died in each other's arms; but the actual effect is to transfer the reader's attention from the lovers to the knight whose rôle is that of a neutral onlooker lost in reverie.

Still more debatable as a structural element is the story of Merlin and Vivian which forms a sort of coda to the poem. As recounted by Iseult of Brittany to her children, this additional legend was obviously meant by the author to

* A similar distinction is made in *A Summer Night*.

reinforce the moral message of the principal narrative. Pretty certainly also, the device recommended itself as a means of externalizing Iseult's perceptions. But again we feel that the poet's too deliberate artifice sacrifices more than it gains. For the ambiguities that arise in trying to establish a direct equivalence between the Tristram and Iseult and the Merlin and Vivian stories fatally impair that "unity and profoundness of moral impression" which Arnold regarded as the indispensable component of all great art. Grant that both Tristram and Merlin are destroyed by reckless love; but what have Iseult of Cornwall and Vivian in common, the one as unrestrainedly passionate as her lover, the other so coolly adept in exploiting Merlin's folly? And how is Iseult of Brittany's situation in any way relevant either to that of Merlin whose faculty for self-delusion she certainly does not share, or to that of Vivian who is as much below as she is above the conventions of romantic love? The fact that the reader even asks these questions, much less that the answers should remain a matter for vague surmise, reveals Arnold's failure here to live up to the ideal of "accurate construction" prescribed in the 1853 Preface.

Iseult of Brittany, as Tristram's wife, is exposed to an emotional climate wholly foreign to her nature. After Tristram's death she withdraws altogether from the world, with only her children to relieve her solitude. Betrayed by her feelings, she experiences the same sense of isolation that sets the tone of Arnold's earlier poems on the subject of romantic love. *Sohrab and Rustum* is also a study in alienation. In this case, however, the line of descent is from *Mycerinus* and *The Sick King in Bokhara*, works in which the individual's estrangement from his fellow beings suggests a wider, cosmic divorce.

Although cast in the form of heroic narrative, *Sohrab and Rustum* develops tension through a series of failures in recognition between father and son, as the two grope through a maze of hostile circumstance. It is fated that they shall not know each other until too late; but the destiny which holds them apart is a blind and unmotivated force, seemingly beyond human comprehension. Sohrab acknowledges the inscrutability of man's earthly lot when he says:

> For we are all, like swimmers in the sea,
> Poised on the top of a huge wave of fate,
> Which hangs uncertain to which side to fall.
> And whether it will heave us up to land,
> Or whether it will roll us out to sea,
> Back out to sea, to the deep waves of death,
> We know not, and no search will make us know;
> Only the event will teach us in its hour.

And again in his death agony:

> Father, forbear! for I but meet to-day
> The doom which at my birth was written down
> In Heaven, and thou art Heaven's unconscious hand.
> Surely my heart cried out that it was thou,
> When first I saw thee; and thy heart spoke too,
> I know it! but fate trod those promptings down
> Under its iron heel; fate, fate, engaged
> The strife, and hurl'd me on my father's spear.

How many of Arnold's earlier and more personal poems invoke in similar terms the enigmatic power of the Zeitgeist to account for the spirit's loneliness and isolation! Rustum accepts his son's reading of life, and on the necessity for submission to an unintelligible order of things builds his philosophy of austere stoicism, which is so closely akin to the temper of mind in which Iseult of Brittany endures her bereavement. But Rustum's resignation is not without the deeper and more bitter perception that he is doomed never to harmonize his violent nature with the general life:

> But now in blood and battles was my youth,
> And full of blood and battles is my age,
> And I shall never end this life of blood.

There can be no doubt that in both *Tristram and Iseult* and *Sohrab and Rustum* Arnold believed that he was working with themes of tragic grandeur. And as the following passage from the 1853 Preface shows, the poet was fully cognizant of the Aristotelian concept of catharsis:

> In the presence of the most tragic circumstances, represented in a work of Art, the feeling of enjoyment, as is well known, may still subsist: the representation of the most utter calamity, of the liveliest anguish, is not sufficient to destroy it: the more tragic the situation, the deeper becomes the enjoyment; and the situation is more tragic in proportion as it becomes more terrible.

Yet there is nothing in the situations of either Iseult of Brittany or of Rustum to purge the emotions. Both are the innocent victims of a fatality which they have in no conceivable way invited. Our sense of their suffering is unrelieved by any intimation that they have transgressed and are undergoing a just punishment. They are, in short, pathetic, but they are not tragic figures. Rustum beside Sohrab's body, grimly aloof in the extremity of his grief, like Iseult hidden from the world in the solitude of her remote castle, exemplifies quite as much as Empedocles the spiritual desolation which "finds no vent in action; in which a continuous state of mental distress is prolonged, unrelieved by incident, hope, or resistance; in which there is everything to be endured, nothing to be done."

The introspective bias which invalidates the epic pretensions of *Sohrab and Rustum* has its formal counterpart in the anomalous conclusion which Arnold attached to an otherwise straightforward narrative. The description of the river Oxus has been justly admired, but the noble qualities of these lines are most apparent when isolated from their context. As an organic part of the poem the passage is hardly more defensible than the self-contained episode which terminates *Tristram and Iseult*. Here again Arnold seems to have been reluctant to let his story stand on its own merits. Out of an impulse to force on the reader a subjective interpretation, the author broke the bounds of artistic propriety. Rustum's tragedy, we must be made to realize, is that of the alienated individual, is in other words Arnold's own tragedy.

To fail to perceive that the poet symbolizes this alienation through his description of the Oxus as "a foil'd circuitous wanderer" is to miss the underlying significance of the entire work as a further revelation of Arnold's imaginative vision.

Having exploited Celtic myth in *Tristram and Iseult* and Persian legend in *Sohrab and Rustum*, Arnold turned for inspiration in his third long narrative poem, *Balder Dead*, to the Norse sagas. The exploits of the gods offered material more heroic in scope than anything he had yet assayed; and in an endeavor to rise to the subject he invested the poem with a full array of epic trappings. Here is an action such as the Strayed Reveller had dreamed of being able to sing; yet in Arnold's hands it undergoes the same tempering down towards pathos that is observable in *Tristram and Iseult* and *Sohrab and Rustum*. Again we sense an ulterior motive which reduces the implications of the action into conformity with some inner and private awareness. *Balder Dead*, along with Arnold's other work in the narrative and dramatic modes, is best understood as a variation on the theme of alienation.

Balder, like Iseult of Brittany and Rustum, is guiltless, and therefore victimized by the circumstances which determine his destiny. Even Odin, father of the gods, does not pretend to comprehend the necessity for the death of his most radiant son:

> But he has met that doom, which long ago
> The Nornies, when his mother bare him, spun,
> And fate set seal, that so his end must be.

There is significance in the fact that Balder had always occupied a place apart among the gods in Valhalla. The mourners at his funeral rites apostrophize him as the composer of strife, the friend of the betrayed, the gentle singer of peaceful pursuits. Almost, we feel, he has been translated because his spirit was too noble longer to endure the barbaric ways of the existing order. Hoder's blindness is a symbol for the general failure to appreciate all that Balder stands for. Like the gipsy boy or Mycerinus or the author of *Obermann*, he is superior to his environment and hence a stranger in it.

His is the loneliness of the individual who lives in a society with the values of which he has no sympathetic correspondence, a society which cannot in any real sense recognize his excellence any more than he can adapt himself to its conventions.

The concluding episode of *Balder Dead*, which was Arnold's original contribution to the story, supports this interpretation. On Hermod's return to the underworld he finds that Balder is not unhappy in his new sphere. He has been reunited with Nanna and Hoder, and his presence consoles the other shades. In a passage curiously reminiscent of Rustum's Weltschmerz, Balder confesses to Hermod his weariness with the fierce turbulence of terrestrial life, and then goes on to prophesy the eventual establishment of a happier and more humane society. There can be no doubt that Balder's vision is an outgrowth of Arnold's own sense of his unsatisfactory relationship to his age:

> But not to me so grievous, as, I know,
> To other Gods it were, is my enforced
> Absence from fields where I could nothing aid;
> For I am long since weary of your storm
> Of carnage, and find, Hermod, in your life
> Something too much of war and broils, which make
> Life one perpetual fight, a bath of blood.
> Mine eyes are dizzy with the arrowy hail;
> Mine ears are stunn'd with blows, and sick for calm.
> Inactive therefore let me lie, in gloom,
> Unarm'd, inglorious; I attend the course
> Of ages, and my late return to light,
> In times less alien to a spirit mild,
> In new-recover'd seats, the happier day.

In 1858, three years after *Balder Dead*, Arnold published *Merope*, his most ambitious attempt to duplicate the manner of the ancients. Sophoclean tragedy was quite beyond his range, and the failure of *Merope* as a dramatic representation illustrates once more how unequal the poet was to the task of putting into practice the theories expounded in the 1853

Preface. The tragedy survives as a shell, competent in form, but entirely lifeless for want of any central fire. Significant in this connection are the opinions which Arnold expressed in a letter to his sister, written in 1858 when he had only recently finished *Merope*. The poet, conscious of a fatal diminution in his imaginative powers, has to resist the impulse to compensate for weakness of conception by relying on structural technique:

> People do not understand what a temptation there is, if you cannot bear anything not *very good*, to transfer your operations to a region where form is everything. Perfection of a certain kind may there be attained, or at least approached, without knocking yourself to pieces, but to attain or approach perfection in the region of thought and feeling, and to unite this with perfection of form, demands not merely an effort and a labour, but an actual tearing of oneself to pieces . . .

Merope would hardly be worth lingering over were it not for the character of Polyphontes, who, as Arnold admitted, usurps the play's interest. The tyrant embodies a further aspect of the poet's interior consciousness. He is, of course, yet another alien, his strength deriving from a lonely temperament which is a law unto itself. Yet Polyphontes is apparently no better able than those most closely associated with him to comprehend his motive force. In *Parting*, it will be remembered, Arnold had asked the twofold question: "And what heart knows another?/ Ah! who knows his own?" The same enigma is posed at greater length by the chorus in *Merope*:

> But more than all unplumb'd,
> Unscaled, untrodden, is the heart of man.
> More than all secrets hid, the way it keeps.
> Nor any of our organs so obtuse,
> Inaccurate, and frail,
> As those wherewith we try to test
> Feelings and motives there.

Polyphontes dies with his secret inviolate; and Merope, as she looks down at his corpse, can only ponder the mystery of individual being:

> O Æpytus, my son, behold, behold
> This iron man, my enemy and thine,
> This politic sovereign, lying at our feet,
> With blood-bespatter'd robes, and chaplet shorn!
> Inscrutable as ever, see, it keeps
> Its sombre aspect of majestic care,
> Of solitary thought, unshared resolve,
> Even in death, that countenance austere!

According to Aristotle's *Poetics* the recognition scene between Merope and Æpytus in the lost tragedy of *Cresphontes* provided the best of all models for handling the technique of discovery. Perhaps this hint helped guide Arnold to his choice of a tragic subject; but in *Merope* the dramatic crux is a *failure* in recognition. Polyphontes, as has been said, is the true protagonist; and Merope's half-sympathetic efforts to understand him give the play such complexity and depth of meaning as it possesses. In fact, all four of the narrative and dramatic works at present under consideration present a romantic inversion of the classic device of recognition. Merlin's betrayal in the final episode of *Tristram and Iseult* results from impercipience; and something of the same sort may be attributed to Iseult of Brittany in her unhappy marriage. Balder dies through Hoder's blindness; Rustum, deaf to the promptings of intuition, slays his son.

The point here is that failure in recognition becomes a further means through which Arnold's sense of alienation carries over as a subliminal motif into poetry from which he had resolutely resolved to exclude all traces of introspection. In the Preface to the original edition of *Merope* the poet declares that the "state of feeling which it is the highest aim of tragedy to produce" resides in "a sentiment of sublime acquiescence in the course of fate, and in the dispensations of human life." Perhaps the capacity for stoic endurance which alike characterizes Iseult of Brittany, Rustum, Balder, and Polyphontes may be accepted as illustrating this "sentiment of sublime acquiescence"; but such is the tone of the poems that the reader is little inclined to assent to so much innocent suffering. The tragic catharsis releases the feelings; but pathos constricts them and wrings a cry of protest. It is because the focal characters in Arnold's narrative and dramatic poetry are delivered out of his own self-consciousness that they seem pathetic rather than tragic. We cannot acquiesce to their plight, any more than Arnold could accept his own. It will be remembered that the poet had with unusual asperity rebuked a contemporary critic for asserting: "A true allegory of the state of one's own mind in a representative history is perhaps the highest thing that one can attempt in the way of poetry." But, the evidence of the 1853 Preface to the contrary, is not this disclaimer factitious? Does it not, in other words, seem to have been provoked by an uncomfortable sense of the statement's relevance to his own practice? Certainly, the poetry which accompanied and came after the Preface becomes fully meaningful only if, like the frankly subjective work of the earlier years, it is interpreted in the light of the author's obsession with self in an age devoid of poetic inspiration and hostile to the creative imagination.

In his search for a way to define the ambiguous tone of Arnold's narrative and dramatic poems, the reader might do worse than adopt the term *elegiac*. He might do so the more confidently because the favorite form of the poet's later career was the elegy. Of the twelve poems, which Arnold gathered in his collected works under the title of "Elegiac Poems," none was written before 1850, and all but four were published after 1853. The fact that many of these poems appeared simultaneously with more ambitious efforts in the volumes of 1853 and 1855 furnishes additional proof in support of the foregoing argument that the poet had set himself a goal in the 1853 Preface that he was temperamentally incapable of achieving. For the elegies of these years sound an insistent note of discouragement; the author is more and more conscious of the distance which divides him from his age, and less and less hopeful of finding artistic means of bridging the gap.

Between *Stanzas in Memory of the Author of 'Obermann'* (1852) and *Stanzas from the Grande Chartreuse* (1855) Arnold had been travelling a lonelier road than might be guessed from a superficial reading of *Tristram and Iseult*, *Sohrab and Rustum*, and *Balder Dead*. In the first Obermann poem the poet's self-engrossment is still counteracted, as in the case of Empedocles, by a reciprocal drive towards the outside world; but the speaker in *Stanzas from the Grande Chartreuse* has made a virtue of estrangement. It must be remembered that the poet is not here seeking out the Carthusians from any innate sympathy for the ascetic life, but rather because he perceives an equivalence between his own isolation and that of the monks whose type of faith is equally anachronistic in the mid-nineteenth century. In analyzing his own situation, Arnold likens himself to a pagan lingering on after the decline of classical culture.* And for the humanist the monastic ideal does not offer an acceptable alternative to the spiritual void of a materialized society. At best, the anchorite and the latter-day Greek participate in a common exile:

> Not as their friend, or child, I speak!
> But as, on some far northern strand,
> Thinking of his own Gods, a Greek
> In pity and mournful awe might stand
> Before some fallen Runic stone—
> For both were faiths, and both are gone.
>
> Wandering between two worlds, one dead,
> The other powerless to be born,
> With nowhere yet to rest my head,
> Like these, on earth I wait forlorn.
> Their faith, my tears, the world deride—
> I come to shed them at their side.

---

* This concept is, of course, a recurrent one in Arnold's thinking. See the letter to Clough, dated 7 June 1852, as well as the lecture "On the Modern Element in Literature," presently to be discussed.

The *Memorial Verses* of 1850 had celebrated the great romantic poets for their lonely but indomitable opposition to the spirit of the times. In *Stanzas from the Grande Chartreuse* Byron reappears. He is no longer in the company of Wordsworth and Goethe; his companion spirits now are Shelley and Senancour. Together they form a trio of defeated voices crying in the wilderness. If messages such as theirs fall on deaf ears, what recourse has the poet of succeeding times but to remain mute? The culminating image of these Stanzas speaks for a lost generation of artists, likening them to

> children rear'd in shade
> Beneath some old-world abbey wall,
> Forgotten in a forest-glade,
> And secret from the eyes of all.

The busy world calls, but the summons is to an alien life:

> Fenced early in this cloistral round
> Of reverie, of shade, of prayer,
> How should we grow in other ground?
> How can we flower in foreign air?
> —Pass, banners, pass, and bugles, cease;
> And leave our desert to its peace!

There is a certain irony in the fact that the 1853 volume, which offered *Sohrab and Rustum* in support of the Preface, should also have contained in *The Scholar-Gipsy* a conclusive refutation of nearly everything that Preface stands for. Little disposed as the poet was to entertain any such notion, the solution to his artistic dilemma lay not in escaping out of himself, but rather in deeper self-immersion; not in ignoring, but in frankly accepting the limitations of individual consciousness. The material of *Sohrab and Rustum* is derivative; we feel how unequal the author was to making it his own. Despite its source in "Glanvil's book," *The Scholar-Gipsy* is a wholly original poem. Just because he apprehended the theme out of his own experience, Arnold here created an action closer to the dimensions of myth than ever resulted from attempts to force his imagination into epic or tragic moulds. In the Theocritan pastoral elegy the poet found an extremely flexible form congenial to his melancholy temper of mind—a form, furthermore, designed to give free play to his faculty for inducing mood through beauty of descriptive language. *The Scholar-Gipsy* is Arnold's closest approximation to that ideal fusion of content and manner contemplated in the Preface.

But what of the theme as the fusing agent? In *The Scholar-Gipsy* the poet imaginatively confronted his dilemma, and as a result called into being a lasting personification of the alienated artist. The lines of conflict between the individual and society are drawn with dramatic sharpness. For once Arnold achieves a complete disassociation between the two halves of the divided awareness, and in so doing emancipates his artistic vision. The central intent emerges only by gradual degrees, however, so cunningly has the poet played variations on the conventional appurtenances of the pastoral elegy.

In the opening stanzas the artist locates himself, and the reader, in peripheral relationship to the workaday world. We are thus prepared to sympathize with the disillusioned Oxford scholar when he forsakes the trodden path and casts in his lot with the gipsies. As elsewhere in Arnold's poetry, the gipsies epitomize freedom from social restraint, but here their way of life holds out an additional inducement. In response to questions about his choice, the scholar answers

> that the gipsy-crew,
> His mates, had arts to rule as they desired
> The workings of men's brains,
> And they can bind them to what thoughts they will.
> 'And I,' he said, 'the secret of their art,
> When fully learn'd, will to the world impart;
> But it needs heaven-sent moments for this skill.'

What this secret art may be is never revealed. It is sufficient that the scholar, like Tennyson's Merlin, believes strongly enough in some ultimate revelation to persevere in his quest. More significant is the nature of the quest which lays on the seeker the necessity of holding himself apart from all habitual intercourse with humanity. This is not to say that the scholar acknowledges no bond with his kind. In his wanderings about the countryside, he is most often to be found where some rural activity is afoot. Yet his rôle remains that of keenly observant, but uncommitted spectator. Like the poet of *Resignation*, he prefers breadth of outlook to specific involvement, because as an artist in training his concern is with the general life, while he waits "for the spark from heaven to fall."

Halfway through the elegy the spell cast by the hauntingly beautiful setting of the scholar's pilgrimage is abruptly shattered. Arnold arouses himself and us to actuality. Having gained our sympathy for the protagonist by the preceding stanzas of idyllic description, the poet now moves on to apotheosize the scholar against a jarringly discordant backdrop of modern life. If devotion to a transcendental vision imposed its burden of loneliness even "in days when wits were fresh and clear," how much more resolutely must the dedicated individual safeguard himself against

> this strange disease of modern life,
> With its sick hurry, its divided aims,
> Its heads o'ertax'd, its palsied hearts. . .

In the process of assuming the immortality which Arnold confers, the scholar sheds his human identity and becomes a figure of myth. While Arnold lapses into the first person as a means of involving both himself and us in "the sick fatigue, the languid doubt" of the here and now, the scholar moves further and further away into the charmed realm of his imaginative life. The first half of the poem had almost persuaded us that we shared this immunity; now our awakening to a truer perception of our situation emphasizes by contrast the scholar's remote felicity. The metaphorical meaning of his quest becomes apparent. Self-centered in his private awareness, the scholar holds true to "*one* aim, *one* business, *one* desire," whereas we, susceptible to the distractions of our external environment, have "tired upon a thousand schemes our wit."

The meaning of the quest is thus expanded into a symbol for the life of the imagination, in terms of which the scholar assumes final status as a representation of the consecrated artist. It does not really signify whether or not heaven will ever vouchsafe its spark to the waiting mind; what does matter is that the individual should maintain his vital energies intact and uncorrupted by the enervating influences of society. Arnold had begun to lose confidence in himself as a creator, but at the same time had come to a clearer realization of the choice which the modern artist must make if his creative impulse is to survive. If Arnold failed to make that choice, *The Scholar-Gipsy* nevertheless testifies to his perception that diffused sensibilities inevitably entail on the artist a loss of sense of direction. And so the elegy ends on a note of despairing admonition to the scholar to protect his dream by estranging himself from the modern world:

> But fly our paths, our feverish contact fly!
> For strong the infection of our mental strife,
>   Which, though it gives no bliss, yet spoils for rest;
> And we should win thee from thy own fair life,
>   Like us distracted, and like us unblest.
>   Soon, soon thy cheer would die,
> Thy hopes grow timorous, and unfix'd thy powers,
>   And thy clear aims be cross and shifting made;
> And then thy glad perennial youth would fade,
> Fade, and grow old at last, and die like ours.*

More than a decade later, after he had crossed his Rubicon into the territory of prose criticism, Arnold cast a nostalgic look backward on the haunts of the scholar-gipsy. Although written in tribute to Clough, *Thyrsis* is quite as much an

---

* The last two stanzas of *The Scholar-Gipsy* are in the nature of a coda, similar to the sections which conclude *Tristram and Iseult*, *Sohrab and Rustum*, and *Stanzas from the Grande Chartreuse*. Here, as in the other poems cited, Arnold enlisted this structurally excrescent device for the purpose of leaving in the reader's mind a vivid objective equivalent to his central theme.

elegy for Arnold's own loss of poetic impulse. This poem also proposes a quest. By revisiting the scenes which he and Clough had loved in youth, the author solicits that lovely landscape to revivify the old artistic response. At first he is unsuccessful in his search for the signal-elm; and his resulting dejection provokes condemnation partly of self, but more particularly of Clough. The old landmarks are gone, but the real betrayal was a human one. The two friends were the first to change. Unequal to the lonely dedication of the scholar, they turned aside into the world. Arnold suggests that while unavoidable responsibilities prompted him to this course, Clough "of his own will went away." And for thus abandoning his native sphere, he paid cruelly, first by forfeiting the spiritual tranquillity so necessary to the poetic faculty, and ultimately by his life:

> It irk'd him to be there, he could not rest.
>   He loved each simple joy the country yields,
>   He loved his mates; but yet he could not keep,
> For that a shadow lour'd on the fields,
>   Here with the shepherds and the silly sheep.
>   Some life of men unblest
> He knew, which made him droop, and fill'd his head.
>   He went; his piping took a troubled sound
>   Of storms that rage outside our happy ground;
> He could not wait their passing, he is dead.

Although his friend is irretrievably lost, Arnold seeks out the scenes of their bygone happiness in the hope of regaining the hopeful spirit of that time. His imaginative being does not respond, however, until, silhouetted against the glory of "the orange and pale violet evening-sky," he at last beholds the elm. The manner in which this fulfillment comes about is thematically significant. A troop of Oxford huntsmen, homeward bound, invades the field where he is loitering; and it is his instinctive revulsion from human society which leads him into a farther field and hence to the sight of the tree "bare on its lonely ridge."

The elm symbolizes everything that Arnold had said in his previous elegy, *The Scholar-Gipsy*. As long as the tree survives, it is possible to have faith in the scholar and his unworldly quest:

> Despair I will not, while I yet descry
> 'Neath the mild canopy of English air
>   That lonely tree against the western sky.
>   Still, still these slopes, 'tis clear,
> Our Gipsy-Scholar haunts. . .

Thyrsis, like the earlier poem, therefore, ends by affirming the life of the imagination, that "fugitive and gracious light . . ./ Shy to illumine," as over against the unpoetical world of actuality. "Why faintest thou?" the ghostly voice of Clough asks:

>   I wander'd till I died.
> Roam on! The light we sought is shining still.
> Dost thou ask proof? Our tree yet crowns the hill,
> Our Scholar travels yet the loved hill-side.

It can hardly escape the attentive reader, however, that a much greater imaginative effort has been required of the poet in order to reach this conclusion. In *The Scholar-Gipsy* the issue of the quest may remain in doubt; but the quest itself takes on a real and immediate symbolic value because the scholar lives his rôle. In *Thyrsis* we are at one further remove from the heart of the matter. The signal-elm has become the metaphorical agent of our apprehension. Its continued existence betokens the reality of the scholar, whose quest, itself a metaphor for the artist's self-imposed isolation, thus carries over the symbolic action of *The Scholar-Gipsy*, but more remotely now, less urgently, in such a way as to imply how the intervening years had relaxed Arnold's hold on his ideal.

IV
"THE DEMAND FOR AN INTELLECTUAL DELIVERANCE"

If the poet in Arnold was reluctant to abandon hope for the spark from heaven, the man found it increasingly difficult to refuse the solicitations of his age that he should assume a conspicuous place in its life. The career of a public servant under an expanding program of government education carried with it responsibilities to Victorian society which could not be ignored. The transformation of the artist into the man of letters was a phenomenon of the times from Carlyle to William Morris; and in Arnold's case the process was materially abetted by a variety of external circumstances, not the least decisive among which was his appointment in 1857 to the Professorship of Poetry at Oxford. His subsequent poetry, nearly all of it in the elegiac mode and much of it purely occasional in nature, reflects the author's final refusal to accept for himself the concept of the alienated artist at home only within the domain of his art.

With the exception of *Thyrsis*, *Rugby Chapel* and *Obermann Once More* are the most memorable poems of Arnold's later period. In them we find the author making the choice henceforth to speak with a public voice. Like others of the elegies, *Rugby Chapel*, dated 1857 but not published until ten years later, directs a retrospective glance on the influences which shaped the poet's faculties. And how noteworthy it is that at this turning point in his career the son should have felt impelled to celebrate Thomas Arnold's memory after fifteen years of silence! For if the scholar-gipsy is correlative to the poet's inner awareness, Arnold of Rugby as certainly exemplifies the ascendency of an outer or social awareness. Here once more Arnold uses setting to juxtapose differing states of mind. He stands in the cold and darkness outside the chapel where his father's body lies buried. And in recollection Thomas Arnold's "radiant vigour" shines out, a bright beacon of spiritual certitude amidst the dreary doubts and perplexities of the age. Like the scholar-gipsy, the elder Arnold was distinguished from other men by firmness of purpose and devotion to a goal; but whereas the scholar must work out his salvation in isolation from his kind, the father served a more altruistic dream. He is to be ranged among the faithful shepherds, the

> souls temper'd with fire,
> Fervent, heroic, and good,
> Helpers and friends of mankind.

In Arnold's tribute to his father the emphasis repeatedly falls on this quality of selfless sacrifice to the needs of one's fellowmen:

> But thou would'st not *alone*
> Be saved, my father! *alone*
> Conquer and come to thy goal,
> Leaving the rest in the wild.

Obermann Once More is Arnold's poetic farewell to the chief literary mentor of his career. Revived in dream, Senancour seems at first to greet his disciple with the old welcome:

> 'And is it thou,' he cried, 'so long
> Held by the world which we
> Loved not, who turnest from the throng
> Back to thy youth and me?
>
> 'And from thy world, with heart opprest,
> Choosest thou *now* to turn?—
> Ah me! we anchorites read things best,
> Clearest their course discern!'

But Arnold has erroneously imagined their meeting as taking place in the context of an earlier and transitional period when withdrawal from the world seemed justified by the disintegration of those traditional values which had made for harmony in bygone ages:

> The past, its mask of union on,
> Had ceased to live and thrive.
> The past, its mask of union gone,
> Say, it is more alive?

In contrast to his method in *The Scholar-Gipsy* and the previous stanzas to Senancour, Arnold can no longer in this elegy keep up the fiction that his protagonist lives on. Obermann's voice now reaches us from the grave; and its accents sound a more optimistic note, as the philosopher contemplates a social order which he did not live to see. The world which was powerless to be born a generation before has come into being; and it is the artist's duty, Obermann says, to associate himself with this world and to make himself its poetic voice, even though his powers have been worn down during the exile from which he returns:

> But thou, though to the world's new hour
> Thou come with aspect marr'd,
> Shorn of the joy, the bloom, the power
> Which best befits its bard—
>
> Though more than half thy years be past,
> And spent thy youthful prime;
> Though, round thy firmer manhood cast,
> Hang weeds of our sad time
>
> Whereof thy youth felt all the spell,
> And traversed all the shade—
> Though late, though dimm'd, though weak, yet tell
> Hope to a world new-made!

And what are the distinguishing characteristics of the change which recalls the artist from estrangement in the depths of self? Arnold is, perhaps intentionally, rather vague on this score; but we are allowed to infer that society is again informed by some all-inclusive cultural idea of a kind to revitalize the creative imagination:

> One common wave of thought and joy
> Lifting mankind again!

It remains finally to account for the shift in intent whereby the poet gave way to the critic and the man of letters. The document most helpful to an understanding of this transformation is Arnold's inaugural lecture as Professor of Poetry at Oxford. Although not published until twelve years later, the address was delivered in 1857. This was the year when he wrote *Merope*; and the difficulties attendant on its composition stirred the poet again to protest to his sister against "this strange disease of modern life," so discouraging to creative endeavor:

> It is only in the best poetical epochs (such as the Elizabethan) that you can descend into yourself and produce the best of your thought and feeling naturally, and without an overwhelming and in some degree morbid effort; for then all the people around you are more or less doing the same thing. It is natural, it is the bent of the time to do it; its being the bent of the time, indeed, is what makes the time a *poetical* one.

To the development of this argument Arnold addressed himself in his first Oxford lecture, in which he proposed to analyze the conditions within contemporary culture which militated against the production of great literature. By opposing these conditions to the ones pertaining in periods celebrated for literary attainment, he hoped not only to point out what was amiss in his time, but also to suggest how this state of affairs might be amended.

What modern man requires above all else, Arnold says, is "an intellectual deliverance." Of the reasons for this demand and of the way that it may be satisfied, the writer makes the following statement:

> The demand arises, because our present age has around it a copious and complex present, and behind it a copious and complex past; it arises, because the present age exhibits to the individual man who contemplates it the spectacle of a vast multitude of facts awaiting and inviting comprehension. The deliverance consists in man's compre-

hension of this present and past. It begins when our mind begins to enter into possession of the general ideas which are the law of this vast multitude of facts. It is perfect when we have acquired that harmonious acquiescence of mind which we feel in contemplating a grand spectacle that is intelligible to us; when we have lost that impatient irritation of mind which we feel in the presence of an immense, moving, confused spectacle which, while it perpetually excites our curiosity, perpetually baffles our comprehension.

Literature, then, when it succeeds in communicating to an age "the complete intelligence of its own situation," is the agent of deliverance; but literature can only serve this function if it is, in Arnold's term, a fully *adequate* literature. For purposes of comparison and contrast, Arnold turns to the writing of classic times. The literature of Greece alone meets his definition of adequacy; with a civilization grander in scope, the Romans failed to achieve comparable heights of literary expression. The disabilities under which Latin writers suffered seemed to Arnold closely to parallel the difficulties impeding artistic creation in his own period; and his criticism of Latin poets will have a familiar ring to any student of his own poetry. For example, although Arnold never wrote his projected poem about Lucretius, the comments on this philosopher in the Oxford lecture make sufficiently clear the reasons why he was so drawn to the subject. Lucretius, like Empedocles, suggested an objective version of his own dilemma. Lucretius, we are informed, fell victim to the "depression and ennui" which are characteristic states of feeling in the modern artist "prevailed over by the world's multitudinousness." In fact, it is hard not to believe that in much that he had to say about the Roman poet, Arnold was motivated by a disposition to rationalize his own similar failure:

> Yes, Lucretius is modern; but is he adequate? And how can a man adequately interpret the activity of his age when he is not in sympathy with it? Think of the varied, the abundant, the wide spectacle of the Roman life of his day;

think of its fulness of occupation, its energy of effort. From these Lucretius withdraws himself, and bids his disciples to withdraw themselves; he bids them to leave the business of the world, and to apply themselves *'naturam cognoscere rerum*—to learn the nature of things;' but there is no peace, no cheerfulness for him either in the world from which he comes, or in the solitude to which he goes. With stern effort, with gloomy despair, he seems to rivet his eyes on the elementary reality, the naked framework of the world, because the world in its fulness and movement is too exciting a spectacle for his discomposed brain. He seems to feel the spectacle of it at once terrifying and alluring; and to deliver himself from it he has to keep perpetually repeating his formula of disenchantment and annihilation.

And again when Arnold says of Virgil that he was "conscious, at heart, of his inadequacy for the thorough spiritual mastery of that world and its interpretation in a work of art," do we not feel impelled to refer these remarks back to their author, and so to interpret them as a personal confession of defeat?

When the lecture "On the Modern Element in Literature" is read with an everpresent sense of its relevance to the speaker's own situation, Arnold's turning away from poetry to criticism becomes fully intelligible. A literature of escape could never effect the intellectual deliverance for which the age was waiting. Once let the need for such a deliverance be admitted and the ideal of the scholar-gipsy was doomed. Yet it was equally unthinkable that the artist should take on the mission of delivering a society which, oblivious to his individual values, could offer in their place none of its own compatible with artistic creation. What was left? For the poet—silence. For the Victorian man of letters, however, there was always the alternative of preaching, even though one could not practice what one preached. The example of Greek literature with its perfect adequacy could always be enlisted to vindicate the theoretical principles of the 1853 Preface. Properly invoked, the Hellenic ideal might yet be made to prevail as "a mighty agent of intellectual deliverance." As Arnold was to argue in his later essays, literary history reserves a place of honor for the critic. In the periods of transition between epochs of creative activity, he is charged with the responsibility of giving currency to the best which has been thought and said, both in the past and in his own time, and so of supplying the impetus for subsequent expansions of imaginative being. Like the Senancour of the second Obermann elegy, the poet turned critic could reveal to his successors the hope of a brighter dawn.

The prose writings of Arnold do not fall within the compass of the present study; yet the importance of the poetry to a proper understanding of the criticism should never be overlooked. The same reservations which apply to the poet's attempts to write in the classical tradition extend to his defense of that tradition in his literary essays. The authors of the standard commentary on the poetry have called attention to the fact that despite his theories Arnold could not escape the romantic temper of his century:

> However much it may at times seem otherwise, the real roots of Arnold's poetry—at least of his power to create poetry—lay not in what was classic and certain and positive, but in what was tentative and romantically obscure. The finish of his poetry and its architecture were classical, as were the limits he put upon it; but its breath and engendering spirit were not. His verses often attained to a statement of what he believed, but they began in what he doubted. His songs arose from what in life was fleeting and lovely, and therefore melancholy and emotional—from the prospect of men set amid beauty and tenderness, looking for some fugitive and gracious light that lost itself among the shadows of uncertain death. Classicist as he was, he knew this secret in his heart.

The foregoing remarks are equally appropriate to the prose criticism. In his important essay, entitled "The Study of Poetry," the writer undertook to define the types of subject and the qualities of style which characterize poetry of the first order. He found that the two essentials of such poetry are truth and seriousness. In order to illustrate the meaning of these terms, he adduced certain passages from epic and dramatic literature to serve as touchstones. All the selections used for illustration share certain thematic and tonal preoccupations which are directly identifiable with similar emphases in Arnold's own poetry. This is merely to say that the poet tended to seek in the work of others elements corresponding to his own sense of tragic conflict. Thus, in each of the touchstones an individual sensibility is subjected to a hostile environment under the stress of alien circumstances. We feel how alone Roland and Hamlet are in the moment of death. Priam suffers Achilles' intrusion with the same helpless passivity that Dante shows under Beatrice's unfeeling gaze. Memories of lost felicity sadden those two exiles: Helen yearning for her brothers, and Satan mindful of heaven. Zeus's lament over the immortal horses consigned to mortal men protests the inscrutable dictates of fate much as does Ceres in her mournful search for Proserpine. For each of these examples parallel situations of a like pathos suggest themselves from Arnold's poems, where also the crux of the action involves some form of failure in recognition.

Arnold carried over into his criticism an aristocratic concept of the artist which is romantic rather than classic in its derivation. Reduced to its central motive, *Culture and Anarchy* is an attack on those Philistine elements in modern bourgeois society which threaten the autonomy of the creative intellect. And in choosing subjects for his critical essays, the author was sympathetically drawn to those writers who had refuged themselves from the Zeitgeist in the life of the imagination. Of Gray, Arnold declared: "He was a man born out of date, a man whose full spiritual flowering was impossible." The same thing might be said of any of those "foil'd circuitous" wanderers about whom he wrote by preference. Arnold was always returning to his dilemma, as he recognized its counterpart in Lucretius or Marcus Aurelius, in Senancour or the two du Guérins or Joubert or Amiel, in Heine or Leopardi, in Shelley or Keats. The dialogue of the mind with itself was not to be resolved in Arnold's prose any more than in his poetry. Yet, the poet's endeavors to deal with the double awareness, however inconclusive, did at least sharpen the perceptions which would later qualify their possessor to become the most penetrating of all critics of the nineteenth-century literary mind.

CONCLUSION

THE introduction to this book suggested that in the poetry of Tennyson, Browning, and Arnold provision must be made for a double awareness. Their problem was to find a middle ground on which to arbitrate the divided allegiance of the modern artist, who, Janus-like, would face two ways at once, both outwards towards society and inwards to the life of the imagination; who would live up to the public responsibilities of the man of letters, while at the same time giving free play to his native sensibilities. To the success of these poets as cultural forces, the Victorian age bears ample testimony. Tennyson, Browning, and Arnold are the last English poets of whom it can be said with any confidence that they widely influenced contemporary thinking and behavior. But once again it may be argued that for the sake of prestige they were willing to capitulate to the superficial values of their world. Readers who hold with this view will maintain that the very nature of the success which the three poets enjoyed as men of letters entailed their failure as artists. To some such verdict the twentieth century has very generally subscribed. Yet one wonders, after all, whether the failure is attributable so much to the poets themselves as to a reading public whose demands were in due course to become so intolerable as to discourage in the serious artist every inclination to compromise.

All things considered, it is remarkable that Tennyson, Browning, and Arnold should have put so much of themselves into their poetry as they did, and still commanded the admiration of their age. Three possible explanations for this popularity may be proposed. Either the Victorians, like Browning's Caliban, were self-infatuated to the extent of making over their poets in their own image. Or we today have inherited a very distorted conception of Victorian habits of mind. Or, finally, Victorian artists were more successful in communicating with their audience on a high imaginative plane than has been recognized. Probably there is a measure of truth in each of these assumptions. In any event, we are

CONCLUSION

left with the realization that a body of poetry, ostensibly aimed at its age, carries in its depths an enormous burden of implication alien to that age.

If the sources of poetic imagination in Tennyson, Browning, and Arnold have been located with any degree of definiteness in the foregoing chapters, then it must surely be agreed that these poets cannot be made to conform to any conventionalized pattern of Victorian thought. Indeed, from their individual points of vantage, each singled out only to repudiate certain alarming tendencies which were shaping contemporary society. Tennyson's mysticism, however vague and ill-defined, was, nevertheless, a direct denial of the cynical materialism, the religion of hard facts that had put power in the hands of the Gradgrinds. By his celebration of intuitive being Browning set his face against the Benthamite psychology, with its teaching that man is a knowable mechanism and hence capable of being tinkered into perfection. The Arnoldian ideal of classical wholeness could not but oppose the emphasis on specialization in a competitive social order, such as had grown out of the Industrial Revolution.

Tennyson, Browning, and Arnold, then, were temperamentally too much at variance with the spirit of their age ever to endorse its basic ideology. As men of letters, however, they were sensible of the need to win public sanction for perceptions which had died stillborn in the too personal idiom of their early poetry. Tennyson, therefore, turned to his English Idyls in an endeavor to invest scenes of everyday life with something of the strange ambiguity which disturbed his inner consciousness. Through his dramatic monologues Browning analyzed familiar types in such a way as to derive a code of behavior from purely intuitive and often anti-social motives. With neither the originality nor the narrative and dramatic talents of Tennyson and Browning, Arnold appealed to tradition, reminding his age that it had lost touch with the best part of its heritage.

Yet, after the problem of communication had been met, there remained the artist's need to give original expression to his imaginative vision. Because their inner poetic awareness

CONCLUSION

sorted so incongruously with the world about them, Tennyson, Browning, and Arnold, the critic is tempted to argue, became conformists from a want of self-reliance; but this imputation is as far from the truth as the rival theory that they were overly conscientious in playing up to their audience and so lost the ability to distinguish between the mask and the face. Either course would have involved an act of self-betrayal, and the consequent drying up of those springs of inspiration whose underground flow we have traced in the work of the three poets. If they assumed the guise of contemporaneity, it was not primarily with the intent to conceal or falsify, but rather to actualize and so inculcate insights which the public had either ignored or reprehended in original, undisguised form.

This process of sublimation, traced through the preceding chapters, is thus to be construed as an artistic endeavor on the part of each poet to assimilate his inner awareness into poetry addressed to the Victorian reading public. This accounts for the curious ambivalence in so much of the writing of Tennyson, Browning, and Arnold. The expressed content has a dark companion, its imaginative counterpart, which accompanies and comments on apparent meaning in such a way as to suggest ulterior motives. However earnestly they address themselves to the normal routines of existence, Tennyson's characters lead a double life; their submerged natures are haunted by dreams, madness, and visionary incitements to unearthly quests. In the same way, the intuitional basis for conduct in Browning's worldly dramas challenges those systems of social convention which warp the individual will to power or love or creativity. And Arnold's myths are really studies in alienation, where the protagonists suffer in all innocence for their superiority to the Time Spirit.

In retrospect we can see that these attempts to bring a double awareness within the compass of a single imaginative vision were destined to failure. Modern society has made the rôles of man of letters and artist mutually irreconcilable without a loss in commitment on one side or the other. The fact of communication presupposes a common language; and as

CONCLUSION

Arnold knew, it is the business of the man of letters to help formulate that language, whereas the artist must speak with his own voice. Under the favoring circumstances of a homogeneous culture (for which Arnold's term was an "epoch of concentration"), the artist may find his public waiting; but when the center falls apart, the dialogue of the mind with itself sustains him. By seeking their audience rather than letting it find them, Tennyson, Browning, and Arnold split their allegiance and partially disengaged themselves from the life of the imagination. The resultant access in prestige and influence involved a fatal loss in artistic status. Their inherent poetic resources only serve to accentuate how great this loss was.

If the uncritical adulation of the age was what they had had most at heart, then, at least, it could be demonstrated that Tennyson, Browning, and Arnold rested on their achievements as men of letters. Like Paracelsus, they were to learn that there are many ways to attain and many levels of attainment. Their later years were embittered by the indiscriminate vagaries of contemporary fame. They were admired, it is true, but for all the wrong reasons; the mask had, after all, got mistaken for the face. Haughtily aloof, Tennyson reverted to his early manner and wrote mysterious poems out of his inner mind. Browning turned crotchety and dissipated his talents in futile disputation, trying to defend the anti-rational on rational grounds. Arnold, wiser, abandoned poetry for expostulatory prose. Meanwhile, the succeeding generation of poets was making the choice that the great Victorians had declined to make. It is arresting to note how unerringly the Pre-Raphaelites and their associates in the aesthetic movement singled out the vital elements in the work of their predecessors. As the early illustrations of Tennyson's poems show, the Pre-Raphaelite painters penetrated to the heart of the poet's imaginative being. One thinks also of Swinburne's admiration for *Maud* and of Edward Fitzgerald's lifelong insistence that the best of Tennyson was to be found in his early compositions. It was Rossetti who discovered and brought *Pauline* back to life after twenty-five

CONCLUSION

years of oblivion, just as it was Browning himself who persuaded Arnold to republish *Empedocles on Etna*.

But the real influence of Tennyson, Browning, and Arnold has operated subterraneously. If their outer awareness took undue cognizance of the surface ripples of Victorian life, they were inwardly aware of the deep ground-swells of change. The individual perceptions, whose concealed operation we have identified in their poetry, were to become the leading motifs of subsequent literary movements. Tennyson's "other life" of dreams foreshadows psychological theories of the imagination and accords with modern thinking about the creative process. Through his reduction of human behavior to its instinctual components Browning anticipates the emergence of modern primitivism. And Arnold's account of the deracinated artist continues to be an obsessive theme in contemporary writing. But such insights were alien to the pretensions of the society which gave rise to them. Because, however hard they tried, they could not simultaneously inhabit the worlds of the imagination and of Victorian society, a split opened, dividing the artistic awareness of Tennyson, Browning, and Arnold. Their failure to close this breach confirmed the alienation of the modern artist.

INDEX OF POEMS

The passages of poetry quoted in this book have been taken from the following editions of the poets' works:

The Poetical Works of Matthew Arnold, edited by C. B. Tinker and H. F. Lowry. London, New York, and Toronto: Oxford University Press, 1950.
The Complete Poetic and Dramatic Works of Robert Browning, edited by H. E. Scudder. Boston and New York: Houghton Mifflin and Co., 1895.
The Shorter Poems of Robert Browning, edited by W. C. DeVane. New York: F. S. Crofts and Co., 1942.
The Poetic and Dramatic Works of Alfred Lord Tennyson, edited by W. J. Rolfe. Boston and New York: Houghton Mifflin and Co., 1898.
Unpublished Early Poems, Alfred Lord Tennyson, edited by Charles Tennyson. New York: The Macmillan Co., 1932.
The Death of Œnone, Akbar's Dream, and Other Poems, Alfred Lord Tennyson. London and New York: Macmillan and Co., 1892.

TENNYSON

Akbar's Dream, 61
Ancient Sage, The, 61, 64-65, 67
Audley Court, 14
Aylmer's Field, 28, 30
Columbus, 60
Day-Dream, The, 15, 26, 40
Demeter and Persephone, 66
De Profundis, 63-64
Despair, 60
Dora, 14
Dream of Fair Women, A, 23, 26
Edward Gray, 14
Enoch Arden, 28, 38
First Quarrel, The, 60
Forlorn, 60
Gardener's Daughter, The, 14, 15
Godiva, 15
Golden Year, The, 15, 37
Hesperides, The, 9, 13
Higher Pantheism, The, 24
Οἱ ῥέοντες, 5, 24
Idylls of the King, 21, 42-59, 60, 63, 84, 119, 120, 187, 188
   The Coming of Arthur, 44
   Gareth and Lynette, 44-45, 46-47
   The Marriage of Geraint, 43, 44, 49
   Geraint and Enid, 43, 44, 49
   Balin and Balan, 42, 43, 47, 49-50
   Merlin and Vivien, 43, 50-51
   Lancelot and Elaine, 43, 51-53, 55, 56
   The Holy Grail, 53-55
   Pelleas and Ettarre, 43, 47, 55
   The Last Tournament, 47, 55-57
   Guinevere, 44, 45, 57-58
   The Passing of Arthur, 46, 47, 57-59
In Memoriam, 16-21, 24-26, 33, 35, 36-37, 97
In the Children's Hospital, 60
Lady Clare, 14
Lady of Shalott, The, 9, 11, 13, 15, 51
Locksley Hall, 12-13, 14, 15, 20, 30, 37, 60
Locksley Hall Sixty Years After, 60, 63
Lord of Burleigh, The, 14
Lotos-Eaters, The, 9-10, 11, 15, 41
Lover's Tale, The, 24, 28
Lucretius, 31-34, 38, 41, 50
Mariana, 30, 52
Mariana in the South, 23
Maud: A Monodrama, xv, 30-31, 219
Merlin and the Gleam, 62-63, 200

INDEX

Morte d'Arthur, 15, 42
Mystic, The, 4
Œnone, 10-11
Outcast, The, 29
Palace of Art, The, 11-12, 19, 36, 44, 59
Perdidi Diem, 4
Poet's Song, The, 15
Princess, The, 15-16, 37-38, 40
Queen Mary, 59
Recollections of the Arabian Nights, 8
Rizpah, 60
Romney's Remorse, 60
Saint Simeon Stylites, 33, 36, 60
Saint Telemachus, 60
Sea Dreams, 28-29
Sea Fairies, The, 9
Sir Galahad, 15, 40
Sisters, The, 63
Supposed Confessions of a Second-rate Sensitive Mind, 4, 13, 30, 34
Talking Oak, The, 14
Timbuctoo, 6-7
Tiresias, 66-68
Tithonus, 13-14, 15, 20, 41, 67
To ——— ("As when with downcast eyes"), 24
Two Voices, The, 7-8, 13, 14, 23-24, 30, 34, 39, 64
Ulysses, 13, 40-41, 67
Vastness, 61
Vision of Sin, The, 23, 26-27, 33
Voice and the Peak, The, 2
Voyage, The, 13, 40, 41-42
Voyage of Maeldune, The, 62
Walking to the Mail, 14-15, 16
Will Waterproof's Lyrical Monologue, 16
Wreck, The, 60

BROWNING

Abt Vogler, 93, 113, 115-116
Andrea del Sarto, 111-112, 113
Any Wife to Any Husband, 103
Balaustion's Adventure, 137, 143
Bishop Blougram's Apology, 98-99, 139
Bishop Orders his Tomb at Saint Praxed's Church, The, 111
Blot in the 'Scutcheon, A, 84, 85
By the Fire-Side, 101, 102
Caliban upon Setebos; or, Natural Theology in the Island, 97-98
"Childe Roland to the Dark Tower Came," 93, 95, 97
Christmas-Eve and Easter-Day, 97, 113-115
Cleon, 97-98, 109
Clive, 140
Colombe's Birthday, 85
Count Gismond, 92, 93
Cristina, 93, 103
Death in the Desert, A, 93-94
Dîs Aliter Visum; or, Le Byron de nos Jours, 106-107
Epilogue (to Dramatic Idyls), 140-141
Epilogue (to Pacchiarotto), 71
Epistle, containing the Strange Medical Experience of Karshish, the Arab Physician, An, 92, 97-98
Evelyn Hope, 93
Ferishtah's Fancies, 140
Fifine at the Fair, 137, 138-139, 142
Flight of the Duchess, The, 101-102, 103-104
Forgiveness, A, 137
Fra Lippo Lippi, 93, 109, 116-118, 135
Glove, The, 104, 106, 140
Grammarian's Funeral, A, 93, 95, 96-97
How It Strikes a Contemporary, 115
In a Balcony, 104-106, 109
In a Gondola, 94, 95, 102, 104
Inn Album, The, 137
Italian in England, The, 96
Ivàn Ivànovitch, 140
James Lee's Wife, 103, 109, 116
Jochanan Hakkadosh, 140
La Saisiaz, 137
Last Adventure of Balaustion, The, 100, 137, 143
Last Ride Together, The, 101, 109
Lost Leader, The, 96
Luria, 85
Master Hugues of Saxe-Gotha, 115
Memorabilia, 119
Mesmerism, 102
Mr. Sludge, "The Medium," 98-99
Muléykeh, 140
My Last Duchess, 92, 96, 111
Old Pictures in Florence, 109, 116
One Word More, 109, 119
Paracelsus, 72, 73-77, 78, 80, 82, 83, 84, 85, 86, 87, 90, 110, 140, 141
Parleyings with Certain People of Importance in Their Day, 140

INDEX

With Bernard de Mandeville, 137
With Daniel Bartoli, 137
With Christopher Smart, 137
With George Bubb Dodington, 137
With Francis Furini, 93, 137
With Gerard de Lairesse, 137, 142
With Charles Avison, 137
Pauline, 72-73, 77, 78, 82, 85, 90, 139, 219
Pictor Ignotus, 110-111, 112
Pied Piper of Hamelin, The, 92, 109
Pillar of Sebzevar, A, 137
Pippa Passes, 86-90, 92, 120, 140
Popularity, 119
Porphyria's Lover, 103
Prince Hohenstiel-Schwangau, Saviour of Society, 137
Prologue (to Asolando), 141
Rabbi Ben Ezra, 93, 94, 97
Red Cotton Night-Cap Country; or Turf and Towers, xv, 137, 139, 142
Respectability, 104, 105
Return of the Druses, The, 85
Ring and the Book, The, 119-136, 137, 138, 187
   The Ring and the Book, 133-135
   Half-Rome, 123
   The Other Half-Rome, 123
   Tertium Quid, 123
   Count Guido Franceschini, 125
   Giuseppe Caponsacchi, 122, 124, 130-133
   Pompilia, 122, 124, 130-133
   Dominus Hyacinthus de Archangelis, Pauperum Procurator, 123-124
   Juris Doctor Johannes-Baptista Bottinius, Fisci et Rev. Cam. Apostol. Advocatus, 123-124
   The Pope, 122, 125, 126-130
   Guido, 123, 126
   The Book and the Ring, 70, 133, 135-136
Saul, 93, 97, 109, 115
Soliloquy of the Spanish Cloister, 92, 96
Sordello, xv, 72, 77-82, 83, 85, 86, 87, 90, 92, 110, 118, 139, 141
Soul's Tragedy, A, 85
Statue and the Bust, The, 93, 107-109
Strafford, 72, 84-85, 86, 90
Toccata of Galuppi's, A, 118-119

Too Late, 104
"Transcendentalism: A Poem in Twelve Books," 109, 116
Two in the Campagna, 101
Two Poets of Croisic, The, 137
Woman's Last Word, A, 102
Youth and Art, 107, 109

ARNOLD

Alaric at Rome, 169
Balder Dead, 169, 187, 193-194, 196, 198
Buried Life, The, 149-150, 155, 162
Dover Beach, 152, 162
Empedocles on Etna, xv, 148, 172-178, 179, 181, 182, 183, 188, 192, 209, 219
Euphrosyne, 162
Farewell, A, 154
Forsaken Merman, The, 148, 161, 167
Fragment of an 'Antigone,' 161
Fragment of a Chorus of a 'Dejaneira,' 161
Heine's Grave, 169
Horatian Echo, 149, 165
Human Life, 156, 157, 162
In Harmony with Nature, 153
In Utrumque Paratus, 160
Isolation. To Marguerite, 150-151, 160
Lines Written in Kensington Gardens, 153
Meeting, 154
Memorial Verses, 171, 199
Merope, 187, 194-197, 208
Mycerinus, 148, 156, 157, 166, 190, 193
New Sirens, The, 164-165, 167, 168, 169, 188
Obermann Once More, 205, 206-207, 211
Palladium, 158
Parting, 150, 152-153, 154, 195
Question, A, 149
Quiet Work, 153
Religious Isolation, 157
Resignation, 148, 168-171, 201
Rugby Chapel, 205-206
Scholar-Gipsy, The, 148, 169, 186, 199-202, 203, 204, 205, 206, 207, 210
Second Best, The, 157
Self-Deception, 155-156
Self-Dependence, 153

INDEX

Shakespeare, 168
Sick King in Bokhara, The, 156, 161-162, 166, 173, 191
Sohrab and Rustum, 169, 186, 187, 190-193, 194, 196, 198, 199, 202
Stagirius, 159
Stanzas from the Grande Chartreuse, 198-199, 202
Stanzas in Memory of the Author of 'Obermann,' 148, 154, 168, 171-172, 193, 198, 207
Strayed Reveller, The, 167-168, 169, 193
Summer Night, A, 153, 189
Thyrsis, 202-204, 205
To a Friend, 168
To a Gipsy Child by the Sea-Shore, 148-149, 156, 193
To a Republican Friend, 154-155
To Marguerite—Continued, 151, 154, 161
Too Late, 162
Tristram and Iseult, 187, 188-190, 191, 192, 193, 196, 198, 202
Wish, A, 153
World and the Quietist, The, 149
World's Triumphs, The, 149
Written in Butler's Sermons, 157
Youth of Man, The, 153, 157
Youth of Nature, The, 153